COMMUNICATION
AS IDENTIFICATION

COMMUNICATION AS IDENTIFICATION:
an introductory view

Donald Byker

Harvard University

Loren J. Anderson

Concordia College
Moorhead, Minnesota

HARPER & ROW, PUBLISHERS
New York   Evanston   San Francisco   London

Sponsoring Editor: Walter H. Lippincott, Jr.
Project Editor: Richard T. Viggiano
Designer: James McGuire
Production Supervisor: Will C. Jomarrón

Communication as Identification: An Introductory View

Library of Congress Cataloging in Publication Data

Byker, Donald, 1936–
    Communication as identification.

     1. Communication.   I. Anderson, Loren J.,
1945–   joint author. II. Title.
P90.B93   301.2'1   74-14097
ISBN 0-06-041111-2

"And may we have neither the mania of the One
   Nor the delirium of the Many—
   But both the Union and the Diversity."

from "Dialectician's Prayer"
by Kenneth Burke

Contents

Preface

In Chapter 1 we define human communication as an ongoing, coactive, developmental sharing of information that creates identification between two or more persons. "Identification" is Kenneth Burke's term. Its presence in our title and definition indicates that Burke's thought is a major influence in our book. Identification comes through understanding another's reasoning, empathizing with another's gregariousness, comprehending another's beliefs, attitudes, and values, sympathizing with another's pleasures and pains, grasping the ordering another uses, interpreting another's verbal and nonverbal codes. Or, more than likely, identification occurs because of a combination of understanding, empathizing, and some of the other factors mentioned.

Our discussion of the various means for creating identification overlaps the time-honored approach of the rhetorical canons. We welcome this addition to our study. Our primary aim in *Communication as Identification* is to set forth theory that improves a student's understanding of interpersonal communication. In our pursuit of this objective we have sought to avoid departmental boundaries and research preferences. We have tried, instead, to weave materials from Burke, traditional rhetorical theory, behavioral communication studies, and other sources into a unified, helpful view of human communication.

Although our primary emphasis is on a thorough analysis of the elements in the communication process, we believe that to study theory alone is not sufficient. Alfred North Whitehead argues:

It is a profoundly erroneous truism, repeated by all copybooks and by eminent people when they are making speeches, that we should cultivate the habit of thinking of what we are doing. The precise opposite is the case. Civilization advances by extending the number of important operations which we can perform without thinking about them. Operations of thought are like cavalry charges in a battle—they are strictly limited in number, they require fresh horses, and must only be made at decisive moments.[1]

Interpersonal communication is an important, highly complex operation. Thinking about it and understanding it are certainly desirable, but one cannot expect to have the time and energy required to think long about all or even most of one's communications. Our overall aim is to have study plus disciplined practice. The practice operationalizes the theory to bring the long-term behavior changes needed for the relatively unconscious, rapid choices required in most interpersonal communication.

Throughout the book we stress the importance of applying communication theory in practice assignments. We include a number of model communications, since we believe that student performance is an essential ingredient as students work to improve their communication.

Communication as Identification seeks an interpersonal emphasis while retaining productive aspects of the public speaking tradition. We see an essential similarity in one-to-one, small group, and speaker–audience settings. We have found that combining the public speaking and interpersonal communication approaches is well suited to the classroom and is well received by our students, who see that this

[1] Quoted in George A. Miller, *Language and Communication* (New York: McGraw-Hill, 1951), p. 223.

blending helps them to improve in a wide range of important communication behaviors. Furthermore, we believe that an interpersonal approach to public speaking provides a more accurate analog to students' nonclassroom communication experiences. We know that our approach has given us and our students unusually enjoyable classes, and we trust that our approach will bring greater vitality to many other communications because of the deeper involvement of the persons engaged.

Writing this book has been most rewarding for us. We have been forced to crystallize and refine our own thoughts about the nature and function of interpersonal communication. Each of us has gained from exchanging ideas in many lively discussions. We are grateful to our teachers, students, reviewers, department colleagues, relatives, and friends, all of whom have made invaluable contributions to our efforts.

Donald Byker
Loren J. Anderson

Part one
INTRODUCTION

1 many and one: communication as sharing: creating identification

To paraphrase John Donne, "Human beings are promontories but not islands." A man is one, but he is also many; and this is the basic factor in interpersonal communication. Without individuality (the many) no person could talk with another or have anything to talk about. Without universality (the one) each individual would be unable to reach other individuals. We base our book on this many–one premise.

Kenneth Burke discusses the concepts of individuality and universality under the terms *autonomy* and *consubstantiality*.[1] If all are together, no one has anything another does not have. In Burke's scheme there is no autonomy, hence no need for communication (Figure 1). If each is completely separate, absolute autonomy prevails; hence no communication is possible (Figure 2). If each is separate yet also joined to others, consubstantiality reigns and communication can occur (Figure 3).

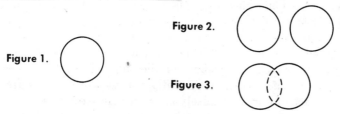

Figure 1.

Figure 2.

Figure 3.

[1] Burke develops and elaborates these ideas in *A Grammar of Motives, A Rhetoric of Motives* (both: Berkeley, University of California Press, 1969), and in other publications. His treatment is profound and well worth the time of one who wishes to explore beyond the material presented here.

DEFINITION OF HUMAN COMMUNICATION

Using Figure 3 as a base, we can define the subject of this book in a preliminary fashion: *Human communication is a sharing of information between two or more persons.* We shall use an illustrative speech to help discuss the terms *sharing* and *information.*

The speech that forms our first example was Vince McGugan's opening speech in the first round of speeches in his class, which had been studying communication theory relevant to Vince's assignment. This chapter as well as Chapters 2, 3, 4, 7, 8, and 9 contain many of the points raised and discussed in our study. (As noted in the preface, the theory and tone of the course emphasize everyday interpersonal transactions as well as somewhat more formal communications. Within this framework, all students prepared material to share with the class. Each presentation would allow the speaker to apply the theory studied, and discussion of each presentation would revisit and amplify the theory.)

Vince was asked to share an aspect of himself that he believed to be an important component of his personality. This assignment explores a significant, usually inescapable, part of interpersonal communication: telling others something about oneself.

Vince and his classmates had seen one another during class sessions, they had participated in open discussion of the communication theory presented, and some had been acquainted prior to enrolling in the course. Since they were fellow students and speakers of the same language, Vince and his listeners were sufficiently consubstantial to share what Vince said about himself as he sat before the class.[2]

When I was a young boy, 13 years old, my father's father   1
died. He died naturally in the middle of winter in Windsor,   2

[2] Vince spoke extemporaneously. The following material was transcribed from the tape recording.

Ontario, which is just across the river from Detroit. It was 3
the same winter that President Kennedy died. It was the 4
same winter that a young girl died on the way home from 5
my school. 6

I wonder if you will understand how these deaths made 7
me realize what people are—what mortality means to me. 8
To explain, I have to tell you about a personal experience 9
related to my grandfather's death. But first you must 10
understand how the President's and the young girl's deaths 11
affected me. 12

The President was remote from my daily life. He was big- 13
ger than life and so in many ways he was bigger than death. 14
His life had a fairy-tale quality about it. He had a young, 15
beautiful, intelligent wife who seemed almost queenlike to 16
me at the time. His background was excellent. He went to 17
school here, he gained the Senate, he earned the Presidency, 18
and he became the national symbol of youth and vitality. 19
He had powerful and deep family roots. Daniel Webster 20
once said, "One may live as a conqueror, a king or a 21
magistrate, but he must die a man." The swiftness and the 22
violence of the president's death frightened me. Here was a 23
man so powerful, yet he was annihilated instantly. Even so 24
at the time I was not moved personally beyond temporary 25
fright. His death didn't make any deep impression on me. 26

About a week after the President died, it was a clear day 27
and beautiful, and school was just let out. I was walking 28
home with a group of friends, as were many other kids. We 29
always walked home in the afternoon. Suddenly, I heard a 30
screech of tires, screams, and as I looked up, I saw a body 31
careening along the pavement, cartwheeling, sort of 32
touching down every few feet on the pavement—much like a 33
stone touches down as it skips over water. I was shocked 34
rigid. When I recovered, I ran toward the person. When I 35
looked down, I saw the face of a young girl totally 36
destroyed. I remember, I felt helpless, and I felt deeper 37
shock when I realized she was dead. I didn't know the girl, 38
but I was terribly afraid at that instant. She was so young, 39
she was only 12 or 13, and she was so destroyed. And in that 40

instant. I saw and I feared human frailty. I saw how weak   41
human flesh and blood is. That accident gave me   42
nightmares for many days after. And in those nightmares I   43
would run and look after I heard the screech of tires, and   44
when I looked I'd see the face of someone in my family. My   45
father, my brother, someone.   46

Just after Christmas that same year, my grandfather be-   47
came very ill. We went as a family in the car to see him.   48
And it turned out that I was the only one of the seven   49
children in our family who was old enough to be allowed   50
into the hospital to see him. I remember everything about   51
that visit, vividly. He lay very still in bed. And he was a big   52
man. I can remember being surprised about how small he   53
looked lying there in bed. There were two racks—one on   54
each side of the bed. Each held a bottle—one clear and one 55
red. Each bottle had a tube leading down from it and each   56
tube had a needle on its end, and the needles were stuck in 57
my grandfather's arms. At the time I didn't understand how 58
he could lie there so quietly with those needles stuck in his 59
arms. I have a terrible fear of needles. I didn't know then 60
that he was in a coma. I kept expecting him to wake up, to   61
tell me one of his great stories. He was really a good   62
storyteller. Like the one about when he and my father built 63
the driveway. When my father was 11 years old, he and   64
Grampa built the driveway from scratch. And my   65
grandfather sent my dad in to get a tool to dig with. My   66
father returned in a few minutes with a teaspoon. He was a   67
real card. My grandfather spanked him on the spot, and   68
when I heard that story from my grandfather, I remember   69
being very surprised because I couldn't really imagine that 70
my father had ever been a boy. He'd always seemed grown   71
up.   72

My grandfather died peacefully and quietly that same   73
night that I visited him. At the funeral home everything was 74
very quiet and somber. I remember looking at my father's   75
face and it was very quiet. I only caught a glimpse of my   76
grandfather in the coffin and he looked white but only as if 77

he were asleep. The funeral day and service were both beautiful, and he was lowered into the grave and we left. 78
79

The next day, returning home from the funeral made his death almost immediately fade from my mind. I can remember that my father went right to work as soon as we got home, and all us kids went to school. I even had a basketball practice that first night. I only thought briefly about my grandfather just before we all sat down to dinner. Afterwards I watched TV, the evening went as it usually did, and I went to bed later on. Another life had come and gone, but this time it was one close to mine. But even yet I hadn't deeply felt its passing. Swift once said: "It is impossible that anything so natural, so necessary, and so universal as death should ever have been designed by Providence as an evil to mankind." My grandfather's death had not seemed evil to me. The President's, yes, the young girl's, yes, but my grandfather's, no. 80
81
82
83
84
85
86
87
88
89
90
91
92
93
94

But that first night home from the funeral, after I'd been asleep for what only seemed a few minutes, I was awakened by the soft voices of my parents across the bedroom wall, I tried to make out what they were talking about, but I couldn't hear it clearly. Then a sound came from the room, and I listened more closely. My father was crying. I froze, stunned. My father never cried. I remember that a cold chill passed through my body as I thought almost in terror, my father was crying. And then a lump grew in my throat, and tears welled in my eyes. I can remember thinking, "fathers never cry." And it hit me in one great flash— Grampa was dead. There would be no more stories. Nothing ever again. The pain of realization that I had not told him all the things that I meant to, that I hadn't appreciated him, that I hadn't told him I loved him, that I had taken him for granted. All those things almost overwhelmed me. A fear grew in me that it might have been my father or mother or brother or sister, and I realized, then, that he was gone forever. I buried my head in my pillow and cried with my father. 95
96
97
98
99
100
101
102
103
104
105
106
107
108
109
110
111
112
113
114

At the same time, I realized then, and have reminded 115
myself often since then, that there isn't a single moment in 116
life that I can afford to lose. I realized that death is 117
absolute. And I saw then, and see now, how it can rob me of 118
the most precious thing that I have—time with the people I 119
love. And I fear it.   120

Sharing

Like other human beings, Vince and his classmates shared a
number of characteristics; this common ground is the
"one"—the consubstantial. At the same time, Vince, like
everyone else, is an individual, with his own special blend of
attributes and experiences; the uniqueness of each human
being guarantees the "many"—the autonomous. Both the
one and the many are needed for interpersonal communication. We all can comprehend what Vince has said, yet
each one responds to the material as an individual. This
shows that the essential overlapping and separation depicted
in Figure 3 does exist.

Because of the many–one postulate, which undergirds the
process of sharing, the sharing process will be *ongoing,
coactive*, and *developmental*. When Vince talks, he continues an *ongoing* process whereby his parents and his society communicated with him about life, death, President
Kennedy, needles, teaspoons, and a nearly infinite list of
other subjects. And Vince's parents, along with others who
have communicated with him in the past, were in turn
acting within a communication process that reached out to
include range upon range of others. Furthermore, each
person who hears or reads Vince's speech becomes involved
in the ongoing process, and each in turn shares with others.
Being many and one, humans perpetually find communication to be necessary and possible.

Since humans are many and one, communication must be
coactive. Vince does not mechanically press buttons and
produce perfectly predictable responses from automatons.

Instead, Vince creates his own, noninterchangeable communication, and he shares it with others; to share with Vince the others must actively interpret and accept what Vince offers.

As Vince decides what to talk about, how to organize his material, what words to use, and which delivery means will be appropriate, he is changing: some aspects of himself are highlighted and become more significant; other parts are passed over and come to have less importance. As others act with Vince, they also change. Thus human communication is *developmental*—each coaction in the ongoing process can influence subsequent communication.

Information

We define information as material one holds in the autonomous sector. This material has the potential to become a stimulus that could have meaning for another. Vince holds material concerning his views of President Kennedy's life and death, the girl's death and his reaction to it, his grandfather's death and other events. Vince encodes the information in a verbal code (nonverbal as well in the face-to-face presentation) and shares this symbolic representation with the listener and reader.

The information, then, is not the words Vince uses; rather, the words are symbolic representations of the information Vince holds. The consubstantial (the one) allows the symbols to be shared; but Vince's coactors attach the meaning. Since persons differ (the many), the meaning attached need not be identical to the information held by Vince. Sometimes the meaning perceived will be a grotesque misrepresentation of what was intended. But one can hope to fare better, and, if some form of contact is maintained, one can always seek ways of sharing information with greater accuracy, meaning, and effectiveness—not a static paradise, but a heaven of sorts nevertheless.

With the foregoing discussion of terms in mind we can

expand our preliminary definition: *Human communication is an ongoing, coactive, developmental sharing of information between two or more persons.*

A Model of the Communication Process

Figure 4 provides a pictorial representation of our definition of communication. The model also introduces further components of the communication process and helps to show the interrelationships of the various components.

We shall discuss this model by returning to Vince and the communication he shared. Think of Vince as person A in the model and yourself as person B. Vince and you probably do not reason exactly alike; on the other hand, you both are one in the ability to reason, and chances are good that Vince and you can understand each other's reasoning. In Chapter 3, which treats this convergence of the many and one in reasoning, we describe the reasoning Vince used in his speech.

Vince's desire for others to understand his views (lines 7–12) is one indication of his gregariousness. His appreciation and love for his grandfather, his concern for his immediate family (lines 42–46), his crying with his father, and his fear that death will "rob me of the most precious thing that I have—time with the people I love," are other indications of Vince's need and love for others. Your relations with others are not precisely the same as Vince's; nevertheless, you and Vince probably can empathize with each other's feelings because you share the consubstantial element that we label gregariousness. Chapter 4 examines this element and its role in communication.

In the first paragraph of his speech Vince states a number of beliefs. We can illustrate this by adding the preface, "I believe that," to some of these statements: "I believe that when I was a young boy, 13 years old, my father's father died." "I believe that he died naturally in the middle of winter in Windsor, Ontario." "I believe that Windsor is just

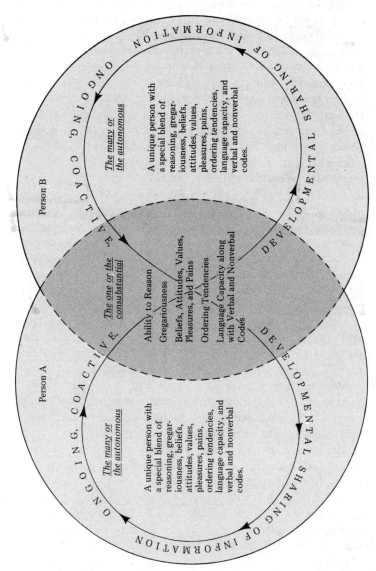

Figure 4. The Byker-Anderson model of communication

across the river from Detroit." A great many such specific beliefs could be pointed out in the rest of the speech.[3]

An attitude is a cluster of beliefs about a certain object. Vince, for example, indicates his attitude toward Harvard when he says of President Kennedy: "His background was excellent. He went to school here, . . ." (line 17). Apparently, Vince's cluster of beliefs or his attitude concerning Harvard is positively weighted. Vince also shows that at 13 he had a cluster of beliefs, an attitude, about fathers showing emotion: "fathers never cry" (line 105).

Vince's fear of death and his affirmation of life and love might also be called attitudes, but these can better be viewed as values. Values are central, enduring beliefs. Since values are basic and stable in one's belief system, they will in some measure determine the less central attitudes and beliefs. Vince's value of life and love influences his attitudes toward dangerous occupations and pastimes and the many specific beliefs relevant to such activities. Influence runs the other way also; one's beliefs and attitudes affect one's values. Values, attitudes, and beliefs are complexly interrelated.

Although human beings in general have beliefs, attitudes, and values (the one), each person has beliefs, attitudes, values and configurations of these that are unique (the many). Surely each reader notices beliefs, attitudes, and values that are similar to Vince's and one would have to search hard to find another with whom no overlapping existed; still, each person has beliefs, attitudes, and values, and interrelations among them that are particular.

All human beings know pleasure and pain. To some extent, individuals can share each other's pleasures and pains. But each person has a central nervous system that is separate from the central nervous system of another; thus in some measure each human being is always alone in experiencing pleasure and pain—a fact that each learns early in life, perhaps while still in the womb. In Chapters 5

[3] We are following the descriptions set forth by Milton Rokeach in *Beliefs, Attitudes, and Values*, San Francisco, Jossey-Bass, 1968.

and 6 we will consider the roles that the consubstantial and autonomous features of beliefs, attitudes, values, pleasures and pains play in interpersonal communication.

Vince's first sentence has 13 words: was I father young years my died when a old father's 13 boy. In random order, these words do not make sense. One can tinker with the ordering of the 13 words as with a puzzle and reconstitute Vince's first sentence as he phrased it: "When I was a young boy, 13 years old, my father's father died." A native speaker of English can quickly and easily follow the sentence that Vince used. Imposing the correct order on the 13 words given at random would be neither quick nor easy, if Vince had begun in this haphazard fashion.

We could have illustrated greater confusion by randomizing the letters in the words, but the point can be made without going that far. Vince and his receivers can communicate readily because they share similar ordering tendencies. These ordering tendencies can be examined within and among sentences as well as among larger units of discourse. For example, after his two opening paragraphs Vince uses chronological order: The president's death comes first, then comes the young girl's death, then Grampa's, and then the aftermath. The ease with which members of our society can follow chronological ordering, as well as other organizational patterns, is evidence of the one. Each person, however, imposes order in somewhat special ways; the many, too, appear again and again in organization.

We will point out another feature of Vince's organization later in this chapter. Other aspects are covered in a subsequent discussion (Chapter 7), focusing primarily on the organization of units of discourse larger than the sentence. Parts of Chapter 8, which deals with language capacity and the verbal code, treat the ordering of words within sentences. In Chapter 8, among many other points, we consider why Vince uses the word "grandfather" during most of his speech but switches to the more intimate "Grampa" at two significant points. Vince chose to sit in a chair facing his classmates. He sat in front of, rather than beside or behind, a table that was in front of the classroom. He could have sat or leaned on the table. If he had stood behind the table, he could have used a podium or done without it. Vince chose to be near and open to his audience—significant aspects of the nonverbal code he transmitted. Chapter 9 introduces spatial relationships and other parts of the nonverbal code.

Vince, of course, makes many choices in the verbal and nonverbal codes besides those just mentioned. Vince's choices show a unique person acting as one of the creators of interpersonal communication. Each of Vince's receivers is also a unique person, and each too, must act to help create the communication. Each person is unique, but communication is possible because the ability to use verbal and nonverbal codes in somewhat consubstantial ways allows symbolization and interpretation to occur in the ongoing, coactive, developmental sharing of information.

The Interaction of Consubstantial Elements

As the random ordering of Vince's first 13 words indicated, words without certain ordering tendencies do not facilitate the coactive, developmental sharing of information. Changes in the order of words will change the sense: "I hit the ball," and "The ball hit me," obviously do not capture the same information. Ordering and wording interact ceaselessly in human communication.

The change in order of "the," "ball," and "hit" requires the change from I to me. If "I" were used at the end of the second statement, a listener could wonder if the resultant statement had an atypical meaning. More than likely, the listener would make other judgments about the language capability and intelligence of the speaker. These judgments indicate interactions between wording, order, and the intelligence dimension (a facet of gregariousness that is investigated in Chapter 4). The interactions of wording, order, and the intelligence dimension are just some of the many interactions among the elements delineated in our communication model. We will mention only a few more here: The reasoning ability one perceives another to have will influence one's attraction to that person (the gregariousness element again); and the attraction one feels for another will influence one's perception of this other person's reasoning ability. Similarly, the beliefs, attitudes, and values one views in another will interact with the reasoning ability and attractiveness the person is thought to have. The same will be true for the pleasures, pains, and ordering tendencies one observes another to have. We elaborate on these interactions and discuss others as we treat the model elements in later chapters.

Our model pictures the communication process. The model also illustrates our book's basic premise: Human beings are many and one. The consubstantial characteristics have been separated from one another for our discussion of each in this section and in later chapters; as we have noted, however, some or all of these consubstantial elements interact complexly as communication takes place.

Communication Creates Identification

Human communication is an ongoing, coactive, developmental sharing of information that creates identification between two or more persons. Two words of our final definition, *creates identification*, are discussed in this section.

We use the word "create" to indicate several related aspects of our view of human communication. To begin, the coactors in a given communication bring something new into existence. This creation may be much like previous ones. For example, the waiter's call to the chef, "One ham and cheese on a roll!" is probably much like many previous orders; still, the call and the receiving of it are a new communication event even though similarities to past ones can be observed.

Furthermore, each coactor in human communication is a

unique person. Thus each act of communication is shaped in some degree by the individuality of the human beings involved, and examples of human communication will not be so closely alike as the products of machines will be. *Create*, then, seems to be a more apt choice than *produce* in considering human communication.

Finally, creation carries a note of unpredictability. The creations of human beings cannot be forecast with the assurance that is possible in estimating the electrical energy a dynamo will produce. To be sure, some persons and some communications are more readily predictable than others, and we do not argue for the chaos of utter unpredictability; yet we affirm that each human being, as a unique individual, creates special and, to a degree, unexpected communication effects. This affirmation leads readily to the following conclusion: *Therefore*, each person is irreplaceable and should be cherished. As one moves further toward the assertion of homogeneity and predictability for human beings, the conclusion, if it occurs at all, comes as an afterthought: *Nevertheless*, each person should be cherished.[4]

Identification is a becoming more alike. When Vince and his audience interact, the coactive, developmental sharing gives them more in common than they had before (i.e., creates identification between them).

This increased commonality can come through understanding another's reasoning, empathizing with another's gregariousness, comprehending another's beliefs, attitudes, and values, sympathizing with another's pleasures and pains, grasping the ordering another uses, interpreting another's verbal and nonverbal codes; more than likely, however, the commonality comes through a combination of understanding, empathizing, and the other factors named. Thus identification describes any or all of the sharings that are possible because of the consubstantial elements in our model. Identification can, then, be used as a shorthand

[4] Kenneth Burke treats the significant change between the therefore and the nevertheless in his *Grammar of Motives*, op. cit., esp. pp. 62–69, 74–79, 112–113.

description of the process of communication: *communication as identification.*

When the waiter calls to the chef, "One ham and cheese on a roll!" an identification is created between the speaker and the listener; they are more alike than before since both now know that the sandwich has been ordered. This identification probably will lead to another; for example, the chef will soon signal that the sandwich is ready. On the other hand, the chef could understand the order but detest the waiter's tone and stalk off the job; identification is created on one level, but the overall result is separation. Identification on one level need not bring more and more identifications: the advertiser uses snob appeal, the prospective customer notices the attempted tug toward a higher social standing but refuses to take the bait; the girl gets her boyfriend to comprehend that she believes he is not for her; the doctor communicates a lack of sympathy, and the patient goes elsewhere.

Vince's speech furnishes an example of identifications leading to other identifications. (Although we could examine the identifications on the level of sentences or even words, we instead will refer to larger units of Vince's communication.) In his first two paragraphs Vince previews the central theme of his speech, and he indicates the order he intends to use in developing this theme. The identifications created facilitate later identifications because Vince's theme is brought into clear focus, and the order for his theme's development can be grasped easily. The identifications created in Vince's first two paragraphs are instrumental identifications: They act as means for reaching further identifications. A large percentage of the identifications humans create are instrumental ones.

Vince arranges the three major incidents of his speech (President Kennedy's death, the young girl's death, and Grampa's death) in an order that allows more easily created identifications to be instrumental in creating a subsequent identification. President Kennedy's death was a public event, widely noticed and discussed. Vince can be confident that his receivers will be able to understand and empathize with his reactions to this man's death. The incident of the young girl's accidental death is sufficiently commonplace to permit Vince to expect this identification, also, to be relatively easy to create. A death in the family is a more rare, more private, and, in many ways, a more complex, difficult experience to talk about. By treating Grampa's death after the other two, Vince can rely on the identifications created through the familiar episodes to help create the more significant identification.

Vince and his receivers probably create a number of identifications and become more alike because of the information they share, but, of course, each continues to be a distinct individual. Two or more persons can create a great number of identifications and become more similar in beliefs, attitudes, values, and other facets; still, each person will be separate and unique. Human beings can continually have both the union and the diversity.

KINDS OF IDENTIFICATION

An identification is created when the robber points a gun and commands: "Give me your money!" Since armed robbery, too, is part of the ongoing process of communication in our culture, both parties know what the gun and command mean, and both can estimate what behaviors are likely to occur. Robber and victim coact, initially, as the first states the command while the other hears and interprets it. Both parties develop with this coaction, and they proceed to the next stage of the robbery, in which the victim probably gives up and the robber takes the money.

Identifications of the highly coercive kind take place despite the unwillingness of one of the parties. Such coactions give very limited choices to the unwillinging party and almost dictate the acceptance of an apparent loss while the coercing party profits (at least in the short run).

Coercive identifications need not be so crassly weighted toward the profit of one party at the expense of the other; for instance, the parent may insist that the child eat a helping of vegetables; when the child eats the vegetables, both parent and child are likely to gain. Furthermore, the proper amount of pressure over a time will bring beneficial results in eating habits, personal hygiene, piano playing, and other behaviors.

Elements of coercion can be found in many identifications. Vince and his classmates, for example, were relatively free in creating their identifications: they chose to join the class and to share what they shared; still, Vince's parents more than likely wanted him to do well in college, Vince probably needed course credits, he had an assignment to fulfill, and he doubtless had other limits on his freedom. And the same held for his classmates.

Since some elements of coercion can be discerned in many identifications, one cannot condemn a given identification just because it has coercive constituents; instead, one must judge whether the degree of coercion is appropriate given the persons, the setting, the purposes, and the other means available for reaching the desired identification.

Granting that coercive elements can be noted in many identifications, we can still distinguish between those identifications that are obviously forced on one of the parties, and those identifications that clearly rely more on free choice than on force. Throughout this book we focus on identifications that are created with relatively free choice by those involved.

Like the more coercive kind, relatively free identifications can benefit one or both of the creating parties. However, since the parties have relatively free choice, nonmutually beneficial identifications must be made to seem acceptable to the party who is being taken for a loss. The encyclopedia hustler, drilled in his pitch that presupposes an upward yearning in his prey, seeks a sizable commission from the "pennies" he asks that the buyer pay "to keep the set up to date." In *The Grapes of Wrath* Steinbeck portrays a used-car salesman who purposely spends time with the Okies because these simple-hearted folk will feel an obligation, stemming from the attention feigned, to buy the junk proffered. These examples sketch the profit-seeking "benefactor." We could all add many examples. The cost of such nonmutually beneficial identification extends beyond that incurred in the immediate transaction. Communication in general becomes suspect—a price too dear eventually for the individual and the community to pay.[5]

In another kind of nonmutually beneficial identification, the losing party is aware of the cost of the transaction yet shares, nevertheless, because of affection for the other, commitment to an ideal, or some other reason not intrinsic to this identification. Parent–child, teacher–student, as well as any number of other identifications may be of this knowingly nonmutually beneficial type. Since, at least for the time being, little comes in return to the primary creator of such identifications, this coactor is drained by the largely one-way process. No one should sustain such a flow continually without opportunity for replenishing; Plato's philosopher-kings were not asked to live that way, nor should the elementary school teacher of today. Another difficulty is that few have the stature to give to one who is behind without pontificating. This will be irritating. Furthermore, the one who takes the subsidiary role, if he does so consistently, will eventually be demeaned because self-expression and consequent validation are discouraged.[6]

Despite the potential dangers, each of us frequently must help create identifications that are known to be nonmutually beneficial. On some occasions or with certain coactors one will know that the identification is largely for the benefit of others. On other occasions or with other coactors the same person will become primarily a recipient as another willingly becomes the major giver. Often two or more persons will alternate in the roles of primary giver and receiver, depending

[5] For a similar point see Erik H. Erikson, *Childhood and Society*, 2nd ed., New York, Norton, 1963, p. 418.

[6] See Kim Griffin, "Social Alienation by Communication Denial," *Quarterly Journal of Speech*, **56** (1970), 347–357.

on time, place, and topic. We should be willing and able to take either role; yet everyone should guard against giving too much or too little.

Ideally, identifications should be the kind that are mutually beneficial; both parties grow as ideas and selves of each are examined, valued, held or changed. Robert Frost attempted this kind of communication with his neighbor in "Mending Wall."[7] He wrote, "Something there is that doesn't love a wall," and he believed that this "something" was the urge for togetherness, which "makes gaps even two can pass abreast." Frost hoped to explore this insight with someone else. If possible, the poet would like his neighbor to see and say "for himself"; that would be mutually beneficial, instead of Frost dispensing to the neighbor. The two would become the "less than two/But more than one" of Frost's "Meeting and Passing." But the neighbor refuses to examine walls; consequently, he fails to evaluate Frost or himself. He secludes himself in darkness behind his father's dictum: "Good fences make good neighbors." Not all attempts at mutually beneficial identification are successful, yet all persons must seek this ideal kind of identification, for in each human being, "Something there is that doesn't love a wall."

Another something in each person—the unique individuality of every human being—ensures that some walls will remain.[8] The perpetual many–one tension, to be unique and yet together, endures as the basic premise of interpersonal communication. Given togetherness (the one or the consubstantial), identifications can be created; given uniqueness (the many or the autonomous), identifications may be created again and again:

Once the realization is accepted that even between the closest human beings infinite distances continue to exist, a wonderful

[7] See Edward C. Lathem, ed., *The Poetry of Robert Frost,* New York, Holt, Rinehart & Winston, 1969. Used throughout courtesy of the estate of Robert Frost and Jonathan Cape Limited, London.

[8] Frost made this point with some care in "Mending Wall," and he spoke directly to it in "Triple Bronze."

living side by side can grow up, if they succeed in loving the distance between them which makes it possible for each to see the other whole against the sky.[9]

QUESTIONS FOR THOUGHT AND DISCUSSION

1. Prepare a list of communication situations that you believe were "nonmutually beneficial." How do these compare with others that you believe were "mutually beneficial"?
2. Think about aspects of yourself that contribute in an important way to the person you see yourself as being. How could you share one of these aspects with your classmates?
3. Study Mario Marchese's speech in Chapter 3 and Juanita Coffee's speech in Chapter 4. What means do these students use in seeking greater commonality with their coactors?
4. What coercive elements exist in communication between teachers and students? How do these affect their communication?
5. To what extent is the presence of violence in our society an indication of communication failure?

SUGGESTED READINGS

Burke, Kenneth, *A Grammar of Motives*, Berkeley, University of California Press, 1969.

Burke, Kenneth, *A Rhetoric of Motives*, Berkeley, University of California Press, 1969.

Miller, Gerald, R., *Speech Communication*, Indianapolis, Bobbs-Merrill, 1966.

Shannon, Claude E., and Warren Weaver, *The Mathematical Theory of Communication*, Urbana, University of Illinois Press, 1964.

[9] Rainer Maria Rilke, *Letters*.

2 the classical bases for improving communication

Chapter 1 introduced our view of communication as identification and indicated that later chapters would present a fuller treatment of various facets of our model for interpersonal communication. Chapter 2 is also an introductory chapter; it allies our study to a traditional method for improving human communication.

For centuries, human beings, especially certain scholars who studied the area, have sought to avoid communication failures by improving communication skills. Underlying this study has been the conviction that communication is not a natural, uncomplicated activity; instead, it is a complex, coactive process. Communicators must choose the correct means to achieve the desired identifications, and to choose intelligently requires careful study and practice.

As the Greeks and Romans developed instruction in effective communication, they set out five major areas for consideration. These areas came to be known as the five rhetorical canons: (1) *invention*—finding ideas to communicate and choosing among them; (2) *organization*—arranging the ideas chosen; (3) *style*—encoding ideas into symbols; (4) *memory*—maintaining control over the ideas, the organization, perhaps even over the exact signs and signals that have been selected;[1] (5) *delivery*—presenting orally or otherwise, the product of the previous canons. Each canon can be viewed as a relatively distinct area for communicators to

---

[1] The fourth canon, memory, is frequently dropped from consideration. We are setting no new course, then, by limiting our coverage to a few small sections in Chapter 9 while treating certain modes of delivery.

master in the search for better and better means to achieve identifications.

Breaking down communication into these components is a useful step in learning; one must keep in mind, however, that in any communication all the parts are intertwined, thus delivery elements cannot be separated completely from the symbolization, and so on throughout the canons. For example, Vince's ideas (invention) cannot be separated completely from the verbal (style) and nonverbal (delivery) encoding of them. Organization within and among Vince's sentences is complexly interrelated with aspects that would usually be placed in other canon.

We shall use a familiar example to illustrate the rhetorical canons. Picture a college student, Joe, with too much term left at the end of his money. Joe would like aid from his father back home. The thesis of Joe's communication with Dad will be: "Dad, you should send me more money!" Joe's appeal for further funding could take many forms. He has a lot of information readily apparent to him: among his deprivations he notes his diminished love life, his curtailed eating choices, his immobile wheels, and his depleted wardrobe; Joe thinks wearily of creditors, fondly of the generally assumed obligation of fathers to offspring, and remorsefully of the shoddy stewardship accorded the last dole from the family pocketbook. Many other items of information might be considered, but the foregoing serve to indicate that Joe is working to bring forth potential bases for his communication with Dad. Joe now must choose among the available pieces of information; he knows he would not do well to discuss last week's poker losses. Joe selects the starkness of his present existence as a useful means of touching on parental sympathies. He decides to underscore, not too boldly of course, the father–son relationship, thus intimating a father–son obligation. He also believes that a direct mention of his bankruptcy is needed; in a more oblique appeal, Dad might miss this crucial issue (or feel too comfortable in appearing to miss it). In trying to find information and choose which items to use in seeking the wanted identification, Joe has labored in the province of invention.

Extending the example to the second rhetorical canon, organization, Joe now thinks of the placement or arrangement of his three points. Should the order be: sonship, stark existence, bankrupt state? This is possible, as are a number of other arrangements. Joe decides that bankruptcy, bleakness, sonship is the best organization to use.

Now the action moves to canon three, style. Joe has decided to send a telegram (primarily a delivery matter that must be considered later in the canon scheme). The telegram medium limits the number of words to be used.[2] Such limitations are often undesired, but on certain occasions, they can be grasped as advantages. Joe's past indiscretions, he hopes, can be hidden judiciously in the shorthand summary that directly tells his financial plight: "No mon." Joe's yearnings for better vibrations, not all of which would reflect well under parental scrutiny, are captured discreetly in "No fun." And the gentle prod to parental obligation is administered neatly by signing off: "Your Son." Joe's little poem

> No mon,
> No fun,
> Your Son.

is, of course, a familiar lament. Joe is probably right in expecting that his father will be well aware of the thesis implied: "Dad, you should send me more money!"

The last canon, delivery, often plays a most important role in communication; this role will tend to be less significant in a delivery mode like the telegram than in the face-to-face oral mode; nevertheless, some elements Joe might have considered are worth remarking here. Delivering his message

---

[2] The choice of the telegraph medium is an encoding in its own right. It connotes urgency and has other factors that are consonant with Joe's appeal; we discuss this further in Chapter 9.

by telegram is quick; hence urgency is suggested by the channel chosen, and Joe hopes his father will recognize the need for a rapid response. The telephone probably would be faster and more intimate, but on this subject Joe prefers the distance. An open line would allow for, even require, amplification, and Joe is uncomfortable with the details he would have to add. Since the telegram may get results with minimum revelation and risk, Joe figures he should try to get by with this delivery device.

As you probably know, the old story we have been embellishing to illustrate the rhetorical canons has an apparently unhappy outcome. Joe's father wires back:

> Too bad,
> So sad,
> Your Dad.

Foiled, Joe tries to figure out where he went wrong. Should he have sent an airmail letter with his poem etched in white on a black background? Perhaps the telegram was too novel and the intended urgency was grasped instead as flippancy, and the identification created by him and his dad became lighthearted rather than serious, as Joe had hoped. After weighing this and assessing still other channels, Joe decides that the telegram was probably all right as a delivery choice.

Now the post mortem can move to the next canon, style. Joe wonders whether the cuteness of his iambic monometer triplet is a flaw. Dad just did not take the little ditty seriously; instead, Dad saw it as a tossing of the gauntlet and gleefully sharpened his pencil to reply in kind. The mimicking of Joe's form gives some weight to this possibility. Joe decides that he will do well in future appeals not to fudge over a point by being flippant and cryptic.

Organization seems to have been sufficiently clear. Dad had no trouble following it to launch a point-by-point rejoinder. Perhaps the organization is *too* clear, suggesting cool, manufactured crafting rather than the agonized utterance of a son in distress. Joe judges that the possible flaws he could find in placement are inconsequential. The undesired identification cannot be blamed on arrangement.

Invention heads the canons. Joe looks ruefully at the relatively rapid and insensitive choices he made. He should have thought more about how well his father knew the justifiable expenses and the sufficiency of the allowance given. He certainly should have been more sensitive to his father's wish for a prudent son. Joe surmises that any future appeal for funds must rely less heavily on his own credibility in the area of supply and demand; he has spent much of his credit on the subject of finances by coming yet again to ask for more. Joe sees that he will have to take a much harder course, now, by confessing past errors and giving a strict account of planned allocations for the new gift. Perhaps through Dad's forgiveness and Joe's improved performance, a good relationship can be rebuilt.

As we leave our extended illustration, we pause to stress a final point. While attempting to improve communication, one often tinkers with delivery when adjustment of style would bring the desired end more efficiently. Long, difficult sentences usually are easier to improve in style than to master in delivery. Virtuosity in vocal and visual elements can hardly cover weakness in wording. Similarly, some quick repairs in organization will save much grief over tortuous transitions and other forms of aimless verbiage in the style. A sure sense of where one is going and what are the right paths will make selecting the appropriate style a far easier task. And, more importantly, strong foundation work in the canon of invention will give the other canons easier, more worthwhile roles. In the finding and choosing of appeals, when one shows sufficient sensitivity to self, others, and the subject, this strength is likely to infuse the efforts made in the other canons. Putting primary effort into invention, then, yields a significant multiplier effect throughout the canons. This does not mean that effects cannot arise from delivery to influence the other canons. Surely this does occur; but the major currents of influence usually flow the other way, from invention to delivery. This indicates that one should parcel out energy accordingly.

Starting with invention and proceeding through organization, style, and delivery the communicators should look into each canon to see what it has to offer for understanding and improving the process of identification. The four chapters of Part Two consider various invention factors. Chapters 3, 4, and 5, respectively, examine consubstantial elements of the Byker–Anderson model: the ability to reason; gregariousness; and beliefs, attitudes, values, pleasures, and pains, as common motivational factors. The fourth invention chapter discusses means for coping with individual differences (the many or the autonomous). Part III has three chapters, one each for organization, style, and delivery, and each one treats its counterpart in the consubstantial realm of the model: organization—ordering tendencies, style—the verbal code, and delivery—the nonverbal code.

QUESTIONS FOR THOUGHT AND DISCUSSION

1. How would you rewrite Joe's message to make it more effective?
2. Why would invention usually be the most important step in preparing a communication?
3. Study Vince's speech in Chapter 1. What are some of the choices Vince makes in regard to each of the canons discussed in this chapter?

SUGGESTED READINGS

Aristotle, *The Rhetoric*.

Benson, Thomas. W., and Michael H. Prosser, *Readings in Classical Rhetoric*, Bloomington, Indiana University Press, 1972.

Plato, *The Phaedrus*.

Part two
FOUNDATIONS FOR IDENTIFICATION

The foundations for identification inhere in the canon of invention. Aristotle split invention into three different kinds of appeal. (1) Communicators could compile and select among appeals to reason: *logos*. (2) Communicators could seek and use appeals to the gregarious nature of human beings: *ethos* (*Rhetoric* 1356a). (3) A similar process of gathering and choosing could be employed for appeals to the emotions: *pathos*.

Although this division of proofs has been widely used, we will not give *pathos* separate treatment. Unlike Aristotle, we do not see the human being split into separate rational and emotional faculties. This is not to say that emotions are not present and influential; on the contrary, emotion permeates all appeals. One can be most rational and emotional at the same time, as, for instance, a mathematician who is suffused with ecstasy over the precise logicality of a newly demonstrated proof. Since all appeals may be tinctured with emotion, we believe it is best not to distinguish *pathos* as an independent grouping for appeals.

Part of Aristotle's division of proofs is, however, reflected in Chapter 3 and 4. Chapter 3, "Identification via Argument," deals with what Aristotle calls *logos*. We want to show that human beings reason in rather similar patterns. In Kenneth Burke's terms, humans are consubstantial in their ability to reason; thus the mastery of coherent reasoning provides a valuable means for achieving identification.

Chapter 4, "Identification via Attraction," presents our thoughts in the area of what is called *ethos*. We try to demonstrate that human beings need, value, and are attracted to one another; this is in line, of course, with the view that men are gregarious. A better understanding of identification via attraction provides another strong means for creating identifications.

In Chapter 5 we depart from Aristotle's classification of appeals and focus on "Understanding Human Motivation: An Aid to Identification." Here we investigate the motivational framework that influences human behavior. Since this framework is shared by all (consubstantial), an understanding of it will aid in creating identifications.

Chapter 6, "Recognizing Individual Differences: A Step Toward Identification," emphasizes the uniqueness of each human being. We show that recognizing and adjusting to individual differences are helpful steps toward identification.

❓ identification via argument

Since human beings share the ability to reason, one way for communicators to create identification is to offer to one another communications that seem to be reasonable. Reason being a generally held and highly important attribute, communicators who improve their ability to reason should find a significant improvement in their chances for creating desired identifications.

TOULMIN'S MODEL

Stephen Toulmin provides a system for studying the sort of reasoning people use in everyday communication.[1] In Toulmin's system communicators who seek identification via reasoning offer to share arguments with one another. In an argument some *claim* is present (either stated or implied) that one person hopes the other person will grant. When the two other basic parts of Toulmin's description of an argument are set forth, the claim will be founded on a *datum* and arrived at from the datum by way of a *warrant*.

We can define the claim as the new (or reinforced old) belief that one of the coactors seeks to have accepted. The datum is the ground or foundation for the claim. The person offering the argument thinks the other will accept this datum (data, if more than one item of foundational material is given) as a legitimate starting point from which to reason toward the claim. The warrant is an inference license. It

[1] Stephen E. Toulmin, *The Uses of Argument*, Cambridge, Cambridge University Press, 1958. Part III, "The Layout of Arguments," is particularly relevant.

permits the passage from datum to claim. The datum is not identical with the claim. If it were, no reasoning would be used because nothing new would arise. If no jump to something new occurs, one has observation or enumeration, but no reasoning. With datum and claim separate, the warrant must be accepted as a viable bridge between them.

When datum, warrant, and claim are laid out spatially to make it easier to follow the reasoning, the result is Toulmin's model. This chapter contains examples of Toulmin's model. To start, we turn to the first model that Vince sketched as he prepared his speech.

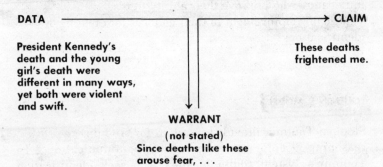

DATA ───▶ **CLAIM**

President Kennedy's
death and the young
girl's death were
different in many ways,
yet both were violent
and swift.

These deaths
frightened me.

WARRANT
(not stated)
Since deaths like these
arouse fear, . . .

Recall that Vince sought instrumental identifications in the President Kennedy and young girl segments of his speech (see p. 17). The model helped Vince clarify and test the argument for himself, thus giving him confidence that his listeners would understand and accept the preliminary argument. These aids show the model's relevance to the key factors that communicators should consider in constructing an argument: (1) the argument should accurately present the position that one of the coactors wishes to take; (2) the argument should do the best possible job of making that position understandable and acceptable to the other coactor.

The Model Is A Tool

Vince's speech in Chapter 1 reveals that the actual communication is considerably more elaborate on the Kennedy
and young girl points than is Vince's Toulmin model.
Models could be sketched for components of the speech
smaller than Vince's first model represents (then Vince
would have had many more models than the five he
sketched; we will reproduce the other four shortly). Vince,
however, uses Toulmin's model to display and test his reasoning for the major identifications he wants his coactors to
help him create. This is as it should be. Toulmin models can
help communicators construct and test communications, but
the models should not become a burden, which could readily
occur if pressed into service at all conceivable times and
places.

As tools for improving ability in creating identifications,
Toulmin models help communicators ask relevant questions
such as: Just what am I asking someone or is someone
asking me to accept? Is the datum (or data) the best possible
grounding for the claim? Would it help to have several
datum–warrant structures that yield the same claim? Is the
warrant a viable bridge? Would another warrant work more
readily?

Note that Vince displays his warrant in the model but does
not state it in the speech. The model, as a tool, helps one
judge what should be made explicit in the presentation and
what one should allow the coactor to supply (this use of the
model is discussed in a subsequent section of the chapter). If
communicators are sensitive to what each coactor should
supply, the identifications created are more likely to be
mutually beneficial than they otherwise would be.

Finally, this tool should be used flexibly as far as arrangement is concerned. Arguments will not always be
presented most effectively in the datum–warrant–claim
order. Claims or warrants can be stated first, and the
placement of the rest can vary. The determining organizational factor should not be the order in which the model is

laid out on paper; instead, the interwoven requirements of the coactors, the subject, the occasion, and the goals should govern the arrangement. Mastering the model as a tool, its users can act creatively within the extant scene to gain the desired ends.

The Rest of Vince's Models

In addition to the model already discussed, Vince laid out the following four models as he was preparing and testing his communication:

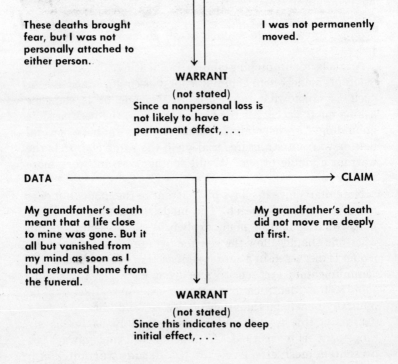

DATA ──────────────────────────────────────→ CLAIM

These deaths brought fear, but I was not personally attached to either person.

I was not permanently moved.

↓

WARRANT
(not stated)
Since a nonpersonal loss is not likely to have a permanent effect, . . .

DATA ──────────────────────────────────────→ CLAIM

My grandfather's death meant that a life close to mine was gone. But it all but vanished from my mind as soon as I had returned home from the funeral.

My grandfather's death did not move me deeply at first.

↓

WARRANT
(not stated)
Since this indicates no deep initial effect, . . .

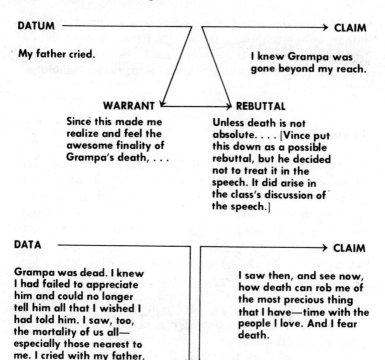

DATUM ——————————————————————→ CLAIM

My father cried.

I knew Grampa was
gone beyond my reach.

WARRANT ←————————→ REBUTTAL

Since this made me
realize and feel the
awesome finality of
Grampa's death, . . .

Unless death is not
absolute. . . . [Vince put
this down as a possible
rebuttal, but he decided
not to treat it in the
speech. It did arise in
the class's discussion of
the speech.]

DATA ——————————————————————→ CLAIM

Grampa was dead. I knew
I had failed to appreciate
him and could no longer
tell him all that I wished I
had told him. I saw, too,
the mortality of us all—
especially those nearest to
me. I cried with my father.

I saw then, and see now,
how death can rob me of
the most precious thing
that I have—time with the
people I love. And I fear
death.

WARRANT

(not stated)
Since the realizations
and the crying are proof
that I know and fear
death's power to rob me
of the most precious
things in my life, . . .

You may have noted that Vince's arguments are not foolproof; they are debatable. Few everyday arguments are
absolutely certain. Observe, carefully, that argument models
for daily communication are not primarily concerned with
strict logicality. The crucial issue in communication is
whether or not the coactors find the arguments to be
reasonable.

Perhaps the term argument has been used in a way that
seems strange. As we use the term, we obviously do not have

in mind a verbal altercation between two or more persons; rather, we use the word argument to denote, minimally, the basic three parts of the model: a claim is made for belief; datum as foundation and warrant as bridge are available.

TOULMIN'S COMPLETE MODEL

Vince's penultimate model has a *rebuttal* feature in addition to the basic three elements. Using Toulmin's system, a communicator can look at an argument and judge what considerations would set aside the progress from datum through warrant to claim. Considerations that could short-circuit the argument can be laid out in the rebuttal position. With the rebuttals foreseen, the communicator can decide: (1) that the rebuttal(s) are so strong that the argument should not even be broached; (2) that the rebuttal(s) are so unlikely or so weak that they need not be given further notice; (3) that the rebuttal(s) can be left alone until someone else raises them, whereupon they can then be discussed (Vince does this with the rebuttal to his fourth model); (4) that the rebuttal(s) should be treated on the spot because they can be overcome and the argument made acceptable.

Perhaps with the third, and rather certainly with the fourth option, the communicator should prepare *backing* for the warrant as a means for overcoming the rebuttals. Backing strengthens the warrant in an attempt to ward off rebuttals. Put in electrician's terms, backing attempts to insulate the warrant against a potential short circuit at the rebuttal stage.

The possibility of a tenable rebuttal leads to a need for the sixth and last feature of Toulmin's complete model: the *qualifier* (Q). Qualifiers are inserted in the claim, and they are frequently expressed by "probably," "more than likely," "quite certainly," and "pretty sure." They can run from an imprecise yet important limitation expressed by way of a

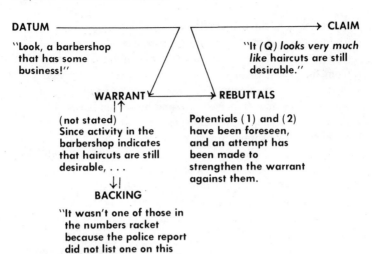

DATUM ⎯⎯⎯⎯⎯⎯⎯⎯⎯⎯⎯⎯⎯⎯⎯⎯⎯⎯⎯⎯→ CLAIM

"Look, a barbershop
that has some
business!"

"It *(Q) looks very much
like* haircuts are still
desirable."

WARRANT ←⎯⎯⎯⎯⎯⎯→ REBUTTALS
   ⌐↑

(not stated)
Since activity in the
barbershop indicates
that haircuts are still
desirable, . . .

Potentials (1) and (2)
have been foreseen,
and an attempt has
been made to
strengthen the warrant
against them.

   ↓⌐
BACKING

"It wasn't one of those in
the numbers racket
because the police report
did not list one on this
street, and the one with
the bar is not in this
town."

Here, as backing, the father argues that the activity can not be taken as a sign of numbers action or a sign of drinking; thus, by the method of residues, the signification asserted in the warrant is made more certain. However, since two rebuttals are considered, plus the likelihood that several other rebuttals could be advanced, the father has sufficient reason for hedging the claim with a qualifier. The realization that the backing given for the warrant is not airtight could be another motivation for the qualifier.

For further illustration of the complete Toulmin model, we turn to another student's speech, presented by Mario Marchese in the opening round of speeches in his class. Mario, like Vince, had been asked to share an aspect of himself that he believed contributed importantly to the kind of person he was. Mario delivered the speech extemporaneously, and the following transcript was taken from the tape recording.

It always happened during the late winter months. Our   1
supply of dried pork sausage would run out, and as we ate   2
the last few pieces, I used to think back to hog butchering   3

day when we had plenty of meat and wine for everyone.   4
And how we had made the sausage ourselves and hung it out   5
to dry from poles suspended from the ceiling of our two-   6
room flat. Now, though, it was late January or early Feb-   7
ruary and the meat supply was running out, and all we had   8
left to eat was macaroni and corn and bread and beans. And   9
I remember getting so sick of beans that just the idea now of 10
eating beans for supper almost makes me sick.   11

We grew the beans and corn and the grain to make the   12
flour for the bread and macaroni on a little 5-acre farm   13
which we had. We worked this farm so well that it provided   14
enough goods for subsistence for 12 of us. Now around this   15
time when the meat had run out, my brothers and I would   16
always get together and decide to get the traps out of storage 17
and do what we had done every year since I can re-   18
member—since I was a little kid. We would dress as warmly   19
as we could, clad in army overcoats and boots, and we'd   20
venture outside each carrying maybe a dozen traps, and   21
we'd all go our separate ways to set the traps in our own fa- 22
vorite little spot. I set my traps very carefully, just as my 23
brothers had taught me to do.   24

When you set a little copper trap, you have to be very   25
careful to hide all the copper parts with the snow so that the 26
only thing that's showing is the little piece of bread crust on 27
the trigger. And when you hide the copper parts, you have   28
to make sure that the snow looks as if it has just freshly   29
fallen, instead of looking as if something was hidden   30
underneath. And if you're not very careful, if you don't   31
cover the traps very thoroughly, the sparrows won't bite.   32

I always made sure that all my traps were set well, but no   33
matter how well I set them, it always seemed to take hours   34
and hours of waiting in the cold to catch enough sparrows to   35
make a decent dinner. You see, you had to catch at least 10   36
or 15 sparrows before you'd have enough meat to make it   37
worth the plucking and the cleaning and the cooking. And   38
even after you did all that, you know, what little meat there 39
was wasn't really a feast, but at least it satisfied the ap-   40
petite or hunger for some meat protein.   41

Now the kind of poverty that leads people to eat sparrows 42
is the kind of poverty I experienced when I was a small 43
child in a small town in Italy—in the southern mountains of 44
Italy. And I believe it was this poverty which is directly 45
responsible for a peculiar characteristic in my personality, 46
and that is that I just insanely, absolutely abhor seeing 47
meat go to waste. For example, whenever I eat a steak or a 48
porkchop, or any piece of meat, I always make certain that 49
I get every single bit of meat off the bone, you know. And I 50
don't do it consciously. I don't consciously think that, well, 51
I have to eat every piece of meat because when I was a child 52
I was deprived. I just do it out of habit. It's a habit that is 53
so ingrained in me from when I was a child and didn't have 54
meat that I just do it, you know, unconsciously. And I'm so · 55
meticulous about this that on more than one occasion my 56
wife has commented that I didn't leave enough meat on the 57
bones on my plate to feed one skinny cat. 58

I remember one time after dinner, my wife was clearing 59
off some plates, and she was just about to throw out a half 60
of porkchop into the garbage, and I got so vehemently 61
angry, and yelled at her so, that she wouldn't speak to me 62
for half a day. 63

I even get angry in restaurants when I see people, you 64
know, leave a half a steak or a meatball on their plate or 65
tray, and I know that that meat is going to be thrown away 66
in the garbage. And I think back to how I would have 67
savored that piece of meat on a cold February evening when 68
I was eating beans and bread. 69

I get very ridiculous about it because I even get angry at 70
commercials on TV. Cat food and dog food commercials, 71
you know, when the announcer comes on TV and tells me 72
that Alpo is made of 100% meat. And I think that dogs and 73
cats eat better in this country than I used to eat when I was 74
back in Italy, and they eat better than many kids 75
throughout the whole world who don't even have sparrows to 76
trap in the winter time. 77

Sometimes, when I think back on some of the ridiculous 78
things I've said and done as a result of this obsession, I have 79

to laugh at myself, but I know that I'll never change. I know   80
it's a real part of me, and I'll always be this way.   81

Mario appeared to his affluent classmates as a handsome, husky contemporary. Some knew he had been a member of the football team. Nothing they had seen or heard of him prior to this speech had prepared them for the unusual narrative of the first 41 lines.

Little in these first lines fits with the life known by the ordinary American college student; hence the story cannot be tested by laying it next to past experience to see if it squares, and thus appears probable. Still the material presented is readily grasped as plausible. Elements in it make sense, and consistency is apparent.

Although the effort may seem to be inappropriate, we can sketch models for various parts of the first 41 lines of Mario's speech. For example:

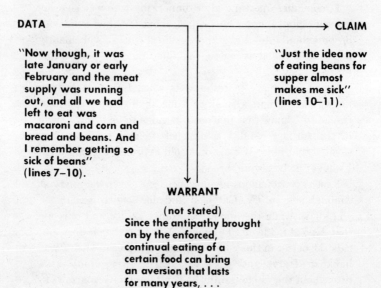

DATA ─────────────────────────────→ **CLAIM**

"Now though, it was late January or early February and the meat supply was running out, and all we had left to eat was macaroni and corn and bread and beans. And I remember getting so sick of beans" (lines 7–10).

"Just the idea now of eating beans for supper almost makes me sick" (lines 10–11).

WARRANT

(not stated) Since the antipathy brought on by the enforced, continual eating of a certain food can bring an aversion that lasts for many years, . . .

We are all so well aware of the warrant from experience at home, restaurant, or college dining hall that Mario does well not to make it explicit. In fact, Mario probably did not pause while outlining his speech to frame these sentences in model form. The same holds for the remainder of the first 41 lines.

Mario is reliving a part of his life that he vividly recalls. And the order evident in the treatment appears to come more from the coherence observed in the flow of events than from Mario's conscious testing of models at the time of composing this speech.

This raises an important side issue about topic selection. If you communicate about a subject on which your experience is extensive, you are usually able to demonstrate a coherence and sensitivity that cannot easily be shown when handling less familiar material. This is because living with and thinking about the familiar subject have brought a clarity and touch that is very difficult to impose in haste on the new. Stated differently, the modeling activity in the familiar subject area has taken place over a period of time and has produced, perhaps frequently tested, an effective communication that now only needs adapting to the specific occasion; but the modeling of the new material must take place in a much shorter time, usually cannot be debugged by trial runs, and thus appears in fairly raw form.

We would argue, then, that Mario's ability to find order in his experience and his disciplined reporting in the first 41 lines show reasoning at work in previous stages of thought and communication. Thus even though the story does not at first seem probable, one is not moved to doubt its plausibility, either because of internal inconsistencies or because of clumsiness in narration.

Even in the opening narrative, therefore, Mario has arguments working for him as he seeks identification. The arguments may be highly automatized; still they are arguments. We could expand more of them into models, but the effort would be gratuitous; the major impetus for going along with Mario's opening narrative does not come from the individual arguments or their conjunction. (Fortunately, these arguments, as interwoven, ally themselves with rather than against the primary proof?) One goes along with Mario's plausible opening primarily because of a reservoir of trust in human beings. Mario can draw upon this reservoir.

We now jump ahead to the subject matter for Chapter 4, to lay out and discuss this model:

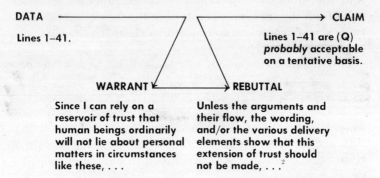

DATA ⎯⎯⎯⎯⎯⎯⎯⎯⎯⎯⎯⎯⎯⎯⎯⎯⎯⎯⎯⎯➤ CLAIM

Lines 1–41.

Lines 1–41 are (Q) *probably* acceptable on a tentative basis.

WARRANT ⟵⎯⎯⎯⎯⎯⎯⎯➤ REBUTTAL

Since I can rely on a reservoir of trust that human beings ordinarily will not lie about personal matters in circumstances like these, . . .

Unless the arguments and their flow, the wording, and/or the various delivery elements show that this extension of trust should not be made, . . .[2]

Without this reservoir to rely on, the communicator could hardly begin. With care, the reservoir can be kept open, the extension of trust justified, and the same or a better trust fund left for another to rely on. Without care, the reservoir may be closed off; or it may be misused and drained, thus hindering those who later need its warranting power.

With the tentative truth of lines 1–41 granted as a foundation, Mario can build the argument he wishes to establish. Mario was using the following model:

[2] Mario did not state the rebuttals, but he showed his awareness of them by the care with which he forestalled each one.

DATA ──► **CLAIM**

Lines 1–41. Lines 42–45 summarize the earlier material and locate the setting in southern Italy. (Once the setting is provided, the narrative becomes much more plausible.)

"I just insanely, absolutely abhor seeing meat go to waste." (Mario states this in his warrant and does not need to restate it here.)

WARRANT ◄────────────────► **REBUTTAL**

"I believe it was this poverty which is directly responsible for a peculiar characteristic in my personality, and that is that I just insanely, absolutely abhor seeing meat go to waste" (lines 45–48).

(foreseen)
Unless time spent in the abundance of our culture erodes the mental set left by childhood scarcity, . . .

BACKING

All the meat off the bones (lines 48–50, 55–58). Angry with wife about the leftover half porkchop (lines 59–63). Angry in restaurants (lines 64–67). Angry at TV commercials (lines 70–77). These are the effects of a habit that was ingrained early, is still operating, and will always be with me (lines 50–55, 78–81).

Mario's warrant is a causal one. He foresees a rebuttal in the possibility that the effect may have worn off. The backing he gives his warrant relies, again, on an auditor's taking Mario's word for the truth of the examples cited. If the backing is accepted, the proof can flow from the warrant through the obstruction of the foreseen rebuttal to the claim.

Mario's claim is made forcefully, without qualification. This seems to be justified on the basis of the data, warrant, and backing he provides. Perhaps qualification creeps in with the frequent use of "you know," the slipping into the indefinite "you," and the charge of ridiculousness in lines 70 and 78–80. Given the coherence of the argument and the believability of the claim, the "qualifying tone" of these parts appears inappropriate.

As intimated in the paragraphs immediately following Mario's speech, building and testing arguments is a commonplace, ongoing activity. People constantly prepare and examine arguments in connection with personal revelations as well as with all sorts of other affairs. The consubstantial ability to reason guarantees that the study of argument in this chapter is not an unfamiliar venture.

Thus laying out arguments in the form of Toulmin models does not initiate one into the use of new forms; rather, the modeling enables the student to examine, probably with more care than is customary, the reasoning that one offers, or is offered, as a means for creating identifications. Careful study of Toulmin's model and disciplined practice with it should improve a person's ability to understand the ordinary scheme for human reasoning (datum through warrant to claim), and such study and practice also should improve one's ability to see how different persons can produce different arguments, because differing experiences and viewpoints are accompanied by variety in data, warrants, rebuttals, backing, claims, and qualifiers. In short, by studying reasoning through the use of Toulmin's model, a person gains a fuller, more productive appreciation of the one and the many in human communication. Having taken apart the process of everyday reasoning and thereby gained a higher level of insight, having practiced at this higher level and thereby improved actual performance, communicators thereafter stand a better chance to create mutually beneficial identifications.

Extending Toulmin's Model

An extension of Toulmin's model allows us to consider a rebuttal to the datum. When the father cajoles, "Look, a barbershop that has some business," the son might snatch away the foundation of the argument with the rebuttal: "Mom sure was right about you needing new glasses; it looked like a beauty salon to me."

Previous questioning of his eyesight or a quick facility in estimating rebuttals would forewarn the father of the son's potential rejoinder. As with the rebuttals to the warrant, the father probably has the choice of allowing his son to state the rebuttal to the datum or trying to head off such a statement with backing for the datum. If the father chooses the latter course both for this rebuttal to the datum and for the two he foresees to the warrant, he would say something like this: "Look, a barbershop that has some business! And don't quibble about my eyesight; I got new lenses in my glasses a few days ago. By the way, it wasn't one of those barbershops in the numbers racket because the police report did not list one on this street. And the one with the bar is not in this town." With abbreviation of some members, the model for this would be:

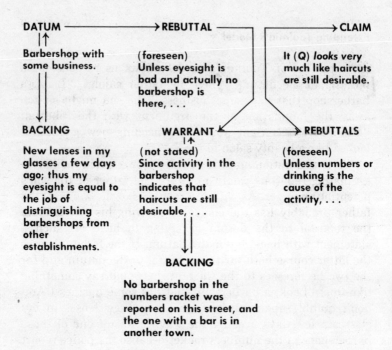

The connection of backing to warrant and datum is more complicated than the model makes it appear. The backing is actually an argument or chain of arguments that yields the supported part as a claim.[3] For instance, the following two-argument chain shows something of what is being argued in support of the warrant regarding the numbers racket.

[3] Toulmin does not develop the connection of backing to warrant; neither does he actually speak of rebuttal to the datum or of backing for it. He does, however, hint at the relationship between backing and warrant shown above, and the treatment we have given rebuttal and backing for the datum is also suggested (see pp. 106 and 97, respectively). The scheme we have given here is nearly identical to the epicheirema Cicero pronounces is the best way of framing a persuasive argument. See Marcus Tullius Cicero, *De Inventione*, trans. H. M. Hubbell, Cambridge, Mass., Harvard University Press, 1949, p. 111.

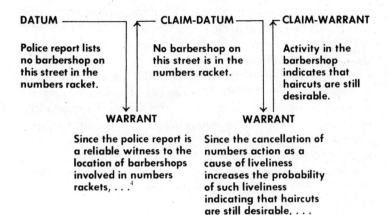

DATUM ────────────┐ ┌── CLAIM-DATUM ────────┐ ┌─CLAIM-WARRANT

Police report lists
no barbershop on
this street in the
numbers racket.

No barbershop on
this street is in the
numbers racket.

Activity in the
barbershop
indicates that
haircuts are still
desirable.

WARRANT   WARRANT

Since the police report is
a reliable witness to the
location of barbershops
involved in numbers
rackets, . . .[4]

Since the cancellation of
numbers action as a
cause of liveliness
increases the probability
of such liveliness
indicating that haircuts
are still desirable, . . .

A model or chain of models could be laid out for the
backing that cancels out the bar as a cause of the activity.
The same could be done for the backing of the datum. We
will not, however, set out these models. Even the rebuttal
features can be, and perhaps on occasion should be,
sketched as a model of three or more parts. The reader can
decide whether chains of models or the elaborated single
model is better for his own uses. The basic three parts of the
model are the primary building blocks. If one masters these,
the assembling of the chains or the elaborated model is not
an essentially new operation.

The modeling in the last several instances may have appeared rather complicated. The flow of reasoning in many
written and oral communications will be at least this complex. Fortunately, however, most communication activity occurs in the one-to-one or small group setting where the coactors can readily alternate roles of speaker and listener. We
would expect the father to decide to state just the datum,
get response from the son, and reply to it; thus the coac-

---

[4] One who hears an argument often has to rely on the other person's report
of his or another's observations. Then this person's capability as observer,
veracity as reporter, and intention as communicator become important
considerations. *Infra*, pp. 79–85.

tion would continue until the claim was granted at some probability level or set aside.

This segmentation of the total model makes each interchange less complicated; still, the parties should know how arguments hang together and what issues are at stake at the various junctures. Imagine that the son broaches the issue of a possible numbers racket and the father triumphantly plays a big card in the wrong suit by revealing the new lenses in his glasses. Perhaps the discussion will survive, but such misplays unnecessarily tax both understanding and affection. If one party continually executes misplays, others probably will turn away because they become discouraged in their communication efforts.

Repeating and extending an earlier point, the models help communicators ask relevant questions, such as: Just what am I asking someone or is someone asking me to believe? Should this be qualified? If so, how and how much? Is the datum or data the best possible grounding for the claim? Would it help to have several datum–warrant structures that yield the same claim? Is the warrant a viable bridge? Would another warrant work more readily? What are the possible rebuttals? Where do they fit? Which are too inconsequential to consider? Which merit real concern? Should these be addressed via backing or allowed to surface in feedback, being handled at that point? Are some rebuttals so strong that a person seems stupid in advancing the argument?

COACTIVE REASONING

When the father says, "Look, a barbershop that has some business!" the son can readily supply what his father means to add. For the father to have stated more would cast him as obtuse or dictatorial. He probably would be leaning too hard on his son, lessening the likelihood of a closeness that could be built through free interplay.

When someone offers only one or two parts of the argument because he expects another to furnish the rest, he is constructing what Aristotle calls an *enthymeme*. We can use Toulmin's model to lay out one of Aristotle's enthymemes:

DATUM ──────────────────────────────→ CLAIM

Dorieus was a victor in
the Olympic games.

(not stated)
Dorieus was given
a prize crown.

WARRANT

(not stated)
Since Olympic victors are
given prize crowns, . . .

If one wished to present this argument to a Greek audience in Aristotle's day, only the datum would have had to be made explicit. Aristotle comments: "It is needless to add that in the Olympic contest the prize is a crown; every one is aware of that."[5] Discussing enthymemes in another place, Aristotle says: "Our statement of what is obvious is mere garrulity."[6]

The two enthymemes we have examined both express just one term—the datum. Other enthymemes may state only the claim or the warrant. Picture two tired Republican campaign workers seeking comfort while looking out into the cold rain of a November election day. One says: "The Democrats' winning margin will be cut." The three part argument would be as follows:

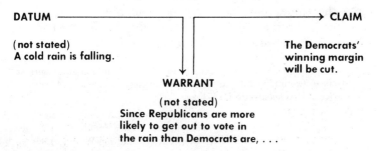

DATUM ──────────────────────────────→ CLAIM

(not stated)
A cold rain is falling.

The Democrats'
winning margin
will be cut.

WARRANT

(not stated)
Since Republicans are more
likely to get out to vote in
the rain than Democrats are, . . .

[5] *Rhetoric*, 1357a. Richard C. Jebb's translation, Cambridge, Cambridge University Press, 1909.
[6] Ibid., 1395b.

Knowing that both campaign workers are sure their candidates will lose, the speaker might risk giving just the warrant to carry the argument. The listener would hear: "Well, Republicans are more likely to get out to vote in the rain than Democrats are." And the reply, "Yes, they may get less than their 60 percent," would show that the implied claim had been understood.

When the auditor has to supply two parts of an argument, the probability of misconstruction or mystification is increased. Even if the argument is presented in complete form, receivers will be prone to misconstrue it. A tendency exists to see an argument as closer to or further from one's own position than it actually is.[7] And these misconstructions become more likely when two parts of the argument are left for the listener to supply. Also, the auditor who finds the argument hard to grasp will probably discount its value as far as logicality, interest, and other measures are concerned.[8]

On the other hand, one coactor can supply too much of the argument. This slights the other as a contributor to the identification. Therefore, the presenter of an argument has to avoid doing too little or too much.

Aristotle saw the same two pitfalls, and he advised that enthymemes not be too difficult or too superficial. Instead, they should "convey knowledge as soon as they are uttered" or be those "behind which the intelligence lags only a little."[9] Plato's requirements for the true art of persuasion fit into the same vein. The wise persuader will be well acquainted with the audience and the subject; thus the correct adaptation of message to audience can occur.[10]

[7] C. I. Hovland, O. J. Harvey, and M. Sherif, "Assimilation and Contrast Effects in Communication and Attitude Change," *Journal of Abnormal and Social Psychology,* **55** (1957), 242–252.

[8] William J. McGuire, "The Nature of Attitudes and Attitude Change." In Gardner Lindzey and Elliot Aronson, eds., *The Handbook of Social Psychology*, vol. 3, 2nd ed., Reading, Mass., Addison-Wesley, 1969, p. 221.

[9] *Rhetoric*, 1410b. Jebb's translation.

[10] *Phaedrus*, 262, 270 ff.

Although one-term enthymemes are not uncommon, two parts are more frequently used. The warrant is usually the unstated member. Fortunately, because a complex world often requires responses, we all have automatized many of the jumps from datum to claim, being able to respond in a split second to the stimuli received.

Unfortunately, however, it is possible to become so accustomed to taking the jump from datum to claim that one seldom or never stops to examine the warrant being used. A result is that in the study of Toulmin's model, the warrant is usually the most difficult part to master. Much more important, communicators often are less adept than they should be at constructing and evaluating messages, since they have failed to develop or maintain their ability to discriminate the warrants in their arguments. This is not to say that communicators should always seek to make their warrants explicit: To do this could often prove too time consuming and pedantic for the circumstances.

One studies the three basic parts of Toulmin's model, then, because the three-part model (like Aristotle's syllogism) delineates the steps used in reasoning. One need not, often should not, express all three parts when advancing a claim for belief. One must be sensitive to what a coactor should be allowed to supply. But even with a careful assessment of the needs and capabilities of others, one can be intelligent about what is made explicit and left implicit only if he or she is clearly aware of what the complete argument is. Aristotle concludes: "He who is best able to see how and from what elements a syllogism is produced will also be best skilled in the enthymeme."[11]

---

[11] *Rhetoric*, 1355a. W. Rhys Robert's translation, Oxford, Clarendon Press, 1952 reprint.

COMMON TYPES OF ARGUMENTS

The warrant used determines the type of argument. In this final section of the chapter we briefly discuss five different kinds of warrants. The discussion should aid communicators in their search for coherent links between data and claims.

Sign Argument

The warrant in a sign argument will say that the datum indicates the claim. Or the warrant will use other terminology to state that the claim is acceptable because the datum signifies it. The following sign argument could appear to be most reasonable to one person while being dangerous nonsense to another:

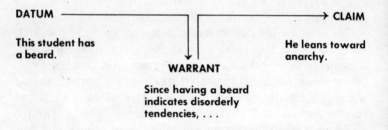

DATUM   → CLAIM

This student has a beard.

He leans toward anarchy.

WARRANT

Since having a beard indicates disorderly tendencies, . . .

And the one who rejects the foregoing series probably would accept this argument from sign:

DATUM   → CLAIM

This student has a beard.

This student is a male.

WARRANT

Since a beard is a sign of maleness.

Some may recall a rare instance of a "bearded lady," but most would grant the claim with no hesitation. A sign argument is accepted as coherent and reasonable, then, if the listener believes that the sign and what the sign is said to signify go together. Perhaps a certain person will see some ties as infallible; usually, however, the correlation will be viewed as a more or less probable one.

Classification Argument

The warrant in a classification argument will say that the datum equals or belongs in the same class with the claim. The often used syllogism concerning Socrates' mortality can easily be set out in model form as a classification:

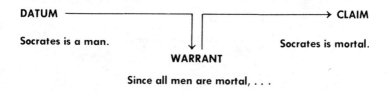

DATUM ─────────────────────────────────────→ CLAIM

Socrates is a man.   Socrates is mortal.

WARRANT

Since all men are mortal, . . .

You may have observed that the last sign argument modeled could be framed as a classification:

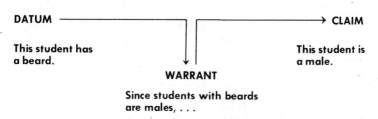

DATUM ─────────────────────────────────────→ CLAIM

This student has   This student is
a beard.   a male.

WARRANT

Since students with beards
are males, . . .

The kind of warrant used determines the type of argument. Frequently, a warrant can be reworked to build one or more other types of argument. Often the type stated or implied will make little difference to the acceptability of the argument. In other times or settings, only one type will serve efficiently.

Cause–Effect Argument

The warrant in a cause–effect argument says that a causal relationship exists between datum and claim. Causal links can be of three kinds: cause–effect, effect–cause, and effect–effect. We will sketch a model for each.

Suppose you see another car back into the your car, hitting the front fender. You would probably set up this cause–effect argument:

DATUM ⟶ **CLAIM**

The car hit my fender.   My car will have a dent.

WARRANT

Since such impact causes
a dent, . . .

Suppose, instead, that you return to your car and see a dent and scratches, and flecks of different-colored paint in the dent and scratches. You would probably set up this effect–cause argument:

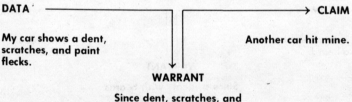

DATA ⟶ **CLAIM**

My car shows a dent,   Another car hit mine.
scratches, and paint
flecks.

WARRANT

Since dent, scratches, and
paint are effects of being
hit by a car, . . .

In an effect–effect warrant, it is reasoned that one effect allows us to claim another because the effects are tied to a common cause. For example, you could reason that the other car will have a dent, scratches, plus paint flecks from your car:

DATA ──────────────────────────────────→ **CLAIM**

My car was hit by
another car and has a
dent, scratches, and
paint flecks.

The other car, too,
shows effects of the
accident.

WARRANT

Since the accident will give
a dent, scratches, and
paint flecks to the other car
as well, . . .

Since the pioneering work of the Greek philosophers, occidental culture has been accustomed to finding causal sequences in the world. Communicators with a ready command of causal reasoning have a dependable means for creating identification via argument.

Aristotle's analysis of causation may prove useful. Aristotle reviews what earlier Greeks have taught about causation and presents his own thoughts. He discerns four kinds of cause: material, formal, efficient, and final.[12] Housing can be used as an example. The material cause is the building supplies. The formal cause is the blueprint supplied by the architect. The efficient cause is the labor expended by the craftsmen. The final cause is the end or purpose that instigated the building process (i.e., the desire for an enjoyable shelter).[13] For each of these immediate causes of housing, antecedent causes can probably be found.

One may not always be able to distinguish all four causes as contributors to a given phenomenon; still, a search for the various causes is likely to build up a supply of available arguments. And more effective communications will be built if the stock of arguments is broad and deep. Holding a wealth of possible arguments, one can select those best calculated to achieve the desired ends. With an impoverished stock, on the other hand, one is forced to settle for whatever is

[12] *Metaphysics*, 982-993.

[13] *Metaphysics*, 996b. Kenneth Burke's pentad is closely allied with Aristotle's analysis of causation. See *A Grammar of Motives*.

available. Any success attending this willy-nilly effort is an accidental rather than a predictable product.

Analogical Argument

The warrant in an analogical argument asserts that observed likenesses allow one to claim another similarity:

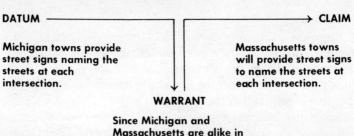

DATUM ———————————————————————→ CLAIM

Michigan towns provide street signs naming the streets at each intersection.

Massachusetts towns will provide street signs to name the streets at each intersection.

WARRANT

Since Michigan and Massachusetts are alike in being states that have towns, streets, cars, and drivers, they will also be alike in the matter of street signs.

Massachusetts, in fact, often does not have the convenience mentioned, and the lack is a source of frequent annoyance to those who expect the foregoing or a similar analogy to hold.

The street signs analogy is a literal one. Analogies range from the strictly literal to the highly figurative. The following highly figurative analogy is taken from a lecture by Robert Frost. The poet was remarking that the process of homogenizing milk had lately come into vogue in his New England town. Like most others in those days, Frost had his milk delivered from the dairy in glass quart bottles. He also followed the popular practice of ordering some homogenized and some only pasteurized. The homogenized was more convenient for drinking and tasted better. The milk that was only pasteurized let the cream rise to the top, and some of this could be snitched for the special uses cream lovers always find for cream. As Frost picked up a bottle of homogenized milk in one hand and a bottle of pasteurized in the other, he thought:

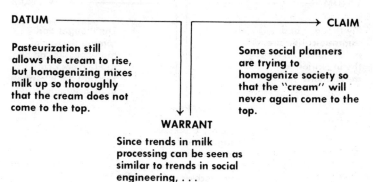

DATUM ——————————————————————→ **CLAIM**

Pasteurization still allows the cream to rise, but homogenizing mixes milk up so thoroughly that the cream does not come to the top.

Some social planners are trying to homogenize society so that the "cream" will never again come to the top.

WARRANT

Since trends in milk processing can be seen as similar to trends in social engineering, . . .

Figurative analogies like this will not convince a doubter; however, such striking associations can put the matter in a memorable fashion. And when an audience is predisposed to move toward a desired identification, a poetic union of this kind can have unusual power. Witness the effectiveness of the lines, "The harpies of the shore shall pluck/The eagle of the sea!" in stating the case for saving "Old Ironsides." Thousands can visit the U.S.S. *Constitution* in the Boston Naval Shipyard because Oliver Wendell Holmes spoke so well for an American audience in the mood to memorialize grandeur.

With the argument just cited, Frost apparently wished to snipe at a trend toward uniformity, but his major thrust was that one's life is divided into facets and enriched through the associating of experiences. Frost's poetry is replete with examples of his ability to conceive parallels, thus producing a new, richer experience for himself and his audience.

Generalization Argument

Frost claimed that his way to enrichment could be followed by others. Let us use this claim for our example of a generalization argument.

Paraphrasing Frost, we have:

DATUM ————————————————————————→ CLAIM

My thought and
communication are
made more rich through
the invention of
associations.

The thought and
communication of
many people can be
made more rich
through the invention
of associations.

WARRANT

Since my processes of
thought and
communication may be
taken as representative of
your processes of thought
and communication, . . .

Generalization moves from an examination of a member or some members of a class in the datum to a claim that covers more of that class. The warrant bridges by asserting the representativeness or typicality of the members examined. The generalization attributed to Frost moves from one to an audience of well over a thousand.

A critic could stand apart and label it a "hasty" generalization, but the adequacy of an argument is not always determined by the extensiveness of the search reported in the datum or data. (Opinion pollsters generalize concerning millions on the basis of a sample of hundreds.) Rather, adequacy often depends on the readiness of the coactor to accept what is offered.

SUMMARY

The ability to reason is shared by human beings. Disciplined study of this shared attribute can lead to better communication.

Toulmin's model enables one to lay out and study the arguments human beings use in everyday reasoning. The model is a useful tool for preparing and testing arguments. Having mastered the model, especially the three basic parts, coactors should be better able to judge what each should furnish while creating identification.

Five common types of argument can be discerned on the basis of the warrant used by each type. The communicator who has trouble identifying the warrants in arguments may profit from a study of these common forms of argument.

QUESTIONS FOR THOUGHT AND DISCUSSION

1. According to this chapter, what is an argument?
2. Select several newspaper, magazine, or television advertisements and lay out models for the arguments they present.
3. Lay out the models for the major arguments in the speeches presented in Chapters 4, 5, and 7. What similarities and differences do you note in the arguments of these communications?
4. Select a recent decision you have made. Analyze this decision by using Toulmin's model. To what extent does the model help to clarify the process you used in making your decision?
5. Lay out a model or models for a communication that you will present.

SUGGESTED READINGS

Ehninger, Douglas, and Wayne Brockriede, *Decision by Debate*, New York, Dodd Mead, 1963, Part III.

McCroskey, James C., *An Introduction to Rhetorical Communication*, 2nd edition, Englewood Cliffs, N.J., Prentice-Hall, 1971, ch. 5.

Toulmin, Stephen E., *The Uses of Argument*, Cambridge, Cambridge University Press, 1958, esp. Part III.

4 identication via attraction

Vince McGugan, who described the steps leading to his attitude toward death (Chapter 1), fears death because it threatens separation from persons he loves. "'I am alone, alone, alone,'" sobs Esteban as he grieves unconsolably over the death of his identical twin in Thornton Wilder's *The Bridge of San Luis Rey*. In some measure, we all fear with Vince and grieve with Esteban, for although each of us is unique, no one is an island.

Besides the shared ability to reason and the obviously similar physiological characteristics and needs, humans also share social characteristics and needs. Being gregarious creatures, humans need one another. On a minimal level each requires others to provide a context within which definition of individuality is possible. Through communication with this social context, each person can find both a concept of self and a rewarding fellowship. (Prisons sometimes use solitary confinement as an extreme form of punishment, and prisoners charge bitterly that prolonged separation from their fellows injures not only the individual's self-concept but also erodes the ties once felt to social groups and causes.)

William Schutz finds three major ways in which human beings need each other: "inclusion, control, and affection."[1] Ideally, in the inclusion-need area of an interpersonal relationship a person feels an interest in others and has this interest returned; a person acts sociably (i.e., includes others), and is included by others; each is gratified by a sense of significance. Looking to an opposite condition in the inclusion area, the individual has little interest in others and is accorded little interest in return; the individual acts anti-

[1] William C. Schutz, *The Interpersonal Underworld*, Palo Alto, Calif., Science and Behavior Books, 1966, pp. 13–33.

socially (i.e., turns others away) and he is turned away, as well.[2]

Ideally, in the control-need sector of an interpersonal relationship a person feels respect for others and is respected; each side acts democratically with the other; each participant is gratified by a feeling of being responsible. Given a much worse situation in this control need sector, a person does not respect others and is repaid in kind; each side becomes increasingly caught up with coercive measures and countermeasures that are mutually unbeneficial; each person feels trapped and persecuted.

Ideally, in the affection-need realm of an interpersonal relationship a person likes (loves) others and is liked (loved); each person develops while creating friendly, personal identifications; each experiences the joy of feeling lovable. With the antipode in the affection need realm, a person dislikes (hates) others and is disliked (hated); communications infused with animosity are sent and received; each person is tortured by feeling unlovable.

In real life one confronts many gradations between the poles described for each of these social needs. Furthermore, although each area can furnish the motivating force for a specific interaction, the inclusion, control, and affection needs will usually work together in complex combinations to initiate and sustain interpersonal communication.

Whether one accepts the three categories Schutz proposes, notes overlapping and combinations, or tries to identify new factors, the basic point holds: Human beings need to coact with each other. Sometimes this need can be met across years and miles by use of written and other codes. Usually, however, social needs are satisfied during face-to-face interpersonal encounters.

The following speech, given by Juanita Coffee to her classmates, gives concrete application to Schutz's theory. Note that society's failure to fulfill legitimate social needs gives this communication its poignancy and power.

[2] Paul Simon's "A Most Peculiar Man" furnishes a sad example.

For you who are younger than I am, let me tell you what 1
life has been like for this black person. For you of a dif- 2
ferent ethnic background than mine, let me tell you what 3
it's like to follow all the rules of this society and still be an 4
outsider. For all of you, let me tell you how prejudice has 5
touched my life—let me tell you my life story. 6

I'm an American hybrid, a mixture of American black, 7
English, and Indian. My name is Juanita Coffee, a 8
Protestant American black; native Detroiter, product of the 9
public schools and a graduate fashion designer. I'm the 10
mother of three delightful children and wife of a handsome 11
dental surgeon. 12

In addition to my all-American heritage, I grew up in a 13
predominantly Catholic, Polish neighborhood, where I ac- 14
quired a basic knowledge of their culture which I incor- 15
porated into my life. This includes many of the foods, a bit 16
of the language, and the polka, which was taught in our 17
schools. 18

I was a happy child in a family of eight children, whose 19
greatest awareness of being different was in the fact that we 20
were Protestant. I lived in this make-believe world for 21
nearly 14 years, except for a frightening interlude when our 22
family experienced Detroit's 1943 race riot in our Catholic, 23
Polish community. I lay on the floor with my family, 24
praying for peace and listening to the news report from the 25
radio as to how close the violence was moving. Our shades at 26
the windows were drawn to ward off any broken glass. My 27
parents stayed busy preparing survival equipment, bottling 28
water, collecting canned goods and blankets, to be prepared 29
for the unexpected. 30

Another experience that I recall was in junior high. My 31
drama-dance teacher took my Greek girl friend and me on a 32
special outing. After seeing a play at the Masonic Temple 33
we were to be treated to a luncheon at a beautiful restaurant 34
in the adjoining hotel. I soon learned that all the patrons' 35
stares in the mirrored walls and from the hotel servants 36
were not in admiration of my fashionable, well-groomed ap- 37
pearance. After more than an hour my teacher was told that 38

the establishment was *not permitted to serve me,* but, if she 39
wished, *I could remain* while she and my friend had lunch. 40

I was given my first trip South as a teenager. My aunt 41
and I were having a delightful time laughing and talking 42
with fellow travelers when we were told that we had reached 43
Cincinnati—which is considered the dividing line for North 44
and South. I asked my aunt why we were getting off the 45
train—this wasn't Birmingham. She whispered, "Because 46
we're colored," and I thought to myself, It isn't catching, 47
why should we be isolated? Isolation would have been better 48
than the dirty, ragged, stinking, squeaking, crowded car we 49
had to ride in all the way to Birmingham, Alabama. 50

In Birmingham I was introduced to Southern hospitality. 51
I remember paying my fare up front on the street car and 52
running to the back door to get on, hoping the conductor 53
wouldn't take off and leave me. I saw the abuse of my 54
people as we crowded in the hot, dirty, rear of the bus. 55
Downtown I was jerked from a "white only" drinking foun- 56
tain by my teenage guide. These things I remember. 57

Graduating from Cass Tech, one of Detroit's finest high 58
schools, I felt prepared to accept any good position that 59
would enable me to earn my tuition for Wayne State 60
University. However, I was able only to secure a job as a 61
stock girl and part-time toilet matron: my reward for all 62
those years in school, all those years of music at the conser- 63
vatory, all the extra training in art, sewing, drama, and 64
dance. Finally, having earned my tuition, I studied in 65
Wayne's Home Economics Department in the division of 66
sewing and family living until I left the university to be- 67
come a fashion designer at a private French school. 68

I married a young man from my neighborhood. While he 69
completed his education at Wayne State University and two 70
years in dental school, I was employed by the government 71
as a map draftsman, simply because designing jobs in De- 72
troit were extremely limited for blacks and I needed a 73
steady nine-to-five. 74

I joined my husband during his junior and senior years of 75
dental school in Nashville, Tennessee. I applied for a job, 76

only to be told that without a degree from college there was 77
no market for blacks with my training except as a 78
dishwasher or a babysitter. This time I just went home and 79
cried. The next day, determined to get justice, I went 80
directly to the Federal Building and presented my papers, 81
showing I was eligible for a job up to a supervisory position. 82
Again the parade of peekers began as I sat in one of the 83
private glassed offices while the white government officials 84
tried to decide what to do with me. Black applicants were 85
not hired in this division of government service in the South 86
except for menial labor—certainly not as draftsmen. 87
Ironically, I was sent their letter of acceptance three years 88
after my husband was in private practice. 89

We were in Nashville when one of my husband's instruc- 90
tors, Attorney Looby's home was bombed; the impact 91
awakened us a half-mile away. Sickened by the horrifying 92
incident, my husband and I joined the hundreds who 93
marched to City Hall. I was in Memphis when James 94
Meredith was shot, and we marched around Memorial Hos- 95
pital that night. And we marched in Detroit in one of the 96
nation's most historic freedom marches led by Dr. Martin 97
Luther King, Jr. 98

As the years passed I came to know prejudice in many 99
forms: in segregated lunch rooms and toilets; in a refusal by 100
the government's Small Business Administration to grant a 101
loan to open my husband's practice; in a refusal of a loan 102
from the bank where my husband had an account since age 103
14; in a refusal to recognize my husband's *state* license for 104
employment as a *city* dental surgeon; in refusal to open ac- 105
counts, or issue insurance policies of any consequence 106
without undue investigation; in refusal to rent commercial 107
property at reasonable rates. 108

On top of all this, when we were ready to purchase our 109
first home we were asked to come at night so the neighbors 110
couldn't see us. Once we came eye to eye with a German 111
shepherd whose master had unleashed him on us. 112

In 1967 during Detroit's civil disorder, I again found 113
myself on the floor with the shades drawn, only this time I 114

was the mother and it was my turn to protect and shield my   115
children. The childhood terror came back and now my   116
children know fear, for they have seen man's inhumanity to   117
man. They have seen their parents join the neighbors in   118
hosing down the houses one night because of a rumor that   119
the whites from nearby Dearborn were on the way with fire-   120
bombs.   121

Today I look back to see that I was raised in a good   122
family, came from a good neighborhood, went to good   123
schools, got a college education, followed all the rules set by   124
the American white society to achieve the American dream;   125
yet, I'm still black and still subject to the same insults,   126
closed doors, and limitations of all blacks. But I'm still   127
marching because my patriotism and brotherly love are not   128
dead. I teach our children the philosophy of a great Negro   129
spiritual: 130

Hand in hand together,   131
We shall overcome some day.   132
Deep in my heart I do believe,   133
We shall overcome some day.   134

Juanita shows early in her speech that she had every right
to expect inclusion, yet again and again she was slighted in a
society that deemed blacks insignificant; lines 38–40, 45–50,
52–57, give just a few examples. Juanita tells how she
followed the rules and gained the credentials that should
have brought fulfillment in the control-need sector, but she
was repeatedly kept from responsibility (lines 61–65, 71–73,
76–89, etc.). The place of the affection-need realm is
perhaps less readily apparent than Schutz's other two social
needs. Probably, though, Juanita's description of her childhood (lines 13–21), of her own family (lines 10–12 and
114–116), and of her faith (lines 127–134), can be taken as
proof that the young woman has and can meet affection
needs. Of course the race riots, the unleashed German
shepherd, and the other cruelties Juanita details would do
little to make her feel that she was lovable to the society at
large.

Prejudices other than racial ones cause some to deny or minimize the social needs and the social value of certain groups of others. A book focusing on interpersonal communication cannot deal directly with the problem of prejudice, although improved ability for communicating perhaps can help to curb racial, ethnic, class, and other biases.

Prejudice in favor of or against a group must also touch the individual, once that individual is tied to the group; however, an individual can be needed, positively valued, and found attractive, or can be unneeded, negatively valued, and found unattractive, with no necessary connection to an existing bias for or against a group. This process of attraction or repulsion without reference to group prejudices is the subject of the next section and most of the remainder of this chapter.

THE RELATIONS BETWEEN NEED, VALUE, AND ATTRACTION

Needing others, each person values them, and valuing leads to attraction. The reasons for valuing and the values assigned will be various, thus the attraction felt will vary also. Possibly, a negative value will be placed on someone; here, instead of attraction one would find repulsion. In more healthy situations, some degree of valuing and attraction exists and provides a force to motivate identification.

Suppose you hear your friend say "You should go to see *Lawrence of Arabia*," and you think back over four movies you have attended because that friend advised you to. If all have been excellent, you could generalize from these pieces of advice and their good consequences to the conclusion that you should again take your friend's advice. Here there is an intertwining of identification via argument as discussed in Chapter 3, as well as the mode of identification we investigate in this chapter. You accept the advice because you value your friend; you value your friend because the advice is good.

These two modes of identification—via reasonable argument and via attraction—often interact. Each mode can function on its own. In rare instances each might succeed despite the contrary impetus of the other; however, both are usually allied in effective communication.

THE ROLE OF ETHOS IN ATTRACTION

Traditionally, many facets of identification via attraction have been discussed under the concept of ethos. From Greek theorists, notably Plato and Aristotle, through a long line of later thinkers, to contemporary writers on communication theory, this concept has been recognized as important and treated accordingly. For our present discussion we define *ethos* as the composite of the impressions one has of another person.[3]

This composite picture or image may be finely detailed and multidimensional for a certain person, and one's representation of another person may be broadly drawn and flat. Usually a family member or roommate would fit the former category, whereas a chance acquaintance or prominent but distant personage would belong in the latter. However well developed the image, if it is sufficiently positive, identification via attraction is possible because one coactor places some value on the other (i.e., one perceives the other as capable of meeting social needs).

The subject another raises has a great deal to do with one's finding a given attraction link to be adequate: Going to a movie is not the same as accepting a heart transplant; nevertheless, the same basic communication process can be noted. Probably the persons attended to will differ, and the mix of identification through reasoned argument and identification through attraction will be altered as the stakes

---

[3] For further development see Kenneth E. Andersen, *Persuasion: Theory and Practice*, Boston, Allyn & Bacon, 1971, pp. 218 ff.

change. One would, no doubt, reason as carefully as possible in the case of a new heart; yet, even here one would find a mixture of identification through reasoning and through attraction. One must, at some juncture, accept the testimony of other patients, other doctors, or still others with relevant experience. One can frame various arguments from this material, yet the result will be a compound of the argument and attraction modes of identification.

The image one person has of another can be well developed yet negatively valenced. (Although clearly possible, well-developed negative composites are less prevalent than well-developed positive ones. This is true because one usually communicates more with and comes to know better persons who are liked, and disliked persons are avoided as much as possible.) If the ethos is wholly negative, no attraction exists, and no bridge to identification can be created via this route. Other motivations for identification may be found, but their effectiveness will be hampered by the negative image. Suppose, for example, that a current prototype of the used-car salesman in *The Grapes of Wrath* greets you on a car lot and gives every evidence of deserving the negative attitude suggested by Steinbeck's incident, mentioned earlier. You would not be moved to buy what he has because of your attraction to him. You might buy a car from him for other reasons: The unsavory salesman may have just the car you want, and you find sufficient arguments for buying despite the negative impact of the salesman's image. Thus you identify with him insofar as buying a car from him is concerned; nevertheless, the transaction is not the most pleasant one you could imagine, and the counterproductive effects of unattractive ethos make such identification much less likely than when the various motives work in harmony.

The ethos factor is like a credit rating system. If the credit rating you give someone is high, you can draw on this credit to carry you to the position the other advocates. If you assign someone a lower credit rating, a withdrawal may be granted with some qualms. If you view someone as ir-retrievably bankrupt, even a small loan will be denied.

If everyone gave everyone else a negative credit rating, mutually beneficial interpersonal communication would be difficult if not impossible. One would find something like Hobbes's state of nature, where each person viciously spars with all others. Any cooperation would have to be imposed and maintained by a power outside the crowd of individuals. Harmony in family or community would be only façade. Fortunately, positive credit, or trust, is possible. Unless crippled by most severe anomie, human beings learn to invest some trust in at least some of their fellows. Personal experience as well as descriptive and experimental measures show that humans are able to value each other positively; thus they can identify via attraction.[4]

The Semantic Differential and the Congruity Hypothesis

The ethos you hold for someone and the ethos that someone holds for you are major influences in your interpersonal communication. You have developed means for ascertaining what you think of someone and what someone thinks of you; the latter is, of course, an important determinant of how well you think of the other person.[5] You note cues in voice, appearance, and action, even though you may often not be conscious of doing so, as you gauge images and estimate their effects.

[4] See Ellen Berscheid and Elaine Hatfield Walster, *Interpersonal Attraction*, Reading, Mass., Addison-Wesley, 1969.

[5] C. W. Backman and P. F. Secord, "The Effect of Perceived Liking on Interpersonal Attraction," *Human Relations,* **12** (1959), 379–384. Also, R. Tagiuri, "Social Preference and Its Perception," in *Person, Perception, and Interpersonal Behavior*, R. Tagiuri and L. Petrullo, eds., Stanford, Calif., Stanford University Press, 1958, pp. 316–336; J. Mills, "Opinion Change as a Function of the Communicator's Desire to Influence and Liking for the Audience," *Journal of Experimental Social Psychology,* **2** (1966), 152–159.

In addition to the everyday assessments, more formal devices for measuring ethos are available. The semantic differential is such a device—in this case, a paper-and-pencil measuring instrument.[6] The respondent is asked to rate someone on a series of bipolar-adjective scales such as:

SENATOR TED KENNEDY

intelligent ____ ____ ____ ____ ____ ____ ____ unintelligent
honest ____ ____ ____ ____ ____ ____ ____ dishonest
kind ____ ____ ____ ____ ____ ____ ____ unkind

The respondent should make a quick decision and check the blank on each scale that best fits the judgment reached for that item. The number of adjective pairs used can range from many (50 or more) to rather few (about a half-dozen), depending on the circumstances and the persons involved.

Suppose the respondent checked Senator Kennedy's scales as follows:

intelligent ____ ✓ ____ ____ ____ ____ ____ unintelligent
honest ____ ____ ✓ ____ ____ ____ ____ dishonest
kind ✓ ____ ____ ____ ____ ____ ____ unkind

One can score these responses on a range from −3 for the negative end of the scale, unintelligent, unkind, dishonest, to +3 for the positive end, intelligent, kind, honest. The middle blank is given a zero. Thus Senator Kennedy would have +2 on the intelligence scale, +1 on the honesty scale, and +3 on the kindness scale. Assuming (just for the sake of illustration) that an accurate picture of the image held for Senator Kennedy can be obtained by averaging these scores, one gets a +2 overall rating for Senator Kennedy.

Besides functioning as a measuring device for ethos, the semantic differential can be used to gauge one's reactions to concepts. The respondent can use the same scales in rating the concept of a national health plan:

[6] Charles E. Osgood, George J. Suci, and Percy H. Tannenbaum, *The Measurement of Meaning*, Urbana, University of Illinois Press, 1957.

NATIONAL HEALTH PLAN

intelligent	✓	___	___	___	___	___	___ unintelligent
honest	✓	___	___	___	___	___	___ dishonest
kind	✓	___	___	___	___	___	___ unkind

Using the same scoring system, one gets a $+3$ rating for a national health plan.

When Senator Kennedy becomes known as the advocate of a national health plan, the respondent perceives a $+2$ source allied with a $+3$ concept. According to Osgood and his associates, the discrepancy in the ratings creates discomfort, since humans prefer congruence.[7] According to the congruity hypothesis proposed by Osgood *et al.*, when someone gives disparate values to a person and something with which that person becomes allied, pressure exists to bring the two into harmony. In our example, the respondent should think a little more positively of Senator Kennedy and a little less positively of a national health plan. If the anchors holding Kennedy's rating and the health plan's rating are equally strong, the ratings would move toward the other by equal amounts, thus congruence would be reached when each stabilized at a $+2.5$ rating. The anchorings may very well be unequal in holding power: Kennedy might move to a $+3$ status for a true believer in national health plans; or, a less ardent member of the national health flock who was certain of the $+2$ rating given Kennedy might switch the health plan rating to coincide with Kennedy's $+2$; various other values are conceivable for the final congruence.

Probably many factors other than his espousal of a national health plan influence Kennedy's image, and many considerations will govern the evaluation of a national health plan besides Kennedy's approbation. In addition, different people will tolerate different levels of incongruity; some

[7] Also see E. P. Bettinghaus, "Operation of Congruity in an Oral Communication Setting," *Speech Monographs,* **28** (1961), 131–142; D. K. Berlo and Halbert Gulley, "Some Determinants of the Effect of Oral Communication in Producing Attitude Change and Learning," *Speech Monographs,* **25** (1957), 10–20.

may be able to accept discrepancies of a point or more, thus feeling no pressure to change the $+2$ and $+3$ ranks, whereas others may be uneasy until a fairly neat harmony is gained.

The congruity hypothesis links up readily with the notion of credit discussed in the previous section. We can illustrate this by returning to the example of the friend who advises you to see *Lawrence of Arabia*. Assume that you rate your friend at $+2.5$, and, since the movie was unknown to you before your friend mentioned it, you must give it a zero rating. The high positive value you accord your friend would be much more securely anchored than the noncommittal position you have on the movie; thus you can borrow a bit from the credit you give your friend, and this loan brings the movie up to $+2$. You attend the movie and like it immensely. *Lawrence of Arabia* rates $+3$ with you. Borrowing on your friend's ethos has paid off. The interest accrued moves your image of your friend up to $+2.75$. But if you attend and find the movie to be merely fair (i.e., only a $+1$), the credit advanced does not seem to have been justified; nevertheless, since your friend is still batting four out of five, you hold the ethos rating at $+2.4$.

Ethos is Dynamic

Several points should be emphasized about our discussion of ethos. First, the composite impression one has of another is dynamic: It changes. Each identification, whether it comes via argument or attraction, is developmental, thus makes an alteration. One need not be aware of the change, and frequently the available measuring instruments are not sufficiently sensitive to pick it up.

Doubtless, everyone is aware that the image held of him by his associates is changeable. We seldom communicate about something completely divorced from ourselves: "Look at me," "Revalue me," or some such personal referent colors each communication. Our questions and statements refer to our intelligence, sensitivity, or other attributes, as well as to the matter ostensibly at hand. We do not like to have our ideas rejected—partly because a rejection of ourselves is intimated. Even "I love you" repeated often in years togetherness keeps a note of courtship.

These attempts to tell of oneself show that a person perceives some control of the image being shaped. In Aristotle's analysis of ethos (*Rhetoric*, 1366a, 1378a ff, 1395b), the speaker chooses at appropriate times to show his love for mother, country, and other tokens he believes the audience esteems; thus the speaker seeks to build a certain character for himself within the auditor.

Aristotle's notion that a communicator may affect ethos by choosing certain rhetorical strategies has been tested in many experimental studies. These studies have demonstrated that a message that is clearly organized,[8] that includes evidence,[9] that expresses a position contrary to the source's self-interest,[10] and that includes discreet references to the speaker's experience (self-references) may contribute to a positive ethos.[11] All of these studies have employed unfamiliar message sources, whose perceived ethos was no doubt quite volatile. Nonetheless, the contemporary studies underscore the validity and importance of Aristotle's claim.

[8] Harry Sharp, Jr. and Thomas McClung, "Effects of Organization on the Speaker's Ethos," *Speech Monographs,* **33** (1966) 182–183; James C. McCroskey and R. Samuel Mehrley, "The Effects of Disorganization and Nonfluency on Attitude Change and Source Credibility," *Speech Monographs,* **36** (1969), 13–21.

[9] James C. McCroskey, "A Summary of Experimental Research on the Effects of Evidence in Persuasive Communication," *Quarterly Journal of Speech,* **55** (1969), 169–176.

[10] William E. Arnold and James C. McCroskey, "The Credibility of Reluctant Testimony," *Central States Speech Journal,* **18** (1967), 97–103; Loren Anderson, "An Experimental Study of Reluctant and Biased Authority Based Assertions," *Journal of the American Forensic Association,* **7** (1970), 79–84.

[11] Terry H. Ostermeier, "An Experimental Study of the Type and Frequency of References as Used by an Unfamiliar Source in a Message and its Effect upon Perceived Credibility and Attitude Change" Doctoral dissertation, Michigan State University, 1966.

The images perceived for some individuals will be more stable than the images perceived for others. The ethos one has for a close friend of many years probably changes very little with a commonplace identification. One has perceived that facet often, and a subsequent encounter reinforces the image already held. (We view reinforcement as one kind of change.) Only a strong, new revelation will bring a significant alteration of the image. On the other hand, the results of a study by Brooks and Scheidel demonstrate that the image of someone who is known but slightly can fluctuate considerably with each identification (see Figure. 5).

Brooks and Scheidel played a tape of a speech by Malcolm X to a group of college student subjects. In the experimental condition (curve e in Figure 5) the tape was stopped at appropriate intervals to allow the students to rate Malcolm X's ethos at that point. Control group b heard the speech but only rated the black leader's ethos at the beginning and the end of the speech; control group a filled out the pretest and posttest instruments, but these students did not hear the speech. Note that line b shows a change in ethos as a result of the communication. The terminal ethos in conditions b and e is about the same, but the fluctuations in the e line illustrate dramatically that ethos is dynamic.

IMAGES DIFFER BUT ALSO OVERLAP

No two people have precisely the same impression of someone else. Each human being is unique and builds original images of others. The means that one person will credit someone, Richard Nixon, for example, and find identification via attraction readily possible; but another person will perceive little or nothing positive in Nixon's account, thus identification via attraction will be difficult or out of the question.

Possibly, a complex society forces each of us to limit interaction with some, to save energy for relating more closely with certain others. Perhaps one presents different image-forming stimuli to those met casually and to those met on deeper, more intimate levels. Robert Browning sets the public show versus the private encounter in these lines:

> God be thanked, the meanest of his creatures
> Boasts two soul-sides, one to face the world with,
> One to show a woman when he loves her.[12]

Figure 5. The Effect of Communication on the source's credibility: solid curve, experimental group; dotted curves, control groups *a* and *b*. (Robert D. Brooks and Thomas M. Scheidel, "Speech as Process: A Case Study," Speech Monographs **35** (1968), 4.)

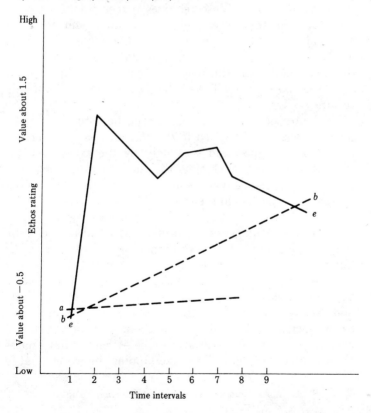

[12] Robert Browning, "One Word More," stanza 18.

The ethos formed for the lover by the loved one is here likely to differ from the ethos formed by someone faced in the outside world.

Granting, for the moment, this public—private possibility, one can see many other possibilities within each of these two categories. In the public and private realms each person assumes certain roles for himself and adjusts to those roles he sees for other persons. Thus, for example, when Oliver Wendell Holmes sketches three Johns: (1) God's John (the actual John), (2) John's John (John as seen by himself), and (3) John as seen by other people, many Johns will exist in the third division.[13] Close relatives perceive John as John the son, John the father, John the brother, and John the husband, to name several of the private Johns. And those who are set apart, comparatively speaking, see John as John the colleague, John the neighbor, John the shopper, and John the sport—just a few of the possibilities in the public sector.

No doubt some truth can be seen in the noting of the different images, but if taken to the extreme, each person becomes jelly, shaped and seen only by the extant circumstances. So at the same time that one sees the possibility that various persons will create a distinct ethos for a given person, one also should see that overlapping of the images is likely to occur.

In the case of images that are prepared and marketed by mass media, some of the overlapping is attributable to the handles the media must devise. Richard Nixon was packaged as "Tricky Dick" for a time; some years thereafter the going labels for Nixon were "consummate politician" and "shrewd statesman."[14] Later still, Nixon was presented as the reclusive "lame duck." Someone met face to face in everyday transactions will also evoke rather similar images from various persons. The overlapping indicates that a

[13] "The Three Johns" from *The Autocrat of the Breakfast Table.*

[14] See *Newsweek*, August 28, 1972, 16–18.

person usually sends out consistent messages relating to personal attributes; the overlapping shows, too, that others tend to assess someone in similar ways. From this viewpoint the public and private selves do not split into "two soul-sides"; rather, a public–private continuum is drawn, and as coactors move toward the private end, deeper glimpses of the same, integrated persons are shared to create richer images.

Dimensions in Ethos

A third point in the elaboration of our discussion of ethos concerns dimensionality in the composite representation. Aristotle observed that the image perceived would have three major dimensions: intelligence, virtue, and goodwill (*Rhetoric* 1378). The intelligence dimension encompasses receiver perceptions of matters such as the communicator's knowledge of the subject, the communicator's ability to reason, the sophistication the communicator shows in adjusting to the audience and the setting. The virtue dimension pertains to the honesty the communicator is seen to use in dealing with ideas and persons—himself or herself included. The goodwill dimension would be the perceived size for sharing. If one sees another as big enough to be giving away something of value in the coaction, one attributes goodwill to this person. If one sees another as unable to give without exacting an equal or larger return, one notes a deficiency in the goodwill dimension.

Although these dimensions seem fairly obvious, and each of us can point to them in various acquaintances, all three have not appeared consistently in research studies aimed at discriminating the dimensions in ethos. The research has supported Aristotle's notion that ethos is multidimensional, but two dimensions generally have been found, rather than three. These two have been "expertness" or "authoritativeness" (similar to Aristotle's "intelligence") and "character" or "trustworthiness" (similar to Aristotle's "virtue," although the connotation of trust may sometimes appear to include goodwill).[15]

Perhaps the one-to-large-group format, a characteristic of much of the research, inhibits both the revealing and the noticing of the goodwill cues. In a like vein, the academic setting for much of the research probably places a premium on intelligence, and this climate may submerge the goodwill features. Also, the goodwill dimension would seem to grow more slowly and probably is less readily intimated by the verbal treatments that are typically set up. Humans seem to need prolonged, tangible evidence of another's willingness to share before allowing the goodwill dimension to grow; whereas the intelligence dimension can be discerned rather quickly in relatively superficial verbal encounters.[16] Doubtless, too, an image of more numerous facets evolves as one person gets better acquainted with another; most research, however, has not been able to focus here, and the present instruments and techniques seem to be ill-suited for such sensitive work. Given the current limitations of research, we can still presume the existence of a goodwill dimension.[17]

We can elaborate Aristotle's three dimensions in ethos by using illustrations drawn from classroom experience.

---

[15] James C. McCroskey, "Scales for the Measurement of Ethos," *Speech Monographs,* **33** (1966), 65-72; Jack L. Whitehead, "Factors of Source Credibility," *Quarterly Journal of Speech,* **54** (1968), 59-63; David Berlo, J. B. Lemert, and R. J. Mertz, "Dimensions for Evaluating the Acceptability of Message Sources," *Public Opinion Quarterly,* **33** (1969), 563-576.

[16] Erik Erikson notes repeatedly in *Childhood and Society* how "basic trust" (goodwill) is nurtured in the family or the intimate social group. A kindred note is frequently evident in Carl Rogers's *Client Centered Therapy.* Also see Edward L. McGlone and Loren J. Anderson, "The Dimensions of Teacher Credibility," *Speech Teacher,* **22** (1973), 196-200.

[17] For a related discussion and conclusion, see Kim Giffin and Bobby R. Patton, *Fundamentals of Interpersonal Communication*, New York, Harper & Row, 1971, pp. 163-171. Also see E. Scott Baudhuin and Margaret Kis Davis, "Scales for the Measurement of *Ethos*: Another Attempt," *Speech Monographs,* **39** (1972), 296-301.

(Pseudonyms are used.) Jim's arguments almost always rambled superficially over the topic at hand, whether the subject was chosen by himself or another; he rarely showed the ability to adjust his thoughts to his auditor or the occasion. The reaction of others to Jim indicated that he was viewed as weak in the intelligence dimension. (Semantic differential instruments were filled out by each class member for the others in class.)

Let us examine another example. Patrick told the group of the multifarious clever strategies he had used to fake his way into college through a supposedly rigorous admissions procedure. He claimed to regret this and other instances of dishonesty. His listeners would have liked to admire the apparent candor he now showed, but no one could escape the suspicion that this was just another in a long line of put-ons. Patrick's image suffered in the virtue dimension.

Gwin worked hard. She was erudite and clear in her communication. She was quick to tell exactly what she saw in her classmates and their efforts. Her discourse was distant, almost supercilious. She scored better in the intelligence and virtue dimensions than in the goodwill one. Part of the weaker rating in the goodwill dimension might be attributable to the loss that usually is suffered by one who ventures to become a "task leader" and show the way for the group.[18] But more was involved with Gwin; her haughtiness probably would have crippled the goodwill dimension even if no group assignment were involved.

Remember, these brief sketches do not presume to capture the true personalities of Jim, Patrick, and Gwin. The sketches only present how each student appeared to his classmates during one semester. And in Gwin's case, the ethos changed remarkably in the final weeks of the term. Gwin saw the results of the semantic differential testing of her image; these results as well as overt class behavior con-

[18] Robert F. Bales, "Task Roles and Social Roles in Problem-Solving Groups," in *Current Studies in Social Psychology*, Ivan D. Steiner and Martin Fishbein, eds., New York, Holt, Rinehart & Winston, 1965, pp. 321–333.

vinced her that the goodwill dimension was weak. Realizing the deleterious effects on her ability to create identifications, Gwin set out to improve this facet. She recreated past experiences that she believed had caused the suppression of goodwill impulses, and she was intensely involved as she gave a moving account of recent shocks to her cold facade. Her resolve to change and the evidence she gave of fulfilling her resolve were well received; the ratings in the goodwill dimension rose to equal those in the other two spheres.

Perhaps the change in most of the class members' images of Gwin was so readily possible because the intelligence and virtue dimensions were relatively strong and could serve as a stable launching pad for the rebuilding effort. The dimensions are interrelated, and perhaps a desire for harmony urges each of us to align them for a given person. Thus the previous composite image of Gwin might have had a special dissonance, since her classmates would have liked to see an intelligent, honest person as being kind, too. With the kindness dimension out of line, an incongruous, discomforting image existed; hence pressure might have been felt to raise the ratings in the goodwill dimension to achieve symmetry.

Each person may experience pressure toward symmetry in the images constructed; yet each of us can and does have composite representations of others in which the various dimensions maintain disparate ratings. Each of us, no doubt, can think of someone who is deemed very bright yet not very honest or kind. Many other combinations of uneven dimensions can be noted for the images created. One probably desires more consonance if such appears to be possible— particularly for those close to oneself, and especially with the goodwill dimension. Self-esteem is threatened if someone who is viewed as intelligent and honest is not perceived as amicably disposed toward oneself.

We can also note, and elaborate on this matter later, that the uncertainty over Patrick's honesty brings special difficulties. With this dimension weakened, almost all other attempts to improve the composite image are handicapped because of discounting in the face of possible deception. This suggests that a positive rating in the virtue (honesty) dimension is critical, since stimuli relating to the other dimensions are judged, at least in part, with regard to this one.

A link appears to exist between Juanita Coffee's difficulty in the inclusion area of social need and the quandary Patrick's classmates faced in assembling a coherent image for him. Juanita shows to her classmates that earlier in life she had been prejudicially defined as insignificant (literally, having no character worth including); thus Juanita and her fellow blacks had, in some cases still have, an intolerably difficult time establishing their legitimate claims to responsibility and affection in white-dominated society. When Juanita displayed the appropriate cues for a wholesome recognition and fulfillment of the inclusion need and for a positive development of the virtue or character dimension, the prejudice tended somehow to insist that she be viewed as of little worth and as one who had sneakily climbed above her place.[19]

Another parallel can be drawn between the control-need sector and the expertness or intelligence dimension of ethos. If one chooses wisely in managing his affairs and if he coacts appropriately with others, his control need is fulfilled and he will be gratified by a sense of being responsible; normally, he will be given a positive rating in the intelligence dimension.

A tie is also clear between the affection-need realm and the goodwill dimension of ethos. When one cares for others and they care for him, the affection need is met, and all involved develop the important sense of being lovable; surely, the goodwill dimension will be seen by those who create such identifications.

The foregoing discussion of the dimensions of ethos seems rather insensitive when one considers the complex images erected for the parties in a close one-to-one relationship. In

---

[19] For a profound discussion of the impact of hierarchy on social interaction, see Kenneth Burke, *A Rhetoric of Motives*, Berkeley, University of California Press, 1969, esp. pp. 141–142, 256–260.

such a relationship the individuals perhaps find entirely new dimensions; they certainly make fine discriminations within the three standard ones: The valued one may be seen as very intelligent in certain ways, about certain matters, under certain circumstances, and less intelligent in other ways, matters, and circumstances. The same refinements will appear in the virtue and goodwill dimensions.

Even though a general slicing of the image pie into intelligence, virtue, and goodwill dimensions may be inappropriate for certain interpersonal relationships, each of us should be aware of dimensionality in ethos. Dimensions, probably the three discussed, exist in the images one creates for others and the images others create for oneself.

Credit is Topic-Bound

Our final point in this exploration of the concept of ethos is that the credit extended because of a positive ethos will usually be topic-bound, at least insofar as the intelligence or expertness dimension is concerned. Chess champion Bobby Fischer may be accorded AAA credit ratings when the subject is chess, but few would view him as an expert on congeniality.

With the continued expansion of areas for specialization, accompanied by dramatic increases in the subject material relevant to each specialty, no one can become an expert without a careful limiting of focus. To be called a "dilettante" was once a compliment to one's refined taste in a broad range of interests. Today the label is usually pejorative and connotes a detached dabbler whose efforts and opinions count for little or nothing.[20]

In a sophisticated society, then, positive values given to the dimensions of a person's ethos do not automatically ensure sufficient credit for the acceptance of pronouncements in any subject area. To be sure, celebrities, mostly

[20] See the etymology of *dilettante* in the *Oxford English Dictionary*.

from the attention-getting yet peripheral world of enter-
tainment, advertisé products that usually are of marginal
importance in our lives. Many people at least attend to these
paid persuaders, and since the relevance is minimal while
the price is relatively small, some of us can muster enough
credit to make the purchase. The success of this advertising
must be adequate for the advertising companies to show the
sellers that their campaign is profitable. Having detoured to
remark this rebuttal, we return to our claim that the credit
for allowing identification via attraction is usually topic-
bound. The omniscience of the parent is soon challenged by
the child's "Teacher says." Shortly, the teacher too is
contradicted as the student recognizes other experts in a
media-crammed environment.

Pity the politician: pressed on one hand to take a position
on a spate of issues, yet having at the same time to project
competence, sincerity, and concern. The politician must
speak out or be fated to obscurity when out of office and
damned for inaccessibility while in. But, while speaking out
on issues of all sorts, the politician can hardly escape being
dubbed idiot, liar, and callous conniver. Credit is topic-
bound, and this assertion seems to need less and less qualification.

BUILDING ATTRACTION

To a degree, this entire book is aimed at building attraction.
Since attraction is such an important factor in interpersonal
communication, and since effective interpersonal communication is such an important factor in attraction, it could
hardly be otherwise. Chapter 1, besides setting out basic
descriptions and definitions, seeks to motivate a willingness
to share with each other. Vince, Mario, and Juanita, the
speakers we have already met, have responded positively to
this challenge, and such a response offers significant

meetings with fellow human beings; through these encounters, attraction bonds can form and be strengthened.

Chapter 2 introduces the rhetorical canons as a means of parceling out the study of communication. Within the canon structure, Chapter 3 concentrates on the *logos* part of invention. However, mastery of argument is closely allied to the control sector (being capable of managing, i.e., being responsible) of social need, thus it is also related to the intelligence or expertness dimensions of ethos and, since one is drawn to identify with a communicator who argues intelligently, mastery of argument is also connected to building attraction. A link to the inclusion area of social need and the virtue or trustworthiness dimension of ethos exists also. One who presents intelligent arguments is more likely to be included (deemed significant) than one who argues unintelligently; thus Chapter 3 is relevant for this area of building attraction. The affection realm of social need (the goodwill dimension of ethos) comes into play as well; a person who thinks and argues poorly is likely to live haphazardly, and to live haphazardly will be expensive both for self and others. Other things being equal, such a person has less chance to develop sufficient size for sharing (doing good works or manifesting real goodwill for others); therefore, the attraction exerted by goodwill has less opportunity to flourish.

The present chapter focuses on identification via attraction, and its aim is a better understanding of this process. Understanding plus disciplined practice should help everyone to build attraction more surely, thereby to communicate more effectively. However, interaction of the various parts in the process of communication has not precluded our isolating relatively discrete elements for study in the chapters and their subdivisions.

We recall our Joe college student from Chapter 2, for some initial observations. Suppose now that Joe has no misappropriations to hide. Joe might call on the attraction his father feels for him more strongly than in the earlier illustration.

He might telegraph only:

> Send money.
> Joe

No attempt at reasoned argument here, no fairly obvious nudge toward shouldering a father's burden, just a reliance on interpersonal attraction. To use so simple an appeal, Joe would have to be sure that his father trusted him with regard to need and use of the family's limited funds. If Dad sends money with no questions asked, one would realize that Joe knew what he was doing and that a remarkably strong attraction appears to exist in the inclusion, control, and affection areas: Dad sees Joe as significant, responsible, and lovable.

When such an ideal attraction bond exists, extensively documented argumentation is probably inappropriate. If Joe launches into a lengthy justification of his request for money while his father is ready to proceed solely on trust, a missing of minds occurs. Perhaps the missing suggests that Joe has begun to betray his end of the bargain, that he is "protesting too much." Perhaps Joe is just not sensitive to how he should communicate. In either case, the inappropriateness of the communication is regrettable: One ought not betray trust extended, and to proceed insensitively is an inefficient way to create the desired identification. Also, continued insensitivities will be costly for the intelligence dimension, possibly for other dimensions as well.

When attraction is high, then, the parties should cherish this relationship (i.e., should not act to strain the trust that exists). Each side should be aware of the kind of communication that will show sensitive reliance on the existing attraction.[21] Building attraction in this situation means careful maintenance so the bonds are continually reinforced.

[21] See Judson Mills and Elliot Aronson, "Opinion Change as a Function of the Communicator's Attractiveness and Desire to Influence," *Journal of Personality and Social Psychology,* **1** (1965), 173–177.

Returning to Joe as sketched in Chapter 2, one can see that the attraction bond between father and son is weaker than the ideal just set out. The great need for strategy shows flaws in the attraction that exists. Either consciously or unconsciously, Joe refers to an image he has of his father while preparing the poem appeal. Joe views his father as sufficiently intelligent to appreciate the poetic form and to decipher the intended meaning. Joe hopes his father will not be sharp enough to see through the form to the indiscretions it seeks to cover. Even if Dad is perceptive enough to read the truth between the lines, Joe hopes Dad's longsuffering in the goodwill dimension will overrule possible urgings from the intelligence and character dimensions: "It is time to help Joe learn an important lesson." Stating the last thought a bit differently, Joe wants Dad's affection for him to be a little shortsighted in order that possible promptings from the inclusion area ("help Joe treat himself and me as significant") and the control sector ("help Joe become more responsible") will be unheeded at this time.

In part of the foregoing strategy, whether Joe is consciously aware of it or not, he is working with what he thinks his father thinks of him. Joe, of course, expects his father to include him as amounting to something—as having significance. "Dad will not just scan this telegram and toss it out of sight and out of mind as he does with junk mail." Joe further assumes that his father does not give him a minus rating in the virtue or trustworthiness dimension; he expects his father to trust him sufficiently to grant the truth of "No mon/No fun." Joe looks for his father to respond as the model shows:

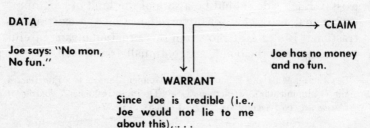

DATA ⟶ **CLAIM**

Joe says: "No mon, No fun."

Joe has no money and no fun.

WARRANT

Since Joe is credible (i.e., Joe would not lie to me about this),.. . .

Joe also believes that Dad loves him and responds with goodwill.

Taken by itself, Joe's use of strategy is not bad. Few coactions can be purely expressive (i.e., an actor simply lets out what wells up within and makes no adaptation to the intended auditor). Individuals usually have to consider the individual or group being addressed, to communicate with accuracy, meaning, and effectiveness. This does not contradict the point made previously that Joe's great need for strategy in the Chapter 2 rendition indicates an attraction relationship that is less ideal than the simple "Send money" ploy sketched above. Even a strong attraction relationship requires sensitive planning and careful performance (strategic concerns), to maintain and strengthen the bonds; still, one can assume that greater credit is available to cover for errors when attraction is relatively high.

Reviewing Joe's chosen strategy in the "No mon/No fun" condition, one can estimate that Dad's attraction to Joe has been shaken and is becoming less positively valenced. Now identification via attraction will be more difficult, and the strategy must be more nearly perfect to avoid failure, which will further damage the already strained tie. Given the weakened attraction, Joe chooses unwisely when he depends on this mode of identification as heavily as he does. When attraction is on the wane, one should not tax it too much because the link will be further strained, perhaps broken; then effective communication will become even more difficult. Instead of causing this dangerous stress, Joe would do well to look very hard for other remedies than the handout. Going without, or seeking the desired end in ways that involve a serious investment on the communicator's part, could help maintain or rebuild the value–attraction bond. Reasonable argument allied with sincere effort will yield better results than the unalloyed appeal to attraction.

Looking back on the "Send money" and "No mon/No fun" conditions, one can see that if attraction is high, the appropriate strategy is to rely on it (sensitively, of course) in the communicated appeal. If attraction is weaker, either because of withdrawals of credit or because the value–attraction ties are in the process of being forged, the appropriate strategy is to avoid a heavy dependence.

Imagine for condition three that Joe's credit with his father is extremely low. If Joe sent his telegram, Dad would receive it as the model shows:

DATA ─────────────────────────────→ **CLAIM**

Joe says: "No mon, No fun."

I do not believe Joe has no money and no fun.

WARRANT

Since Joe is not credible (he probably wants extra money to spend for an expensive party or for some other foolish fling), . . .

Attraction is indeed low, and Joe's attempt to communicate any need becomes perilously difficult.

Continuing to assume that Joe's misdeeds have brought about this estranged state, we contend that Joe now will have to work extra hard to make up the ground he has lost. Probably, Joe should go to talk with his father, like the Prodigal Son. The face-to-face encounter will give Dad both verbal and nonverbal cues on which to judge the sincerity of Joe's commitment to change. Whether Joe uses the face-to-face, written, or another channel, he will do well to reveal his mistakes honestly and to show a real willingness to attempt a difficult reform program.

No doubt we are all aware of repentances that have been short-lived and plans to rebuild that have gone agley. Admonitions probably should and do come, but this is not the place for such counsel. We can, however, touch on three points of specific relevance to this section on building attraction:

1. The regret–repair appeal can be used again and again, provided the forgiveness quotient discussed in the Epilogue maintains a plus sign; but the more often this appeal must be reused with a given partner, the less likely are the

chances for a healthy, mutually beneficial relationship:

> He comes unfailing for the loan
>   We give and then forget;
> He comes, and probably for years
>   Will he be coming yet,—
> Familiar as an old mistake,
>   And futile as regret.[22]

2. The regret-repair approach can be used for communications ranging from the opening of an overdue letter to the contrite pleading that follows a major injury of one person by another. The broad application and the apparent effectiveness of such an appeal can lead to overuse. General overuse diminishes the utility of this important means for rebuilding interpersonal attraction because the plea and promise become commonplace. Clearly, the best means to avoid overuse is to maintain strong attraction bonds by sensitive control of words and deeds.

3. Knowing the effectiveness of the regret-repair appeal, one may be tempted to fake it. The remorse is pretended, the promise insincere. Self-aggrandizing deception in interpersonal communication is always injurious, especially when the damage is to this final recourse in rebuilding an attraction bond.

To some extent the regret-repair plea is allied to the offering of "reluctant evidence."[23] In presenting reluctant evidence, the communicator testifies against actions and interests the auditor knows the communicator to have favored previously. Joe, in admitting his previous errors, is giving reluctant evidence: He testifies against previous pleas or presumptions of innocence. The witness who breaks down on the stand (under cross-examination by Perry Mason, Owen Marshall, or whoever plays the role of defender of the truth) and admits guilt is offering reluctant evidence. Such

---

[22] "Bewick Finzer" by Edwin Arlington Robinson.

[23] See Douglas Ehninger and Wayne Brockriede, *Decision by Debate*, New York, Dodd, Mead, 1963, p. 115.

evidence is unusually persuasive because the communicator seems to have no vested interest in having it accepted. Unsurprisingly, then, researchers have found that low-credibility sources can be persuasive if they offer reluctant evidence.[24]

Low credibility is a facet of an already formed image; that is, the low credibility is a dimension of an existing ethos. The use of reluctant evidence can still bring identification in this tenuous attraction condition because the attending coactor does not see the other grasping for selfish advantage (Aristotle's *Rhetoric*, 1417a). A related case can be made for using something like reluctant evidence in a newly forming attraction link. The person who seeks quick advantage by flashing certain honors and excellences is not pursuing an intelligent course for building interpersonal attraction. Vince and Mario could have talked about how wonderful they were and how well they had done in various competitions (we all know people who treat us to such dessert when an unimposing entrée would be a much more welcome first course); instead, Vince and Mario reveal significant aspects of themselves that do not obviously clamor for praise. By risking more of themselves and asking less from the delicate new attraction relationship, Vince and Mario build intelligently.

To begin by risking more of oneself and asking less of another indicates awareness of the fragility of the newly forming attraction bond. In addition, an initial coaction depends in a critical way on a reservoir of interpersonal credit that others have helped to create.[25] For some persons the reservoir may be nearly full when one comes to depend on it; for others the reservoir may be nearly dry. Whatever the supply of interpersonal trust, one should not draw on it any more than is necessary. As the attraction continually strengthens, one can depend on it more and more.

[24] See Elaine Walster, Elliot Aronson, and Darcy Abrahams, "On Increasing the Effectiveness of a Low Prestige Communicator," *Journal of Experimental Social Psychology,* **2** (1966), 325–342.

[25] See Reinhold Niebuhr, *Man's Nature and His Communities*, New York, 1965, pp. 106–109.

SUMMARY

Human beings are gregarious—they have social needs; this unifying factor underlies our chapter on "Identification via Attraction."

William Schutz sets out three major areas of social need: inclusion, control, and affection. The existence of social need and the acceptability of Schutz's trichotomy are illustrated by Juanita Coffee's speech about the racial discrimination she has experienced.

Need brings value, and one is attracted to what one values. The need–value–attraction progression yields attraction bonds that can serve by themselves as a means for creating identification; usually, however, identification is sought through an alliance of the argument and attraction modes.

Ethos, the composite of impressions one person has of another person, is a term that is frequently used in the study of attraction. The ethos or image may be positively or negatively valenced, and valencing has a great deal to do with the success or failure of the identification process. One can use the semantic differential and the congruity hypothesis both for explaining the concept of ethos and for assessing its effects in communication.

Although some images are more stable than others, all images change as identifications occur. Moreover, no two persons have precisely the same impression of someone else. Each person has a unique way of perceiving and structuring stimuli; hence each person will form original images of others. At the same time the images will overlap. The overlapping occurs because human beings are consubstantial, to some extent, in their processing of image-forming cues, and the overlapping occurs because the cues given have a measure of consistency.

Intelligence, virtue, and goodwill are three dimensions that commonly exist in ethos. These dimensions seem to be closely related to the control, inclusion, and affection areas of social need. Finally in our discussion of ethos, we note that the credit extended because of a positive valuing will be topic-bound.

Building attraction can be seen as a general task to be kept in mind throughout the book. More specifically, some advice can be given here for building attraction under various conditions. If attraction is high, the communicator should rely sensitively on the bond to achieve the desired identification and to strengthen the bond even more. If attraction is weaker (because of waning or still growing bonds), each of us should be careful not to overtax the bond. If attraction is low because of rash expenditure, the regret–repair appeal may furnish a means for rebuilding attraction. If an attraction bond is just beginning to form, communicators may wish to use something akin to reluctant evidence. This low-keyed approach probably will not be a serious drain on the existing reservoir of interpersonal trust.

QUESTIONS FOR THOUGHT AND DISCUSSION

1. Identify a public figure who is currently unattractive to you. What dimension suffers the most? How might this person begin to build attraction?
2. Consider your relationship with a close friend. How has your view of that person changed as you became better acquainted? Did you ever have a more positive view of your friend than you now have?
3. Read Vince's speech in Chapter 1. Do you feel attracted to Vince? Why or why not?
4. Compile a list of subjects on which you have considerable expertise relative to the rest of the class. How might you use your expertise in communicating with your class?
5. How important is the attraction of a teacher? Does the degree of attraction students feel for a teacher affect learning?

SUGGESTED READINGS

Andersen, Kenneth E., and Theodore Clevenger, "A Summary of Experimental Research on Ethos," *Speech Monographs,* **30,** 1963, 59–78.

Berscheid, Ellen, and Elaine H. Walster, *Interpersonal Attraction,* Reading, Mass., Addison-Wesley, 1969.

Schutz, William C., *The Interpersonal Underworld,* Palo Alto, Calif., Science and Behavior Books, 1966.

5 understanding human motivation: an aid to identification

Much time each day is spent making choices. One chooses to go to a movie rather than study, to go to college rather than enlist in the army, to vote Democratic rather than Republican, or pie rather than cake for dessert. Daily activities involve choices that require virtually no attention and choices that call for lengthy deliberation. Some choices have great importance for oneself and others, and some are very trivial. Summed together, one's choices show not only what one believes and values but also who one is.

The concept of choice is central to our discussion of human motivation; for example, some of the above-mentioned choices could be rephrased as follows: Why is one motivated to attend a particular movie? Why is one not motivated to study? Why is one motivated to attend college? Theories of human motivation attempt to describe the motivational forces that explain the direction, vigor, and persistence of behaviors.[1] The theories attempt to explain the choices a person makes.

In Chapter 1 we described communication as an ongoing process in which coactors share information to create identification. When an identification is achieved, the coactors become more similar: They share something new. In this chapter we want to illuminate human motivation as an aid to seekers of identification by examining the shared belief,

[1] John W. Atkinson, *An Introduction to Motivation*, New York, Van Nostrand, Reinhold, 1964, p. 4.

attitude, and value systems, and by looking at the universal feelings of pleasure and pain. This discussion, too, is based on the many and one premise. Humans have in common the possession of a motivational framework, but each person remains unique and autonomous.

A FRAMEWORK FOR VIEWING HUMAN MOTIVATION

Human behavior is extremely complex; thus, unsurprisingly, a complete explanation of human motivation has yet to be formulated. One can argue that the continuing existence of autonomy precludes the development of such a theory; nevertheless, perceptive and useful explanations have been advanced.

It is difficult to develop a comprehensive explanation for human motivation because so little is known and, paradoxically, so much opinion is available. Few subject areas are devoid of conjecture regarding human conduct. The literature of religion, philosophy, English, sociology, psychology, speech communication, and other fields is replete with explanations for human actions; but amid this wealth of information, little agreement exists on the theoretical model that best integrates and explains this wealth of data. The description of motivation presented in this chapter must be understood as representing only a sample of available materials. We believe, however, that the theories we discuss provide a useful view of human behavior, and we think that the various explanations of human motivation share, to a significant degree, a model of behavior.

Each of the theories conceives of human behavior in terms of two more or less polar states or conditions. One of these conditions is sought, the other is avoided. The positive or preferred state can be described as a condition of harmony. One is at peace with oneself. One's system is at rest. The negative state represents a condition of disequilibrium or discomfort and results in pressure for the restoration of internal harmony. The greater the disequilibrium, the greater the pressure to restore harmony. One is, in short, motivated to achieve and maintain a state of harmony and to avoid or relieve a state of disequilibrium. Consistency theories underscore the preference for balance (consistency) among beliefs, attitudes, values, and actions. Hedonistic theories of motivation are based on the pleasure–pain principle. We all strive for the pleasurable and prefer to avoid the painful.

These theories suggest that communicators who seek identification may employ several different approaches to arouse motivational pressure: (1) they may present material that will result in a state of disequilibrium, then offer solutions that will restore a state of harmony; (2) the participants may try to demonstrate that the action proposed will preserve a positive state; (3) conversely, they may try to show that a failure to act as proposed will result in imbalance. In the sections that follow, we detail the applications of these approaches.

PLEASURE AND PAIN

The view that human behavior can be explained by considering two polar conditions has its roots in hedonistic philosophy. For centuries hedonistic theories have attempted to predict behavior on the basis of pleasure and pain. Human beings, it is reasoned, will engage in activities that tend to maximize the pleasure–pain ratio.

This notion typically is attributed to the Greek philosopher Epicurus, in whose writings hedonism is presented as a self-centered philosophy.[2] The desire to seek pleasure and avoid pain is seen as an innate feature of all men. Although Epicurus is usually viewed as the founder of he-

[2] *Epicurus: The Extant Remains*, trans. Cyril Bailey, London, Oxford University Press, 1926.

donistic philsophy, the notion that human beings seek pleasure and avoid pain was a commonplace in Greek thought.

In relatively modern times, the most extensive and appealing statement of the hedonic position has been offered by Jeremy Bentham.[3] Bentham outlined a more altruistic hedonism in which pleasure and pain are considered for individuals as well as with reference to the greatest good for the greatest number.

Critics of hedonism maintain that the pleasure and pain categories do not provide a complete explanation for human actions. Because of each person's uniqueness, perceptions of pleasure and pain in any situation are difficult to predict. Individuals may perceive the pleasant and the painful in extremely different ways. Nevertheless, the general principle that humans pursue the pleasurable and avoid the unpleasant seems to hold true.

Recent behavioral research on fear-arousing appeals provides examples of pain avoidance as a motivational force for creating identification.[4] In the laboratory, fear appeals related to the need for dental hygiene and the dangers of cigarette smoking, to take just two examples, have been effective in producing attitudinal changes. The subjects are told that a failure to act will result in pain; for instance, if one continues to smoke cigarettes, one may contract lung cancer. If one adopts the advocated position, he presumably avoids the uneasiness (pain) that the appeal to fear caused. This research, as well as widespread experience with the effectiveness of appeals based on pleasure or pain, lead to the conclusion that communicators can create identifications by relying on the hedonic principle.

Although everyone probably likes pleasure and dislikes

---

[3] Jeremy Bentham, *An Introduction to Principles of Morals and Legislation*, Oxford, Clarendon, 1907. First published in 1789.

[4] This research has been summarized by C. William Colburn, "Fear Arousing Appeals," in *Speech Communication: Analysis and Readings*, Howard H. Martin and Kenneth E. Andersen, eds., Boston, Allyn & Bacon, 1968, pp. 214–223.

pain, merely knowing this elementary condition does not give foolproof control of human motivation. The fear-appeal research shows, for example, that the creation of the identifications depends partly on the degree of interpersonal attraction between the coactors, the perceived importance of the issue discussed, and various personality traits of the participants.[5] Furthermore, when certain fear appeals are pressed too strongly, some people may simply refuse to consider them.[6] Thus although the shared desire to maximize pleasure and minimize pain provides some insight for one seeking identification, one must not proceed as if a simple pleasure–pain explanation is adequate.

EXPOSITION OF CONSISTENCY THEORIES

The speech we use in our discussion of consistency theories demonstrates that consistency theory can be directly applied by those who aim to create identification. The speech was developed using Milton Rokeach's belief, attitude, and value model (elaborated later) and the *homeostatic principle* (i.e., that humans prefer a state of balance or harmony to a state of imbalance or dissonance), which is accepted in all consistency theories.

Steve Long presented the following speech to his classmates, who knew that Steve was participating in a program designed to procure a more highly educated police force. Steven had discussed his police affiliation in an earlier speech, and he told of the hostility he faced from other students because of his police work. Steve knew from the class's reactions in earlier communications and from the questionnaire responses he received that his auditors were less in favor of police professionalization than he was; in

[5] Ibid., pp. 218–222.

[6] Irving L. Janis and Seymour Feshbach, "Effects of Fear-Arousing Communications," *Journal of Abnormal and Social Psychology,* **48** (1953), 78–92.

fact, Steve was sure that several classmates were rather strongly opposed to any measures that would improve the police.

Steve presented the speech extemporaneously, and his words were transcribed from a tape recording.

Recent studies by the National Crime Commission indi- 1
cate that somewhere between 6 and 8 percent of this 2
country's law enforcement officers have a college degree. It 3
is nonsense to assume that the enforcement of the law is so 4
simple that it can be done best by those unencumbered by a 5
study of the liberal arts. The men who go into our streets in 6
hopes of directing or controlling human behavior must be 7
armed with more than a gun and the ability to perform 8
mechanical movements. Such men as these engage in a dif- 9
ficult, important business that most people just read about 10
in their living rooms. The intellectual and professional 11
armament of the police, so long restricted to the minimum, 12
must be no less than their physical prowess and protection. 13

I would like to invite you to join me on a routine patrol 14
shift. The reading that I take from the log is based on actual 15
incidents; only the names have been changed to protect the 16
innocent. 17

As we leave the police station at 4:00 P.M., the first radio 18
report comes as follows: "Unit 43: Have an 1183 at Mon- 19
tana and Sycamore. Proceed code 2." An 1183—all we know 20
by that is that a no-detail accident has just occurred. We 21
don't know if an injury is involved or not. Code 2 is an ur- 22
gency alert, which means that we get there as quickly as 23
possible without using sirens or lights. When we arrive on 24
the scene, suddenly we are aware that we no longer have a 25
no-detail accident. It becomes an 1184, a serious accident. A 26
child on a bicycle has been struck by a car. He was thrown 27
from the bicycle, skidded across the street, and he is now 28
lying against the curbing, his neck broken and his brains 29
strewn on the street. Immediately, we send in an 1141 30
report: "We need an ambulance." Not long after that it be- 31
comes an 1144, a coroner's case, and we make a routine 32

1146, which is a death report. Unfortunately, our first taste 33
of law enforcement has to be with something that is difficult 34
to stomach. 35

The patrol turns to the light side quickly. At 5:45 P.M. 36
with our thoughts still on the accident, we get another radio 37
report: "Unit 43: We have a 417 just occurred at 1119 West 38
Sixth Terrace. Proceed code 2." Once again we are not sure 39
what the situation is. A 417 only tells us that we have a 40
threat with a weapon. As we proceed, code 2 (in a rush, not 41
using lights or siren) we keep thinking the four words, 42
"threat with a weapon." How serious could it be? We arrive 43
at the scene—it's a residence—knock at the door, and find 44
out that it's nothing more than a husband and wife ar- 45
gument. The wife has thrown a mixing bowl at her husband. 46
The adrenalin can stop flowing now. We give a warning to 47
the wife because the man isn't ready to press charges. 48

At 6:20 P.M. we observe a child on a bicycle run a stop 49
sign. It's an automatic citation, but under most circum- 50
stances we'd probably ignore it—except we can still see the 51
boy at 4 o'clock lying against the curbing with his head split 52
open. We stop the boy to give him a citation. In the process 53
his mother comes out of the house about three doors down 54
and proceeds to chew us out. His mother is irate because we 55
are not out rounding up the real criminals. We're stupid 56
enough to fill our quotas by giving citations to little boys on 57
bicycles. If we were comical, we might tell her that we don't 58
have a quota; we can give as many tickets as we like. But 59
we're not humorous at this point, so we simply tell the 60
mother that it is against the law to run a stop sign on a 61
bicycle and that the boy deserves a citation. And it's for his 62
own good. 63

At 7:20 P.M. we receive another alert: "Unit 43: We have a 64
possible 187 in progress, beach area at State. Screams were 65
heard, be advised. Proceed code 3." A code 3 is the most ur- 66
gent message. As we are driving along talking about who we 67
want to be president, the silence is shattered by the an- 68
nouncement of a possible murder in progress. It's not often 69
that we have a murder in progress. We change from 40 70

miles per hour to 100 miles per hour. It's about 7:30 at night   71
and we speed through busy intersections. "Units 61, 42, 40   72
copy last message." En route we begin wondering what the   73
situation will be when we arrive. Is it going to be a gang   74
fight on the beach? Is it going to be simply that someone has   75
pulled a gun and is threatening someone else? En route we   76
receive another message: "Unit 43: 1023." This is a "stand-   77
by" message. Here we are at 100 miles an hour, a possible   78
murder in progress, and now the idiots at the police station   79
want us to stand by for a further report. "Your call is now   80
confirmed; change to 261 [no longer a murder, we have a   81
rape now], code 3 still advised. Units 61, 42, 40 copy."   82
When we arrive at the scene, we find a lady at the side of   83
the bamboo shoots on the beach, naked, with blood all over   84
her body. A man runs from the bamboo shoots and down   85
the beach. I chase him for a while and am not able to catch   86
him. I pull my weapon, identify myself as a policeman and   87
ask him to halt. He continues to draw away. Now I have to   88
make a quick decision, the man will probably get away if I   89
don't fire. I fire a warning shot, but that does not stop him.   90
It's a tough decision to make whether or not to shoot some-   91
body, especially with the idea flashing through my mind that   92
the woman is lying there perhaps dead already.   93

This decision, I think, needs to be made by someone who   94
is at least a professional. Not some of the amateurs who are   95
on the force today.   96

At 8:45 P.M. we have another radio report: "Unit 43: Have   97
a 417 at 942 South Ninth Street. Proceed code 2." [One of   98
the more open members of the class interrupts to blurt out   99
the question all the others are asking themselves as well: 100
"What was the decision?" "Well," Steve said, "I made a   101
mistake, and I fired the weapon and shot the man in the leg,   102
and you're not supposed to do that. That's why I didn't put   103
it in; I hate to make mistakes." When the reaction has   104
subsided, Steve picks up smoothly by repeating the last   105
report.] "Unit 43: Have a 417 at 942 South Ninth Street.   106
Proceed code 2." Another 417. You remember that's   107
another threat with a weapon. The last one turned out to be   108

a laugher. We arrive at the scene and find out it's not at the 109
address we were given after all. It's in a parking lot next 110
door. No weapon appears to be involved. It's simply a minor 111
argument between two groups of juveniles in cars. We 112
should run a standard 1029 on the subjects, which is a 113
"check for wants" process, to make sure that none of them 114
are wanted. It's a computer system that runs national. 115
However, we receive a lot of flak from the subjects. They 116
are very upset and tell us that we want to run a 1029 on 117
them simply because they have long hair. That forces us to 118
go ahead and run a 1029. All the subjects are 1129, which is 119
no record; however, one, J.D., has a code 37f. We've been 120
told a felony warrant is out one of the individuals—J.D. We 121
have to decide how we are going to make an arrest. We don't 122
know if the boy has a gun on him or any other weapon. Also, 123
he doesn't know that we know he's wanted. It's another dif- 124
ficult decision. The shakedown produces a knife and a 125
silencer unit for a .44 caliber gun. A .44 caliber gun is the 126
most powerful hand weapon in the world. A moment ago we 127
were trying to make a decision on whether or not to run the 128
standard 1029. It would have been a heck of a lot easier just 129
to forget the situation and go·on our coffee break. Once 130
again, I say, it's a difficult decision to make. 131

At 10 P.M. we receive another radio report: "Unit 43: 132
Have a 415 family at 33 Louisiana Street. Be advised 133
possible 314." A 415 family is a public disturbance of a 134
family argument nature. The 314 possibility is indecent ex- 135
posure. We arrive, knock on the door, and the woman 136
answers. She is cut above the lip, blood is coming down. We 137
ask the woman what's happened, and she says her husband 138
has struck her. We try to get her to press charges. She 139
refuses. The man comes from the kitchen—obviously had a 140
few drinks. He's naked and starts shouting obscenities at us 141
pigs and tells us to get out of his house. It's another difficult 142
decision to make. Actually, there is not much we can do. 143
Certainly, what should be done cannot be done by someone 144
unskilled in the art of psychology. If we were psychologists 145
we might be able to persuade the guy that he should dress 146

and leave the house for a period of time. Clearly, the woman 147
is not in safe circumstances; however, once again, we have 148
nothing that we can really do unless we're something more 149
than poorly trained police officers. 150

A few minutes after we leave the home, we observe a 151
23103, which is a reckless driving citation. We stop the man 152
and give him a field test. He fails the field test, and we 153
proceed with the drunk driving arrest. Suppose that you are 154
putting him in the car, and he spits in your face. It's 155
another very difficult situation to handle. 156

We'll end our patrol shift here, and I'd like to return to 157
the issue I raised at the beginning and several times along 158
the way. The issue concerns professionalizing our police 159
forces. I have been concerned with this issue for some time, 160
and I've been especially troubled over it since I got your 161
responses to my questionnaire. One-half of the students in 162
this class are opposed to making steps toward a more 163
central and professional police organization throughout the 164
country. That fact scares me. As Ralph Nader has chosen to 165
professionalize the citizenry, so should we decide to 166
professionalize our police. A felony is committed every three 167
seconds in this country while a policeman is shot every 168
three days. It takes a very long time to make the hard de- 169
cision to face a patrol shift. While on patrol, many difficult 170
decisions must be made, often with very little time. To even 171
begin to do the job well, the police officer and the police or- 172
ganization must be pros and not pigs.   .   173

The Belief-Attitude-Value System

We said earlier that Steve Long wanted to create an identification with the notions of a common belief-attitude-value
system and a common desire for homeostasis in mind. In
discussing Steve's speech, we turn first to the manner in
which it illustrates the role of the belief-attitude-value
system in creating identification.

Milton Rokeach, who has outlined a comprehensive depiction of a person's belief, attitude, and value system says: "A belief is any simple proposition . . . inferred from what a person says or does, capable of being preceded by the phrase 'I believe that.'"[7] Attitudes are more complex. They represent, Rokeach says, "an organization of beliefs around a common subject."[8] Values are enduring beliefs regarding the conduct of life and the end goals of life. As central enduring beliefs, values have the capacity to influence decisions and actions in a wide variety of situations.

Rokeach's description of the belief system (see Figure 6) has been widely accepted and it is consistent with several earlier models. The components of the system—beliefs, attitudes, and values vary along a central peripheral or a general-specific continuum. Beliefs are specific and peripheral; values are central and general. Attitudes fall between the more peripheral beliefs and the more central

Figure 6.   Rokeach's model of the belief system.

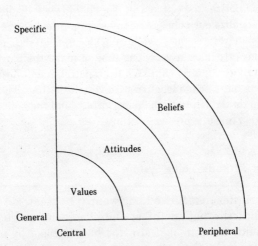

[7] Milton Rokeach, *Beliefs, Attitudes and Values*, San Francisco, Jossey-Bass, 1968, p. 111.

[8] Ibid., p. 116.

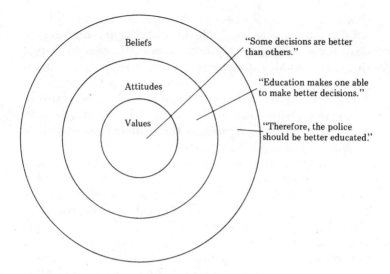

Figure 7. A Rokeach Model for Steve Long.

values. Although attitudes, beliefs, and values are thus distinguishable in terms of their scope and centrality, it is important to note that their characteristics and functions are similar. Moreover, beliefs, attitudes, and values are closely linked and related to one another.

One of Steve's intentions was to create an identification at the belief level. When the communication was completed, Steve hoped to share with his listeners the belief that "the police should be better educated." In seeking this identification, Steve assumed that his audience shared the basic value he operated on ("Some decisions are better than others."). No doubt Steve was safe in this assumption. Only someone who was an exceedingly thorough absurdist would have a contrary value. But such a believer in the absurd could hardly dispute Steve's assertion, because any urge to argue would undercut the absurdist's position. After all, why argue if any decision (or assumption) is as good or bad as any other?

Steve's message also incorporated an important attitude

that, once again, he assumed was shared by the audience ("Education makes one able to make better decisions."). The audience might have had more inclination to dispute this than the value statement, but none of Steve's classmates raised any objection in this realm. Probably their presence in a college classroom made any serious challenges of this attitude statement unlikely. Figure 7, a Rokeach model for Steve, schematically represents the relative positions of the beliefs, attitudes, and values.

If one grants that some decisions are better than others, that police are needed to handle trying situations and to make difficult decisions (that police as a rule are not well educated: lines 1–3 and elsewhere), and that one would like the police to decide as competently as possible, one has the data for Steve's major argument. Next, the attitude statement, "Education makes one able to make better decisions," serves as Steve's warrant. The conclusion, "Therefore, the police need to be better educated," is not easy to avoid. This argumentation will probably be more clear if we set it out as Steve's major argument model:

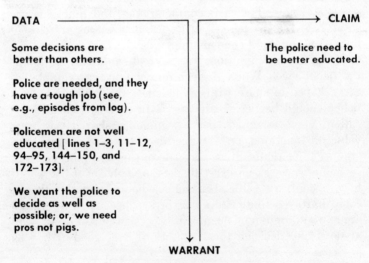

DATA ──────────────────────────────────→ CLAIM

Some decisions are
better than others.

Police are needed, and they
have a tough job (see,
e.g., episodes from log).

Policemen are not well
educated [lines 1–3, 11–12,
94–95, 144–150, and
172–173].

We want the police to
decide as well as
possible; or, we need
pros not pigs.

The police need to
be better educated.

WARRANT

Since education makes one able
to make better decisions, . . .

Steve's reliance on the shared value and attitude, plus the related argumentation he provides, is a potential challenge to the previously expressed antipolice and anti-police-professionalization attitudes and beliefs of some of his listeners. In this way Steve relies on the consubstantial element–humans are alike in having belief-attitude-value systems—in trying to create identification.

The Consistency Principle

We have said that Steve's effort to create identification also relies on the consistency theory premise (homeostatic principle) that human beings prefer a state of balance or harmony to one of imbalance or dissonance. This consistency principle has been the basis for a number of useful explanations for belief and attitude change. The explanations assume that humans strive to maintain consistency among the elements of their belief systems. Consistency represents a state of harmony—the pleasant condition. Inconsistency, being an unpleasant condition, will motivate one to change beliefs and attitudes, to find or restore consistency.[9] We will discuss one such consistency theory, and then we will return to Steve's speech for further application.

Leon Festinger's theory of cognitive dissonance describes the desire to maintain consistency among all of one's "cognitions."[10] (A *cognition* is "any knowledge, opinion, or belief about the environment, about oneself, or about one's behavior."[11]) Whenever a person perceives "nonfitting" or inconsistent cognitions, he experiences cognitive dissonance.

[9] Several balance or consistency theories have been formulated. See Fritz Heider, "Attitudes and Cognitive Organization," *Journal of Psychology,* **21** (1946), 107–112; Theodore M. Newcomb, "An Approach to the Study of Communicative Acts," *Psychological Review,* **60** (1953), 393–404; Charles Osgood and Percy Tannenbaum, "The Principle of Congruity in the Prediction of Attitude Change," *Psychological Review,* **62** (1955), 42–55; Leon Festinger, *A Theory of Cognitive Dissonance,* New York, Harper & Row, 1957.

[10] Festinger, *A Theory of Cognitive Dissonance.*

[11] Ibid., p. 3.

"The existence of dissonance, being psychologically uncomfortable, will motivate a person to try to reduce the dissonance and achieve consonance."[12] The magnitude or strength of the dissonance is a function of the number and the importance of the cognitions that one perceives to be existing in an inconsistent relationship. Festinger further hypothesizes that humans actively attempt to avoid dissonance.

At one level, the desire for consistency can be understood as testimony for a rational view of man. At another level, the means by which consistency is achieved and maintained are not necessarily rational. Dissonance theory predicts that humans will deliberately avoid some information, selectively seek other information, and even distort information, to maintain consonance. These behaviors could easily be described as irrational.[13]

Whether a given behavior appears rational or irrational, human beings do possess a strong desire for consistency, and this desire operates as a potent motivational force. This is true even though total consistency among values, attitudes, beliefs, and actions is an unreachable ideal. Most of us are willing to tolerate a certain number of inconsistent relationships. Even so, the high value that is placed on consistency is shown by the hundreds of research studies that have supported predictions derived from dissonance theory.

What happens when one advocates ideas or engages in activities that are inconsistent with beliefs, attitudes, and values? Dissonance theory predicts that participants will change their evaluation of the idea or activity.[14] This principle may be illustrated by the persuasive campaign, either for a political candidate or a charitable organization. One strategy used in these campaigns is to actively involve as

[12] Ibid.

[13] Robert B. Zajonc, "The Concepts of Balance, Congruity and Dissonance," *Public Opinion Quarterly,* **24** (1960), 280–296.

[14] A summary and review of research in this area is given in Ralph L. Rosnow and Edward J. Robinson, *Experiments in Persuasion*, New York, Academic Press, 1967, pp. 297–345.

many persons as possible. The hope is that someone who has spent time and energy working for the cause will become more committed to it. If you spend several evenings urging your neighbors to support the United Fund, your belief in this charity is likely to be strengthened. You can only justify your increased expenditure of time and effort if you have a more positive attitude toward the organization.

A similar effect has been observed when individuals are placed in decision-making situations and required to choose one of two attractive alternatives.[15] Assume that you are shopping for a new car. The choices are a Ford and a Chevrolet. You like the Chevrolet best, but the Ford can be purchased at a $300 reduction. Whichever car you choose, you will experience dissonance because your action will be inconsistent with the attractive features of the unchosen alternative; thus if you choose the Ford, you can restore consonance by strengthening your belief that the $300 price differential was very significant, and you are likely to minimize the cost difference if you choose the Chevrolet. In either case, you have modified your beliefs to relieve dissonance.

Dissonance theory also predicts that individuals seek information that supports their attitudes and avoid information and situations that are likely to produce dissonance.[16] This prediction is consistent with the general notion that the human "intake" system carefully screens and filters reality. Filtering may occur at four stages: exposure, attention, perception, and recall. Research has demonstrated that each stage may operate to limit the amount of unpleasant, discrepant, dissonance-producing information that is received.[17]

Dissonance theory treats the selection of information at

---

[15] Festinger, *A Theory of Cognitive Dissonance*, pp. 48–83. Additional research in this area is summarized by Jack W. Brehm and Arthur R. Cohen, *Explorations in Cognitive Dissonance*, New York, Wiley, 1962.

[16] Festinger, *A Theory of Cognitive Dissonance*, pp. 123–176.

[17] A very clear summary of these filtering processes may be found in James McCroskey, *An Introduction to Rhetorical Communication*, Englewood-Cliffs, N.J., Prentice-Hall, 1968, pp. 42–44.

the exposure level. Clearly, selective exposure occurs: Individuals are more likely to listen to a candidate of their own party than to one from the opposition; one's friends probably hold attitudes similar to one's own; people choose to belong to groups that embody their private attitudes. Perhaps all these actions cannot be explained merely by the desire to avoid cognitive dissonance. We all select our friends, our groups, and the speakers to whom we listen for a wide variety of reasons. Although one may argue that dissonance avoidance is not an adequate explanation for all selective exposure, dissonance avoidance probably is a significant factor.[18]

A third application of dissonance theory has been in communication settings where one person attempts to change another's attitude. The first person presents information and arguments that support a chosen position. When this position differs from the other person's, the presentation should result in dissonance. The listener may avoid this dissonance or restore consonance in a variety of ways. The listener may choose to derogate the communicator: "He doesn't know what he is talking about." The listener may simply refuse to listen, or he may distort the speaker's message (selective attention or selective perception). Or, as the source hopes, the listener may change the beliefs and attitudes related to the issue being discussed. Aronson, Turner, and Carlsmith have shown that selective attention or selective perception are unlikely in small group, face-to-face settings, and that the most likely modes of dissonance reduction are (1) derogation of the communicator, (2) attitude or belief change on the issue, or (3) some combination of derogation and attitude change.[19] If the speaker is highly at-

[18] Jonathan L. Freedman and David O. Sears, "Selective Exposure." In Leonard Berkowitz, ed., *Advances in Experimental Social Psychology,* vol. 2, New York, Academic Press, pp. 57–97; Chester A. Insko, *Theories of Attitude Change,* Englewood Cliffs, N.J., Prentice-Hall, 1967, pp. 198–284.

[19] Elliot Aronson, Judith A. Turner, and J. Merrill Carlsmith, "Communicator Credibility and Communication Discrepancy as Determinants of Opinion Change," *Journal of Abnormal and Social Psychology,* **67** (1963), 31–36.

tractive, derogation is very difficult, and attitude change is more likely. If the speaker is unattractive, derogation is the most likely outcome. Figure 8 illustrates this effect. Whether the communicator's message is slightly, moderately, or very discrepant, the attractive (high-credibility) source is more likely to succeed in securing the desired change in attitude.[20] The result of such attitude change is an identification between the persons involved.

These applications of dissonance theory illustrate how, in a variety of situations, one's desire to maintain a consistent relationship among values, attitudes, beliefs, and actions may serve as a motivational force. Communicators should harness the power of the desire for consistency in a manner that will aid in creating identifications.

Steve Long attempted to create dissonance within his listeners' belief-attitude-value systems. One illustration

Figure 8. Dissonance reduction in the speaker–audience setting: solid curves, observed; dashed curves, theoretical. (Elliot Aronson, Judith A. Turner, and J. Merrill Carlsmith, "Communicator Credibility and Communication Discrepancy as Determinants of Opinion Change," Journal of Abnormal and Social Psychology, **67** (1963), 31–36.)

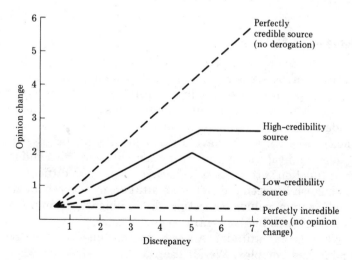

[20] Ibid.

comes from the argument we discussed earlier. Steve assumed that he already shared two important premises with his listeners: (1) Some decisions are better than others, and (2) education makes one better able to make decisions. Throughout his message, Steve used examples to demonstrate that the policemen must make many important decisions. If the police must make important decisions and if education helps to make better decisions, it seems to follow that the police should be better trained. To believe the opposite would appear to be inconsistent, thus dissonance producing. Steve, then, attempted to create a new identification with his listeners by demonstrating shared premises and employing the consistency principle to motivate the change desired.

Steve spoke to a group who had expressed antipolice attitudes. His presentation contained several incidents revealing policemen as concerned, thoughtful, and humane. These positive qualities are apparently inconsistent with the listeners' antipolice attitudes. Steve hoped that as a result of his communication, the listeners would associate these more positive qualities with policemen, thereby coming to hold a less negative attitude toward the police.

Recognizing Attitudes

As each of us seeks to create identification, there will be many opportunities to apply the principle of consistency. We believe, however, that such applications are more readily made by focusing on the concept of attitude. We make this choice because, as we have already mentioned, beliefs, attitudes, and values are similar in their characteristics and in their function within the belief system. It is often difficult to distinguish between a belief or an attitude, or between an attitude and a value. Reflecting this ambiguity, communication research has concentrated on attitudes.

What is an attitude? Answers to this question can be simple and complex. We all use the term frequently when discussing how we feel toward the government, toward chemistry, or toward women's liberation. People often characterize others in terms of their "attitudes" toward persons, ideas, or policies. Our frequent, easy use of the term "attitude" perhaps belies the complex and lengthy study during which investigators have tried to make the concept more precise.[21] Within this more refined treatment, we define attitude as *a predisposition to respond evaluatively toward a person, an institution, or an idea.*[22]

Attitudes are difficult to define precisely because they are hypothetical constructs: No one can see, hear, touch, taste, or smell an attitude. One can only infer the existence of attitudes by observing behavior. One who fails to salute the flag is said to have a negative attitude toward his country. By the same token, statements of praise regarding the United States are interpreted as indices of a positive attitude. The attitude must be inferred from the behavior. But it is often possible to make incorrect inferences. People fail to salute the flag or praise the United States for a variety of reasons. Fortunately, however, attitudes can be measured rather accurately by asking individuals to report their predispositions. This is most commonly accomplished with a paper-and-pencil measure such as the semantic differential (Chapter 4, pp. 72–74). These self-report measures have been extremely useful in operationalizing attitudes and in monitoring attitudinal changes.

All attitudes have certain characteristics. First, attitudes are learned; they are the result of experience. Imagine, for

[21] Gordon W. Allport, "Attitudes," in *A Handbook of Social Psychology,* C. Murchison, ed., Worcester, Mass., Clark University Press, 1935. A stimulating critique of the concept attitude may be found in Daniel Katz and E. Stotland, "A Preliminary Statement to a Theory of Attitude Structure and Change." In *Psychology: A Study of Science,* Stanley Koch, ed., New York, McGraw-Hill, 1959, pp. 423–475.

[22] This definition is condensed from Allport's description of attitudes. He defined an attitude as "a mental and neural state of readiness, organized through experience, exerting a directive or dynamic influence upon the individual's response to all objects and situations to which it is related." Allport, "Attitudes," p. 810.

example, that you were bitten by the first dog you ever encountered. The second dog you met growled and frightened you. Almost certainly you developed negative attitudes toward dogs. As you grew, you met both friendly and hostile canines. After a time you thought you saw that unfriendly dogs shared certain physical traits. They were, you learned, called German shepherds. You found that dogs lacking the shepherd characteristics were very friendly. Your attitudes toward dogs were modified and became more complex. Now you have negative attitudes toward certain breeds and, perhaps, very positive attitudes toward others. Similarly, those listening to Steve's message who have had lengthy and close association with the police are likely to hold more complex attitudes than those who have not had such experiences.

As this illustration suggests, attitudes can be thought of as abstractions from experience(s). The more numerous the experiences or the more complete the data about the attitude object, the more complex and well developed will be the attitude. An attitude that is based on a large number of experiences is less likely to change. But an attitude is always a generalization; it always represents a summation of previous experiences with the attitude object.

Second, attitudes vary both in direction and in intensity. Directionally, attitudes will usually be positive or negative. Attitudes can also be neutral; most attitudes, however, tend to be valenced to some degree. The extent to which attitudes are valenced refers to their intensity (i.e., from a slight positive or negative feeling to a very strong feeling of approval or disapproval).

Third, attitudes vary in salience or importance. This characteristic has been described in depth by Sherif, Sherif, and Nebergall.[23] The importance or salience of an attitude often correlates positively with intensity. One is more likely to hold an intense attitude regarding issues that are very im-

---

[23] Carolyn W. Sherif, Muzafer Sherif, and Roger Nebergall, *Attitude and Attitude Change*, Philadelphia, Saunders, 1965. An earlier statement of this principle appears in Muzafer Sherif and Carl Hovland, *Social Judgment*, New Haven, Conn., Yale University Press, 1961.

portant, but in some instances attitudes may be intense yet unimportant. One may strongly condemn the actions of a foreign dictator, even though his actions do not strongly affect oneself. Occasionally, attitudes that are neutral, or nearly so, are very important.[24] In most cases, however, importance and intensity are correlated.

Finally, attitudes are relatively enduring states. Once a given attitude is developed, people tend to maintain the position it represents for a considerable period. In part, of course, resistance to change is a function of the complexity, intensity, and importance of the attitude. Because attitudes tend toward stability, a communicator should usually not expect that a single coaction will bring radical changes. The skillful communicator will usually seek an identification that calls for only a modest amount of attitude change. If a communicator takes a position that is very discrepant from the listener's, the attempt may boomerang and cause a strengthening of the listener's current attitude. This effect is illustrated in Figure 9. A change in attitude requires that the

Figure 9.   The relationship of message discrepancy and attitude change.

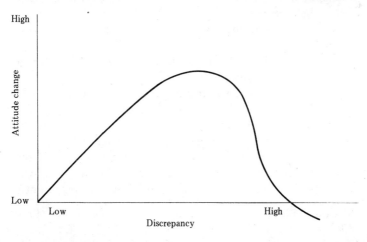

[24] James C. McCroskey, "Latitude of Acceptance and the Semantic Differential," *Journal of Social Psychology,* **74** (1968), 127–132.

source endorse a position that is discrepant from the receiver's. Trumpeting a discrepant position, however, may hinder or even reverse the identification process. Such reversals may help account for a "generation gap."

The Relations Between Attitudes and Behavior

In the foregoing discussion we have maintained that attitude change is an important way of creating identification. However, attitude change is seldom more than an instrumental goal in communication. For although one may seek attitude change, the usual ultimate goal is to influence behavior. The activist tries to rally the crowd to demonstrate. The advertiser wants people to not only like the product but to buy it. Joe wants Dad to send money. Steve wants his listeners to support police professionalization.

An attitude, as defined earlier, involves a *predisposition to respond*; hence, when an attitude changes, the response (behavior) toward the attitude object should be affected. Attitudes, in other words, are an important motivating factor because behavior reflects attitudes.

The relationship between attitude change and behavior change has frequently been questioned. It is claimed that people often behave in a manner that appears to be inconsistent with their privately held attitudes. LaPiere surveyed hotel and restaurant owners regarding the provision of service to Chinese.[25] A vast majority of the owners indicated they would not provide such service. However, when Chinese visited these businesses, only a very small percentage of owners refused to provide service.[26] The owners seemed to be acting in a manner inconsistent with their expressed attitude. The assumption in this argument is

[25] Richard LaPiere, "Attitudes vs. Action," *Social Forces,* **13** (1934) 230–237.

[26] Ibid. See also, Melvin DeFleur and Frank Westie, "Verbal Attitudes and Overt Acts: An Experiment on the Salience of Attitudes," *American Sociological Review,* **23** (1958), 667–673.

that behavior can be understood as the reflection of a single attitude. However, each of our actions is influenced by a group or cluster of attitudes.

During the late 1960s demonstrations against the war in Vietnam were a common event on college campuses. Students were frequently involved in influencing their friends to attend and participate in these demonstrations. Student leaders were sometimes frustrated, particularly during the later stages of the war, by the small number of students who attended antiwar functions. These small numbers seemed to be contrary to the knowledge that a majority of students on most campuses held strongly negative attitudes toward the war. The decision to participate in rallies and demonstrations, however, was influenced by factors in addition to this single attitude. Figure 10 indicates how the decision to protest the war may have been influenced by four different attitudes.

Surely the decision to participate in antiwar activities

Figure 10.   The relationship of attitudes and behavior.

Attitudes Favoring Participation	POSSIBLE ATTITUDES TOWARD PARTICIPATION				
	Student A	*Student B*	*Student C*	*Student D*	*Student E*
I oppose the administration's war policies.	Agree	Agree	Agree	Agree	Disagree
Demonstrations are effective.	Agree	Agree	Agree	Disagree	Disagree
I trust the demonstration leaders.	Agree	Agree	Disagree	Disagree	Disagree
I am willing to sacrifice some of my study time.	Agree	Disagree	Disagree	Disagree	Disagree
Likelihood of participation	Very high	Probably will	Uncertain	Probably will not	Very low

could be influenced by a number of additional attitudes. The attitudes that are perceived as relevant varied with each individual. The decision to participate was also affected by the importance and intensity of the attitudes. If the need for study was particularly acute, this single attitude might have been the primary determinant of behavior. Although the illustration does not account for these effects, it clearly displays the complex relations between attitudes and behavior. When all the relevant attitudes are valenced in a single direction (students A and E), one is able to predict with some assurance the behavior to follow. When individual attitudes suggest opposite behaviors, prediction is nearly impossible (students B, C, and D). In all cases, however, the student would be acting in a manner consistent with some or all of the relevant attitudes.

The communicator's task is made more difficult because behavior is usually influenced by a number of attitudes. The source who aims to affect behavior cannot limit his focus to a single attitude. If he does, he may succeed in changing that attitude, while failing to secure the desired behavioral response. Many students who were opposed to United States actions in Southeast Asia also believed that protests were ineffective in influencing government policy. Involving these inactive students probably would have required, first, a change in their attitudes regarding demonstrations. This change might have then been followed by an active expression of their antiwar sentiments.

Attitudes may also fail to result in actions if the threshold of behavior is too high. By *threshold of behavior* we mean the amount of effort that a particular action requires. The skillful communicator seeking to elicit a behavioral response will attempt to minimize the response threshold. Consider the case of subscribing to a magazine. Few of us are likely to decide that we need a particular magazine, thereupon, writing to the publisher requesting a subscription. Thus magazine publishers engage in mailing campaigns. In addition to offering a subscription at a reduced rate, the mailings may include a "bill me later" clause, a stamped envelope, and sometimes even a pencil with which to fill out the order form. All these techniques are designed to make the response easier. Subscribing thus requires less effort. Similarly, we are more likely to attend an antiwar activity if it requires us to walk a block instead of a mile. The higher the response threshold, the less likely it is that an attitude will be expressed in overt behavior.

SUMMARY

Theories of human motivation attempt to explain and predict behavior. Because human behavior is extremely complex, a complete theory of human motivation is not possible. Each person's uniqueness (the many) precludes such a theory; however, sufficient similarity (the one) exists to allow useful explanations of human motivation.

Hedonistic and attitude change theories all begin with a similar model of human behavior. Human beings, it is reasoned, strive for an idealized state of internal harmony. Deviations from this state are unpleasant, and they motivate persons to act in a way that will achieve or restore harmony.

Hedonistic theories apply this model in terms of pleasure and pain. Humans are motivated to pursue pleasure and avoid pain.

Attitude change theories assume that consistency among beliefs, attitudes, values, and actions is the preferred state. The presence of inconsistency is psychologically uncomfortable. Dissonance theory, as one of several consistency theories, has been applied in a wide variety of situations and has demonstrated the importance of consistency as a motivational force.

QUESTIONS FOR THOUGHT AND DISCUSSION

1. Have any of your attitudes changed recently? How do you explain these changes? Is consistency theory helpful in explaining the changes?
2. Select several short articles or editorials that incorporate fear appeals. How do you respond to these appeals?
3. Can you recall instances in which you acted in ways that were inconsistent with one or more of your values? Did you experience dissonance?
4. Read the speech presented in Chapter 7. Does this speech illustrate elements of consistency theory?
5. Do you agree with the authors' claim that attitudes are usually consistent with actions, provided one is aware of all relevant attitudes?

SUGGESTED READINGS

Festinger, Leon, *A Theory of Cognitive Dissonance*, New York, Harper & Row, 1957.

McGuire, William J., "The Nature of Attitudes and Attitude Change," *The Handbook of Social Psychology*, 2nd ed., vol. III, Reading, Mass., Addison-Wesley, 1969, pp. 136–314.

Rokeach, Milton, *Beliefs, Attitudes and Values*, San Francisco, Jossey-Bass, 1968.

Sherif, Carolyn W., Muzafer Sherif, and Roger Nebergall, *Attitude and Attitude Change*, Philadelphia, Saunders, 1965.

6 recognizing individual differences: a step toward identification

Stereotypes are frequently used in describing groups. Some politicians express the belief that all college students are "long-haired radicals." Many citizens stereotype politicians as deceitful, ruthless individuals. Republicans are stereotyped as conservative, Democrats are liberals. In one sense, such stereotypes are comforting. They provide one with the secure, albeit false, feeling that he really knows college students, politicians, or Republicans. A close look, however, reveals that because they are based on a minimum of information, stereotypes can be very misleading and are potentially harmful. In short, stereotypes ignore individual differences.

Communicators who seek to create identification on the basis of stereotypes will have little success. The professor who develops a stereotype of "college freshmen" and uses the same teaching methods with every class, soon learns the inadequacy of his approach. The lobbyist who approaches every senator on the basis of party affiliation rapidly finds that the "liberal" or "conservative" stereotype is inadequate. Thus skillful communicators attempt to identify actual individual differences, and they adjust to those differences.

In the last three chapters we have explored the creating of identification on the basis of human beings' shared qualities (the consubstantial). Interpersonal communication is possible because humans share an ability to reason, because we all are concerned with interpersonal attraction, and because we all have a common motivational framework. However, each of us is also an autonomous, unique individual. To be effective, communicators must be sensitive to both the shared and the unique qualities of human beings. This chapter explores several key sources of individual difference and the process of building communications that reflect those differences.

Studying and adapting to individual differences can be labeled "audience analysis." This term is frequently used in communication literature, but it can be misleading. Because interpersonal communication often involves small groups or only two persons, the term "listener analysis" may be more appropriate. One's concern with individual differences cannot be limited to large group situations. Whichever term one prefers, the activity can be defined as *the process of analyzing individual differences and building communications that reflect listeners' unique qualities.*

The importance of a thorough study of individual differences varies greatly from one situation to another. Generally the importance of a formal receiver analysis, and the extensiveness of this analysis is a function of (1) the degree to which the persons involved are familiar with each other, (2) the number of persons concerned, and (3) the importance of the communication.

If you are preparing to coact with a single individual whom you have known well for several years, it is likely that little analysis will be required. The worker who seeks a salary increase may, for example, be well acquainted with the supervisor's likes, dislikes, attitudes, values, and even his usual mood on Monday morning. A fledgling politician, however, may benefit by an extensive voter analysis before selecting the issues on which to base a campaign. The simple point is that previous acquaintance with an individual or group of individuals should provide at least part of the data necessary to select and refine communications; thus little formal analysis of one's coactors is necessary.

As the number of persons involved increases, analysis and

adjustment become more difficult. In many cases, a large group is more diverse than a small group. The interests, attitudes, and needs of a large group can be extremely diverse, indeed. Nevertheless, it is possible to identify shared and unique qualities of even very large groups. Advertisers are careful in selecting the magazines in which they promote their products. Readers of *The Farm Journal* differ in many ways from the readers of *Playboy*, although both publications may be read by more than a million individuals. Yet on the whole, the larger the group the greater the diversity of knowledge, interests, attitudes, and personality; as the number decreases, more homogeneity is likely.

The importance of a communication may be thought of as the "stakes" involved. When the defense lawyer pleads for the acquittal of a client, the stakes are high. Failure to convince the jury could result in a long prison term. When one asks neighbors for small contributions to the United Fund, the stakes are relatively small; thus a thorough analysis of one's neighbors may be judged unnecessary. On the other hand, the importance to counsel of thoroughly analyzing jury members and attempting to make the proper adjustments is obvious.

Listener analysis must be understood as an ongoing component of the communication process. The first stage of analysis occurs before a coaction begins. In some cases the primary analysis must occur at this stage. This is the case when the communication setting precludes adjustment during the communication event. When the president announces and defends a policy decision, the announcement and the arguments cannot be ad-libbed. Similarly, a careful preanalysis is necessary when the communication is transmitted via the electronic or printed media because response to the message is delayed. Often the president must await the outcome of a public opinion poll before the reaction to his message can be gauged. The author of a book usually faces a delay of months or even years before the reaction of readers is known. Thus when the communication setting precludes adjustment during the interaction, the analysis and adjustment must precede the communication event.

In face-to-face communication settings, the process of analysis and adaptation continues during the communicative act. In two-person or small group settings, all the participants can be overtly coactive. In larger face-to-face settings, the apparent coaction is often limited to nonverbal cues (e.g., facial expressions posture, restlessness). Here the speaker must be sensitive to the cues, attempt to interpret them, and adjust accordingly. Whether in the small or large group, the alert communicator is engaged in a continuing process of audience analysis.

Listener analysis may also occur after a communication event is concluded. Usually one is interested in knowing the outcome of his communication. Thus the president watches public opinion polls, the actor waits for Nielsen ratings, and the author watches book sales. This post analysis is particularly important when communications are not one-shot attempts but involve a continuing dialogue with an individual or group. In these cases, the outcome or development from one coaction becomes an important input for following encounters.

The skillful communicator begins, then, with a sensitivity to individual differences. This sensitivity is aided by studying the listener in order to adjust wisely. The key sources of individual differences, and the means for identifying these differences are discussed below.

KEY SOURCES OF INDIVIDUAL DIFFERENCE

Merchandisers have long recognized the importance of adapting their products to consumer needs and preferences. During the 1950s and early 1960s American automobile companies emphasized the "style" of their products. Flashier and more powerful cars were the result. However, increasing costs, the success of foreign compacts, and the energy crisis have led to greater production of economy cars by all American manufacturers. The availability of numerous models and options means that each customer is more likely to purchase a car that is adapted to unique and individual desires. The process of adapting a product to consumer needs is not unlike the process of adjusting a message to one's listeners.

The differences to which the communicator may turn in an attempt to distinguish one individual from another, or one audience from another, are legion. A complete understanding of these differences is not possible. Psychologists may work for months attempting to understand a single individual; still their understanding is limited. The communicator, then, cannot hope to begin with a comprehensive list of individual differences; rather, certain differences that will have maximum influence must be identified.

One way of identifying key individual differences stems from a consideration of the communicator's goals. Hovland, Janis, and Kelley describe these goals as (1) attention, (2) comprehension, and (3) acceptance. They argue that these goals may be thought of sequentially.[1] Attention is a necessary prerequisite for comprehension, while both attention and comprehension must precede acceptance. Each goal suggests an important source of individual differences.

Securing Listener Interests

Attention is a selective process. At any given time there are available an almost infinite number of stimuli on which one could concentrate. A person tends, however, to focus on only one or a very few of these stimuli. One of the communicator's objectives is to focus the listener's attention on the message.

[1] Carl I. Hovland, Irving L. Janis, and Harold H. Kelley, *Communication and Persuasion*, New Haven, Conn., Yale University Press, 1953.

Attention is, to a large extent, governed by interests. One sorts out, selects, and focuses on matters that are of some interest. The uninteresting, the unimportant, and the irrelevant are ignored. The communicator thus should attempt to assess the interest value of a message for particular listeners. If the subject of a communication is one of little interest, the communicator must devise strategies that will heighten the listener's interest. If the subject of communication is closely linked to the listener's interests, the goal of attention may be easily achieved. In any case, giving attention to the subject under discussion is an essential step in building identifications.

The Information System and Comprehension

"Information system" designates the individual's knowledge about the topic under consideration. The extent of this knowledge is always a product of experience. Because communication is a process of information sharing and exchange, the knowledge held by the participants is an important variable. It is important, first, because information that is already shared by the coactors provides a means for creating identifications. The information can function in various roles (data, backing, warrant) in the development of an argument. If the communicator overestimates the shared information, the argument may collapse (see Chapter 3, pp. 50–53).

The information system is important, second, because often beliefs, attitudes, and values are built on and reflect the information that one possesses. An attitude based on extensive information and experience tends to be less susceptible to influence. A person's beliefs, attitudes, and values will probably rest on the sort of information that lends ready support to those views. One will not comprehend another's beliefs, attitudes, and values without some understanding of the information the other person depends on.

Finally, the information system may be related to the goal

of message comprehension. A message that is too complex may not be understood by the listener. The receiver becomes lost amid too much new information that is too far removed from known ground. The communicator must share new information that at the same time is intelligible to the listener. Achieving this objective requires a sensitive assessment of the listener's information system.

The Belief System and Acceptance

The belief system consists of one's beliefs, attitudes, and values. As we described in Chapter 5, beliefs, attitudes, and values perform similar functions but differ in specificity and centrality. We told how attitudes may vary in direction, intensity, and salience, also maintaining that humans strive for consistency in their belief systems.

The goal of acceptance suggests that an accurate understanding of listener attitudes is essential. One person's attitudes may be so far from another's that a direct confrontation of these differences would lead to a "boomerang" effect: Instead of the desired identification, the listener would recoil from what was advocated, becoming more entrenched in the old position. In addition, research has shown that one's listener sometimes selectively perceives the communication in terms of his prior attitudes; thus if a communication is only slightly discrepant, the listener may perceive it as more similar to his position than it actually is. Also, if the communication is too discrepant, the listener may perceive the source's position as further removed from his own position than it actually is.[2] The communicator, therefore, should consider very carefully the existing listener attitudes and their likely effect in the coaction.

To this point, we have focused on receiver attitudes toward the concept or policy endorsed by the source.

[2] Carl I. Hovland, O. J. Harvey, and Muzafer Sherif, "Assimilation and Contrast Effects in Communication and Attitude Change," *Journal of Abnormal and Social Psychology,* **55** (1957), 242–252.

Another key individual difference is the listener's attitude toward the communicator. In Chapter 4 we described the importance of personal attraction. If a listener perceives the source to be highly attractive or credible, the listener is more likely to accept the communicator's recommendation. This general research finding has been specified in several studies. Aronson, Turner, and Carlsmith found that a high-credibility source is able to take a more discrepant position than a low-credibility source.[3] McCroskey has demonstrated that whereas a low-credibility speaker must use evidence to support claims, a high-credibility source has no such need.[4] Miller and Hewgill found that a high-credibility communicator can effectively employ a high level of fear appeals, but a low-credibility source is more successful with low-fear appeals.[5] Anderson learned that a low-credibility source will be less effective if his listeners suspect an intent to persuade. No similar effect was isolated when the source was perceived to be highly credible.[6] Taken together, these findings support the conclusion that high credibility or attraction is a great boon for the communicator as well as for the coaction. If credibility or attraction is low, very different choices must be made if the encounter is to be productive (see pp. 81–83, 86–92). Clearly then, the goals and the strategies of the communicator are affected by audience attitudes toward the source.

[3] Eliot Aronson, Judith A. Turner, and J. Merrill Carlsmith, "Communicator Credibility and Communication Discrepancy as Determinants of Opinion Change," *Journal of Abnormal and Social Psychology,* **67** (1963), 31–36.

[4] James C. McCroskey, "A Summary of Experimental Research on the Effects of Evidence in Persuasive Communication," *Quarterly Journal of Speech,* **55** (1969), 169–176.

[5] Gerald R. Miller and Murray A. Hewgill, "Some Recent Research on Fear Arousing Message Appeals," *Speech Monographs,* **33** (1966), 377–391.

[6] Loren J. Anderson, "An Experimental Study of Perceived Intent to Persuade, Source Credibility, and Topic Salience in Persuasive Communications." Doctoral dissertation, University of Michigan, 1971.

Examining Personality

Unlike interest, knowledge, and attitudes, personality is so complex and global a variable that precise research findings are elusive. As Erwin P. Bettinghaus explains:

> For personality research to be of major help in understanding persuasive communication situations, it should enable behavioral scientists to make predictions ... about the reactions of a receiver possessing certain characteristics as he listens to a message given by a source having a specified set of personality characteristics. The available research, however, cannot be stretched that far.[7]

Nevertheless, certain individual personality differences that affect the manner in which receivers respond to communication have been identified.

The most comprehensive investigation of the role of personality in communication has been reported by Hovland and Janis.[8] After extensive research, they reported the identification of a general persuasibility factor. Some individuals, regardless of topic or situation, are more likely to change their beliefs or attitudes than others are. The authors conclude, "The results support the hypothesis of a general factor of persuasibility and indicate that the predisposition to change opinions is not wholly specific to the topic or subject matter of the communications."[9] The strength of this general persuasibility factor is difficult to estimate.

Several studies support the conclusion that self-esteem affects persuasibility. An individual who is high in self-esteem feels more positive toward himself or herself than a low-self-

[7] Erwin P. Bettinghaus, *Persuasive Communication*, New York, Holt, Rinehart & Winston, 1968, p. 83.

[8] Carl I. Hovland and Irving L. Janis, eds., *Personality and Persuasibility*, New Haven, Conn., Yale University Press, 1959.

[9] Ibid., pp. 226–227.

esteem person does. Unsurprisingly, people low in self-esteem have been found to be more subject to influence.[10]

Rokeach has identified open- and closed-mindedness as personality variables. Open-minded individuals are more likely to accept new information and ideas. Closed-minded listeners are more likely to respond to authority than to new information, generally preferring the status quo. The communicator who supports change is more likely to succeed with an open-minded listener.[11]

Although personality differences surely are important in communication, the variable is difficult to manage. The research findings are limited, and application of limited findings is difficult. This is particularly true when the group is rather large and the source is relatively unacquainted with the listener(s). When the communicator is well acquainted with the listener, however, some applications will probably be possible. As the number of listeners increases, these personality traits are likely to be distributed throughout the group in a manner that makes generalization impossible.

ASSESSING INDIVIDUAL DIFFERENCES

The dimensions of individual difference just described help to define the objectives of audience analysis. The communicator wants to learn about the interests, knowledge, attitudes, and personality traits of the audience. We turn now to the techniques that a source may use in specifying these differences. The methods available range from those requiring little time and effort to methods calling for much time and a great deal of money.

[10] Ibid., pp. 55–68, 102–120, 121–140.

[11] Milton Rokeach, *The Open and Closed Mind*, New York, Basic Books, 1960; Frederic A. Powell, "Open and Closed-Mindedness and the Ability to Differentiate Sources and Message," *Journal of Abnormal and Social Psychology*, **65** (1962), 61–64.

The most commonly suggested approach to listener analysis involves an indirect assessment of the listener's interests, knowledge, attitudes, and personality. Such an analysis requires that one infer conclusions about the listener on the basis of observable traits and characteristics. The traits include the listener's age, sex, race, religion, education, occupation, and income level. In most situations the communicator is able to assess the receiver(s) with regard to some of these characteristics; nevertheless, the source must guard against the temptation to reach hasty conclusions based on these observable traits. Surely, the source should resist a judgment based on a single characteristic. The simple fact that someone is young or old or male or female provides little help. Yet by considering all or a number of such traits, the communicator may develop a reasonably accurate "picture" of the listener(s).

A second approach to audience analysis involves the use of paper-and-pencil surveys or direct interviews. This method is more precise; one inquires specifically about the audience's interests, knowledge, and attitudes. In many cases a speaker cannot interview or survey all potential auditors; then the communicator must choose a sample of the audience for study. The interview method can yield the most in-depth information about receivers, but it is relatively time-consuming and can be very costly. The survey method is usually more efficient, but as a rule it is limited to more superficial information. The survey is particularly appropriate to situations involving a large number of listeners.

The questions that may be included in an interview or a paper-and-pencil survey are limited only by the creativity of the source. As a general guideline, we have already suggested that the speaker specify the listener's interests, knowledge level, and attitudes. It follows that both the interview and the survey should contain questions designed to identify these sources of individual differences. We believe it is particularly crucial to include items that measure listeners' attitudes. In Chapter 4 we showed how the semantic differential scale may be used for this purpose. Frank Barron's questionnaire in Chapter 7 (see p. 142) furnishes another example.

A final approach to gathering listener data is the pilot study. In its most elementary form, the pilot study is simply a previewing of one's message for an individual, or a small group who represent the auditors. The feedback from the pilot audience then serves as a basis for adjusting the message. In mass communications a pilot study may be conducted on a community- or city-wide basis. Again the reaction of the pilot audience is used to evaluate the source's communication strategy. Often a pilot study is employed to supplement information gained from a survey, an interview, or a study of audience traits. The usefulness of the pilot study depends on the representativeness of the members of the pilot audience and on the closeness with which the pilot study's conditions approximate those of the actual communication.

These commonly used approaches to assessing individual differences represent only a sample of the methods available to a source. A variety of approaches is often best. As you acquire additional information about your auditors, you should become more aware of their unique qualities and more successful in adjusting your communication.

LIMITATIONS ON ADJUSTMENT

National political candidates are frequently accused of "overadjusting" their communications. Candidates are criticized for "saying one thing in the North and another in the South," or "saying one thing to labor and another to big business." No doubt these allegations are sometimes true. "Overadjustment" is possible. Any communicator who hopes to endorse and support new and different ideas can adapt the message to a certain point only. If such a communicator says only what the listeners want to hear, beneficial change is unlikely to occur.

The communicator's ability to adjust may also be limited by past statements. A speaker may, because of previous statements, be closely linked with a particular position on an issue. In subsequent communication efforts, however, the source cannot abandon that position to achieve favor with present listeners.

Ethical considerations should place further constraints on the source. Although a speaker may find rhetorical advantage in advocating a position that is not overly discrepant, a moral imperative exists against prostituting one's private positions.

At first glance these limitations may appear to minimize the importance of listener analysis. You may ask, Why is listener analysis important if I am unable to adjust my communication fully? The answer to this question requires us to distinguish between adjusting one's basic position or idea and adjusting one's approach in seeking the desired identifications. The limitations outlined previously apply to the source's position. Even though you should not lie about your beliefs, various adjustments of the approach used in explaining and defending your position are usually possible. Thus a senator who has just voted against revenue sharing cannot adjust this position when explaining the vote to a gathering of state and local government officials. The senator can, however, select, organize, and support ideas in a variety of ways. A careful study of the audience should provide a basis for developing an appropriate method for sharing.

SUMMARY

Effective communication requires sensitivity to the differences that distinguish individuals. Listener analysis is the process of identifying individual differences and building communications that adjust to the listener's unique qualities. The importance of a formal and extensive listener analysis varies with different communication settings.

A communicator's study of the listener is inevitably limited; nevertheless, one can profit from analyzing the listener's interests, knowledge, attitudes, and personality. A study of the listener's observable traits and characteristics, an interview or survey, a pilot study, or some combination of these techniques can be used in learning about him.

The desire to advocate new ideas, past statements, and ethical considerations will limit your opportunities to adjust the message to listener predispositions. These limitations should not, however, obviate the requirement to represent your truth as competently as possible.

QUESTIONS FOR THOUGHT AND DISCUSSION

1. Pick a close friend or a member of your family. Given what you know about this person, can you predict his/her behavior? Does your knowledge help you communicate more effectively with him/her.

2. Select two advertising campaigns and describe how these campaigns reflect an awareness of individual differences?

3. Are there factors, other than those identified in this chapter, that could function as important individual differences in certain communication settings? List some of these.

4. To what degree have the speeches presented in your class reflected an awareness of individual differences?

5. Have you ever witnessed a communicator who "overadjusted" to the listeners? How did this affect the outcome of the communication?

SUGGESTED READINGS

Clevenger, Theodore, *Audience Analysis*, Indianapolis, Bobbs-Merrill, 1966.

Holtzman, Paul D., *The Psychology of Speaker's Audiences*, Glenview, Ill., Scott, Foresman, 1970.

Hovland, Carl I., and Irving L. Janis, *Personality and Persuasibility*, New Haven, Conn., Yale University Press, 1959.

Hovland, Carl I., Irving L. Janis, and Harold H. Kelley, *Communication and Persuasion*, New Haven, Conn., Yale University Press, 1953.

Part three
IDENTIFICATION THROUGH ORGANIZATION, STYLE, AND DELIVERY

The four chapters of Part Two dealt with invention's role in the process of identification. Part Three emphasizes the means to identification that should be considered in the canons of organization, style, and delivery. The focus is on the effects of organization, language, and delivery choices. The communicator should study these effects to increase the probability of achieving the desired identification.

The human tendency to impose order is a manifestation of the one, a consubstantial basis that allows the conceiving of theories for effective organization; the theories, in turn, aid the planning for certain order effects. Since each person is unique, however, each will impose orders that are to some degree particular (the many).

Human beings share a capacity for language and an ability to use the verbal and nonverbal codes of one or more language groups. This capacity and ability reveal the consubstantial binding that we have emphasized as a necessary condition for communication. Humans are one in the ability to use language and the various codes; but each person interprets experience in ways that are to some degree unique, and each person uses symbols in ways that are to some degree unique. These persistent signs of individuality are proof of the many. Chapter 8, "Identification Through Style," and Chapter 9, "The Nonverbal Code: Identification Through Delivery," expand this discussion.

7 identification through organization

We accept as axiomatic that human beings prefer order to chaos; hence organization is an important canon to consider. Although organizational concerns may be more obvious in longer, more formal communication efforts, placement (we use placement, arrangement, and organization rather synonymously) is also significant in relatively brief, informal interactions (recall Joe and his plea for money in Chapter 2, pp. 25–27). Wherever the communication comes in the long–short or formal–informal descriptions, we can discuss its organization as being source-centered, scene-centered, or receiver-centered.

The organization of a communication may be dominated by the needs and interests of the source, the dictates of the situation (scene), or the response capacities of the receiver. This chapter is primarily about receiver-centered organization, but source-centered and scene-centered arrangements, plus mixtures of the three modes, are discussed from time to time.

SOURCE-CENTERED ORGANIZATION

The newly married young man who blurts out: "Got 75 scratches on my back!" on meeting one of his wife's acquaintances for the first time has not chosen a smooth way to open conversation. His allergy problems and the tests he has just undergone are clearly uppermost in his mind, and he reveals his predominant concern in an expressive way (like a young child, or a person preoccupied with a great emotion). However, such communication is not appropriate for the persons and the situation, and the announcement of the 75 scratches causes an awkward pause, since the listener is caught off guard and suspects that further awkwardness will result if the matter is pursued. The abrupt notification of the 75 scratches illustrates a source-centered organization. Source-centered arrangement is not necessarily bad. We all allow for it and are sometimes happy for it, for example, in the unique vision of the world that a child's conversation will show.

SCENE-CENTERED ORGANIZATION

One can also think of organization that is dominated by the situation or, to use Kenneth Burke's language, the "scene" controls the organization.[1] The chemist who is carefully reconstructing an experiment must follow the order established by the work that was done; thus the elements, their properties, and their interactions dictate the placement, rather than the psychological demands of the chemist or the observers. Using another example, a speaker's narrative about a past experience may follow the time sequence that was established in the actual happening. By sticking to the chronological ordering, the communicator is governed by the established environment or scene and not, first of all, by immediate internal impulses. As we pointed out in connection with source-centered organization, the scenically dominated arrangement need not be bad: The relating of the precise physical process may be fascinating, and the unfolding of the historical scene may have fine coherence and drama. Juanita Coffee's speech in Chapter 4 uses chronological organization to its advantage (see pp. 64–67); however, everyone has suffered while the relentless plod of "and then, and then, and then . . ." overcame both teller and listener.

[1] See Kenneth Burke, *A Grammar of Motives*, Berkeley, University of California Press, 1969, esp. pp. 3–11, 127–170.

RECEIVER-CENTERED ORGANIZATION

The organizer of a receiver-centered speech looks to the audience's need for coherent and interesting development of the message. The father in the barbershop example of Chapter 3 might have begun his attempt to talk the son into getting a haircut by saying, "I've got new lenses in my glasses, and the barbershop with the bar is in another town." Perhaps the son could gather from this that his father was asserting that haircuts were still desirable. Perhaps, too, the father and son could set the matter straight through an exchange of questions and answers. Probably, though, the communication between father and son would flow more efficiently if the father began as he did in Chapter 3 by saying, "Look, a barbershop that has some business!"

When the father chooses the organization that we judge to be more efficient, he is arranging his ideas with his son's capacity to respond in mind. Efficient communication is more likely when the source organizes according to what the audience appears to require.

Receiver-Centered Organization: An Application

We use Frank Barron's speech to aid our study of receiver-centered organization. (To meet an assignment in his class, Frank used a detailed outline but spoke extemporaneously; the words below were transcribed from tape.) Among other requirements, the assignment required the communicator: (1) to locate an important belief, attitude, or value—probably a combination of two or three of these—about which the audience appeared to differ from the communicator and seemed to be open to worthwhile change, (2) to use an appropriate means of listener analysis for gathering data to be used in learning the listeners' positions and in mapping the possible avenues for creating the desired identifications, and (3) to bring to bear insights relevant to the process of communication, to make the best possible choices while preparing and presenting the speech.

Frank had discussed his subject frequently with small audiences, ranging from one to three persons. No doubt, these previous treatments were similar to pilot studies, and Frank learned to see from the encounters which appeals and organization would have a good chance for success in his new effort. But Frank did not rely on the insights gained from earlier engagements. He used the following questionnaire to survey his present audience's knowledge and beliefs. Since the questionnaire was filled out in class two periods before the date that Frank had chosen for his oral presentation, he had time to analyze the results and to plan accordingly.

You may wish to check your own responses to this questionnaire while you consider the possible impact of the tabulated responses on Frank's organizing of the speech.

FRANK BARRON'S QUESTIONNAIRE AND THE RESPONSES

1. What is your concentration [major]? 3 Nat. Sci.   10 Soc. Sci.
2. If asked, which of the following could you identify?

    3   Edward Jenner   3   Paul Dudley White

    0   Joseph Price   6   Atherosclerosis   6   None of these
3. Have you ever had a friend or a relative who died of a heart attack or a stroke?   YES 8   NO 5
4. Which of the following do you think are related to heart disease? (Check as many as you wish)

10 Old age	9 Pollution	11 High Blood pressure
10 Heredity	12 Cigarette smoking	12 Obesity
9 Occupation	5 Male sex	0 Chlorinated water
10 Inactivity	4 Place of residence	11 Cholesterol

5. Which *three* of the following groups do you think have the highest incidence of heart disease? (Check the three answers)

1 Ancient Romans	0 American Indians	0 Modern Chinese
13 Modern Americans	0 Eskimos	1 Aborigines
8 Modern Japanese	10 Modern Europeans	1 Modern Africans

6. At your present age, how much greater do you think your life

expectancy is than your grandfather's was at the same age?
  <u>0</u> less than a year   <u>0</u> 1 year   <u>2</u> 2 years
 <u>1</u> 5 years   <u>8</u> 10 years   <u>2</u> 20 years

7. A prominent scientist has remarked that with Einstein's discovery of relativity, we now have the basic structure of all scientific knowledge; all we have to do now is "fill in the outlines." Do you agree?   YES <u>0</u>   NO <u>11</u>   (2 undecided

8. Do you believe that any scientific community would deliberately keep knowledge of a lethal and insidious poison from the public if they knew about it?   YES <u>9</u>   NO <u>4</u>

9. Do you know why or how a heart attack takes place in the human body?   YES <u>3</u>   NO <u>10</u>

FRANK BARRON'S SPEECH

Heart disease is an epidemic in America today. Heart at- 1
tacks kill one-half million Americans every year—many 2
times the number of persons killed by all serious infectious 3
diseases combined. In fact, the heart attack, known scien- 4
tifically as coronary thrombosis or myocardial infarction, is, 5
by a substantial margin, the number one killer of Ameri- 6
cans today. Almost everyone knows someone—a friend or 7
relative, or a public figure—who has died from a heart at- 8
tack. And, of course, in addition to deaths, there is the vast 9
toll of nonfatal heart attacks, the skyrocketing costs of 10
medical care, the loss of wages and jobs, and the incal- 11
culable mental and physical anguish of maimed patients 12
and their families. Most frighteningly, the death rate from 13
this cause is still rising despite massive expenditures on re- 14
search and treatment programs. Yes, heart disease is truly 15
an epidemic. 16

In order for you to understand what I am going to say 17
later, it is necessary for you to understand what a heart at- 18
tack is. The heart is a hollow muscle about the size of your 19
clenched fist. And of course it serves the life-sustaining 20
function of pumping blood to all parts of the body. What is 21
not understood by most nonmedical persons is that the 22
heart muscle itself cannot use any of the blood that is within 23

its pumping chambers. Instead, the heart is supplied 24
entirely by two little vessels called coronary arteries, which 25
arise from the aorta and enter the heart to feed it. If one of 26
these arteries or one of their branches becomes blocked off, 27
the portion of the heart supplied by that artery dies. If the 28
part is small, then the tissue will gradually be replaced by 29
scar tissue, and the patient will likely recover. If a large 30
part is involved, death may come within a matter of 31
minutes or hours. 32

Now what causes the blocking off? Well, while the actual 33
occlusion of a coronary artery which results in a heart at- 34
tack takes place very suddenly, it only occurs in previously 35
diseased arteries affected by a pathological process known 36
as atherosclerosis. Atherosclerosis is a particular kind of 37
hardening of the arteries characterized by the gradual accu- 38
mulation of certain fatty substances on the inner wall of the 39
arteries, slowly making their diameter smaller and smaller. 40
A heart attack occurs when spontaneous bleeding in or 41
around an atheromatous deposit causes a clot to form which 42
blocks the flow of blood through the coronary artery. 43

The heart attack is by no means the only outcome of 44
atherosclerosis. A stroke occurs when the clot forms in a 45
brain artery. High blood pressure and senility are the more 46
nondramatic results of atherosclerosis. 47

While the actual heart attack or stroke is one of the most 48
dramatic events known to medicine, the underlying disease 49
process of atherosclerosis is quite the opposite. In fact, the 50
infiltration of the artery walls begins in most cases at least 51
10 to 20 years before any overt symptoms are evident. 52
Medical science does not acknowledge a definite causal 53
factor for atherosclerosis. The only clues to its causes are 54
certain correlations. A correlation simply means that two 55
things exist together, but, contrary to popular belief, does 56
not necessarily mean that one causes the other. If this were 57
so we could safely infer that eating corn flakes causes the 58
sun to come up. 59

The most widely accepted theory both within and outside 60
the medical community holds that atherosclerosis is caused 61

by the excessive consumption of foods containing choles-   62
terol. As a result of the widespread acceptance which this   63
theory has enjoyed, there has been, over the last few years,   64
an informal, nationwide campaign to discourage the   65
excessive consumption of foods high in cholesterol. And the   66
sales of margarines and oils high in the so-called polyun-   67
saturated fats have increased sharply. Obviously the im-   68
plication is that if we control our diet we reduce the chance   69
of heart attacks. This theory is amazing in one particular   70
respect; it is amazing because there is little if any direct evi-   71
dence which proves that lowering blood cholesterol by any   72
method possible will decrease the risk of heart attack or   73
stroke or even affect the underlying atherosclerosis. The so-   74
called evidence seems to be entirely circumstantial.   75

But science always hates to admit that it does not know   76
the answer to a problem, so it proposes a tentative or   77
hypothetical solution, really an educated guess; and that's   78
fair enough, because a scientist needs some sort of starting   79
point. Unfortunately, though, for lack of anything better,   80
these educated guesses often attain the status of established   81
theory—not because anything has been proved, but rather   82
because these guesses fill what would otherwise be a scien-   83
tific vacuum. Thus in scientific history, well-organized igno-   84
rance has often passed for wisdom.   85

There is plenty of evidence against the acceptance of the   86
cholesterol theory. Consider the following. I have referred to   87
heart disease as an epidemic. This of course implies that   88
heart disease has not always been with us. And, indeed, this   89
seems to be the case. If all humans were and always had   90
been subject to heart attacks and strokes with the same   91
prevalence as found in the United States today, the hope of   92
finding a definitive solution would be dim indeed. For if this   93
were so, we would have to admit that atherosclerosis is an   94
inevitable part of aging. But, even the staunchest   95
proponents of the cholesterol theory realize that atheroscle-   96
rosis is a disease process which is by no means universal,   97
and therefore is at least theoretically capable of being   98
retarded and possibly even reversed.   99

Actually, heart attacks were virtually unknown until 100
early in this century. Now many physicians will im- 101
mediately challenge this hard-to-believe statement, but in 102
pure and simple terms, the first clinical description of 103
coronary thrombosis was made in the year 1912. The great 104
Canadian-American physician, Sir William Osler, did not 105
mention the existence of the heart attack in his 106
comprehensive lectures on heart disease in the year 1910. 107
And the world-famous heart specialist, Dr. Paul Dudley 108
White, who treated President Eisenhower for his heart at- 109
tack in the 1950s, did not see his first heart attack until 110
after 1920. Moreover, the heart attack did not reach suffi- 111
cient proportions to affect statistical tables on mortality in 112
America until 1930. 113

Now if we remember that the development of atheroscle- 114
rosis to its acute stages takes 10 to 20 years, we may infer 115
that some environmental factor or factors of critical im- 116
portance began to affect Americans in the early part of this 117
century. This could not have been cholesterol. Cholesterol 118
has been with man as long as there has been man. 119

To get more directly to cholesterol, consider the following 120
facts: (1) A careful investigation of the literature has shown 121
that in England at the end of the nineteenth century almost 122
one-third of the population consumed dietary fats in 123
amounts that would be considered excessive by modern-day 124
standards. And yet, heart attacks and other evidence of 125
atherosclerosis were apparently nonexistent. (2) There are 126
no reports of heart disease in China; 700 million people and, 127
as far as we know, no heart attacks. (3) While atheroscle- 128
rosis seems to be virtually nonexistent among most 129
primitive peoples of the world, there is no better example of 130
high dietary fat intake coupled with the absence of athe- 131
rosclerosis than the Eskimos. The dietary fat intake of the 132
Eskimos is simply hard to believe. A single adult may eat 133
several pounds of blubber, which is about as saturated a fat 134
as exists, in a single sitting. This fantastic dietary pattern is 135
followed for a lifetime, and yet there are no heart attacks or 136
strokes from atherosclerosis. If there were no other evidence 137

than this, any thinking man would have questions about the   138
cholesterol theory. Nevertheless, there is more. For instance,   139
if you want something a little closer to home, a few years   140
ago there was an article in a popular magazine about a   141
small town called Roseto in the hills of Pennsylvania. The   142
people of this town are of Italian descent; they tend to be   143
obese and to eat a diet abnormally high in animal fats. Yet,   144
they seem immune to heart attacks—as long as they do not   145
move out of their community. That's a little more food for   146
thought.   147

By now you are probably wondering, if cholesterol is not   148
the factor, do we know what is? Well, we suspect that it is   149
something that is not only less than 75 years old, but is even   150
today confined to peoples under the influence of modern   151
Western civilization. Dr. Joseph Price, M.D., contends that   152
the culprit is the ubiquitous chlorine in our drinking water.   153
The experimental use of chlorine to purify water supplies   154
began in the late 1890s, and chlorination gained relatively   155
wide acceptance between 1910 and 1920. Once again, if we   156
remember that it takes 10 to 20 years for atherosclerosis to   157
reach the stage where a heart attack may occur, it becomes   158
evident that there is a correlation between the introduction   159
of chlorine into water supplies and the origin and increasing   160
incidence of heart attacks that is exceedingly difficult to   161
explain away. Furthermore, consider the following: (1)   162
There was no chlorinated water in England during the last   163
century. (2) The Eskimos may consume huge quantities of   164
dietary fats, but their drinking water is pure melted snow.   165
(3) Chlorinated drinking water is unknown among prim-   166
itive peoples; the so-called primitive Chinese spread their   167
sewage on the ground and get worms in their guts from   168
drinking contaminated water and eating filthy food. We in   169
the Western world are much more civilized: we take our   170
sewage, dump it into our rivers, drain it into our water sup-   171
plies, strain it, and inject chlorine into it; we don't get   172
worms, but it seems that we may be getting something else.   173
(4) The inhabitants of Roseto, Pennsylvania, drink water   174
straight from flowing mountain springs, but when they   175

move to the big city and drink chlorinated water, they seem 176
to be subject to the same retribution. What's more, the 177
Japanese, a modern technological society in significant 178
respects except for chlorinated water, normally have a very 179
low heart attack rate, but when they move to Hawaii and 180
drink chlorinated water, they have heart attacks at the 181
American rate. Coronary disease was unknown among a 182
group of 500 poor Irish farm workers studied by Paul 183
Dudley White, while being widespread among their 184
chlorine-drinking brothers in the United States. And 185
contrary to popular belief, high-level business executives, 186
who are supposedly under a great deal of stress and thus 187
prone to heart attacks, actually have a lower incidence of 188
heart attacks than their subordinates. When a business 189
executive reaches the highest echelons in America, he drinks 190
nonchlorinated, bottled water at the office and has more 191
chance of living in a house in the suburbs, which may have 192
a private, nonchlorinated well. 193

Finally, to get to some more direct evidence, during the 194
Korean War autopsies were performed on otherwise healthy 195
soldiers killed in battle. In an article published in the 196
Journal of the American Medical Association, it was 197
reported that among the soldiers, whose average age was 22, 198
over 75 percent showed gross evidence of coronary ar- 199
teriosclerosis. These results, which have also been found in 200
Vietnam, have been widely discussed. The usual conclusion 201
is that coronary artery disease is far more common and ex- 202
tensive than had been thought, especially in young men. 203

Dr. Price questions this conclusion. He asserts that 204
anyone who was either in Korea or in Vietnam, as he was, 205
will tell you that the drinking water of the American troops 206
was so heavily chlorinated for sanitary reasons that it was 207
almost undrinkable; yet it was the only thing to drink in the 208
miserably hot jungles of Southeast Asia. What's more, heart 209
disease was virtually unknown among the natives of these 210
countries who were still drinking unchlorinated water. 211

Being a scientist, Dr. Price was not satisfied with this ar- 212
ray of admittedly circumstantial evidence, as impressive as 213
it seemed. He set out to conduct a controlled experiment 214

using chickens as subjects because of the similarity of their 215
circulatory systems to those of humans. He took 100 day-old 216
cockerels and divided them into two groups of 50 each. The 217
two groups were placed in identical conditions, the only dif- 218
ference being the presence of chlorine in the water and 219
mash of the experimental group and its absence from the 220
food and water of the control group. The results were 221
nothing short of spectacular. Within three weeks there were 222
grossly observable effects on both appearance and behavior: 223
the experimental group became lethargic, huddling in 224
corners except at feeding time. Their feathers became 225
frayed and dirty, and their pale combs drooped. Meanwhile, 226
the control group was the picture of vigorous health. They 227
were larger, cleaner, and more active. Within seven months 228
almost all of the experimental cockerels were dead. 229
Autopsies were performed on each one, and in more than 95 230
percent of them there were readily visible yellow plaques of 231
atherosclerosis protruding into the aortas. At the end of the 232
seven months one-third of the control group were sacrificed, 233
with not one abnormal aorta being found. Dr. Price reports 234
that the total cost of this experiment was $100. 235

Dr. Price does not go so far as to contend that chlorine 236
alone causes heart attacks, but he suggests that chlorine 237
may be a necessary, but not sufficient factor in the etiology 238
of heart disease. We know that everyone who drinks chlori- 239
nated water does not suffer a heart attack; but it seems 240
likely that with all other factors held constant, chlorinated 241
water may increase the chance of heart attack. 242

By now you are probably a little uneasy and perhaps a 243
little angry about the water you drink. What can you do 244
about it? Well, in terms of long-range action, it is a known 245
fact in the scientific community that both ultraviolet light 246
and a process called ozonation may purify water as effec- 247
tively and as cheaply as chlorine. You could write your 248
congressman and demand action or at least an investigation. 249
But in the meantime, I would recommend that you boil all 250
of your drinking water and put it into the refrigerator before 251
you drink it. Boiling will drive off all the chlorine. 252

I don't have time to deal extensively with the critical 253

question of why you did not already know what I've just 254
told you and your own doctor probably still doesn't know. I 255
can tell you that to the best of my knowledge no one in the 256
medical community has confirmed or denied Dr. Price's 257
findings, or even admitted the existence of Dr. Price's work, 258
even though he has published a book on this subject. 259
Perhaps it will suffice for now to point out that unusual 260
scientific discoveries have never been accepted easily. From 261
the beginnings of science, men like Galileo, Galen, La- 262
voisier, Jenner, Pasteur, the Curies, and even Einstein, have 263
confronted a disbelieving and hard-to-move scientific com- 264
munity. Science has always had its sacred cows, and chlori- 265
nated water may be one of them. There is little reason to 266
believe that our generation of scientists, or for that matter, 267
our generation of men, is any different from these previous 268
generations. If anything, the medical research community 269
today seems to be even more monolithic and immovable 270
than the Royal Academy of Sciences in Paris ever thought 271
of being. 272

Medical research has become a big business, with corpo- 273
rate identities and corporate spokesmen and even public 274
relations men vying for the funds needed to maintain the 275
existing superstructure. Fewer and fewer people are exer- 276
cising control over the flow of information from specialized 277
fields. And, of course, the funds which the corporations need 278
depend on the promise of results; perhaps this partly 279
explains the tenacious grasp on the cholesterol theory and 280
the reluctance to admit the existence of a man who 281
threatens to smash the corporate ego by disproving its worth 282
with a $100 experiment. 283

There may be problems with Dr. Price's findings, but 284
until somebody takes the trouble to tell me what they are, I 285
think that I will continue to boil my water. 286

It is not difficult to follow the thread of Frank's argumentation. Regardless of whether source, scene, or receiver
motivates the arrangement in this speech, we can safely
assert that a definite pattern of organization exists. Even if

the order were less evident than it is, the listener could figure out and impose structures (although the receiver-centered approach seeks increased efficiency by requiring less of this kind of effort by the auditor). However, an auditor comprehends less when chaos abounds in a presentation; also, an auditor is less likely to be persuaded when the message is severely disorganized.[2] Unsurprisingly, the ethos of the communicator becomes less positive when the listener perceives disorganization.[3]

We doubt that comprehension, persuasion, or attraction suffer because of Frank's placement. His organization is consistently strong because it is so solidly audience-centered. Frank's own idiosyncrasies are certainly represented, since no two people having the same knowledge of the subject and the audience would come up with exactly the same arrangement. But the organization is not speaker-centered; otherwise, Frank might begin testily by announcing: "Your questionnaire responses show that you don't know it, but chlorinated water is closely related to heart disease." And throughout the speech Frank would arrange ideas as they suited him, not as listener coaction and development would seem to require. Clearly, Frank proceeds as he does mostly because this way appears to be best adapted to the audience's needs and responses. The scene has some impact as well on the organization; for instance, the form of presentation of the second paragraph (lines 17–32) largely reflects the existence of those physical properties and

[2] See K. C. Beighley, "A Summary of Experimental Studies Dealing with the Effect of Organization and of Skill of Speakers on Comprehension," *Journal of Communication,* **2** (1952), 58–65; E. Thompson, "An Experimental Investigation of the Relative Effectiveness of Organizational Structure in Oral Communication," *Southern Speech Journal,* **26** (1960), 59–69.

[3] H. Sharp, Jr., and T. McClung, "Effects of Organization on the Speaker's Ethos," *Speech Monographs,* **33** (1966), 182–183; J. C. McCroskey and R. S. Mehrley, "The Effect of Disorganization and Nonfluency on Attitude Change and Source Credibility," *Speech Monographs,* **36** (1969), 13–21.

processes, which should be detailed in the way chosen. But the overall organization is not scene-centered.

PROBLEM–SOLUTION ORGANIZATION

One clear showing of an audience-centered placement is the "need–satisfaction" or "problem–solution" structure. The opening sentence and paragraph underscore an important problem and raise a significant need; the rest of the speech, all the way to "boil my water" at the end, seeks to solve the problem and satisfy the need. The need–satisfaction or problem–solution organization has been preached and practiced for millennia. Contemporary theory and research affirm the effectiveness of this receiver-centered approach.[4]

ONE-SIDE–BOTH-SIDES ORGANIZATION

Frank shows a second feature of audience-centered organization in his handling of the "one-side or both-sides" question. This rather complex matter is not, at least in the early stages of its discussion, strictly an organizational concern. (The one-side–both-sides question could be treated under invention, since it advises *what* the communicator should select for appeals. However, the development of this question leads into matters of placement, thus it is appropriate to consider the question here.) In his defense of the choices he made in preparing his speech, Frank states:

> My major purpose in this speech is not a treatment of the honesty, competence, or beneficence of the medical research community, although I find that I do, out of necessity, touch on those matters. Rather, I am primarily interested in convincing others that there is sufficient cause to avoid drinking chlorinated water for the sake of their own health and that there is sufficient cause to agitate for alternative methods of purifying our water

[4] A. R. Cohen, "Need for Cognition and Order of Communication as Determinants of Opinion Change," in *The Order of Presentation in Persuasion*, C. I. Hovland et al., eds., New Haven, Conn., Yale University Press, 1957, pp. 79–97.

supplies. I cannot absolutely prove the chlorine theory, but I believe that I can raise sufficient doubt concerning the cholesterol explanation, and those who support it, to convince my listeners to investigate for themselves and to take precautionary measures until they are convinced otherwise.

Since Frank's major purpose is to convince his listeners to stop drinking chlorinated water, he might have presented only this side of the case. The speech would proceed as it does up to line 52, skip to pick up the sentence on lines 100 and 101, then go to "the first clinical description . . ." on line 103, continuing to line 118, then take "Dr. Joseph Price . . ." from lines 152–153 on to line 162, jump over to include lines 177–252, and end with lines 284–286. This one-sided version of the speech shows quickly and simply that chlorinated water appears to be a cause of heart disease.

Experimental work demonstrates that a one-sided treatment can be more effective with an audience that is poorly educated and unfamiliar with the subject under consideration.[5] Suppose that after careful audience analysis, Frank had found that his listeners had little education and were ignorant of the various theories about the causes of heart attacks. His desired ends—to persuade these listeners to stop drinking chlorinated water and to work for change in the methods of water purification—perhaps would be gained more efficiently with the one-sided approach.

If Frank had used only the chlorinated-water side of the heart disease case in his talk, he might have been more effective in changing the behavior of some in the short run; yet this one-sided approach might have proved less effective in the long run than a both-sided (chlorine versus cholesterol) case. The reason is that a person convinced by the one-sided chlorine case may later hear arguments favoring the cholesterol theory. Since the cholesterol side was not raised and

---

[5] C. I. Hovland, A. A. Lumsdaine, and F. D. Sheffield, "The Effects of Presenting 'One Side' versus 'Both Sides' in Changing Opinions on a Controversial Subject," in *Experiments in Persuasion,* R. L. Rosnow and E. J. Robinson, eds., New York, Academic Press, 1967, pp. 71–97.

questioned, Frank's convert might be more ready to switch than Frank would like. Thus Frank would have to weigh the short-run benefits against the possible long-run losses in deciding to use the one-sided or the both-sided approach.[6]

In the classroom situation Frank did not meet this problem. He knew that his audience was composed of college students, and the responses to item 4 of the questionnaire revealed a wide range of awareness of the theories about the causes of heart disease. This audience would be more positively affected by a both-sided (or many-sided) approach.[7] The one-sided presentation would not treat material that these auditors know to be relevant. As a result, the listeners would have been preparing rebuttals as Frank proceeded, and the conceiving of counterarguments would have drawn attention away from Frank's points. Furthermore, whoever prepared a counterargument would have some interest in maintaining that position; therefore, this person would be less easily changed than if Frank could have proceeded without triggering the urge to rebut. And by allowing or encouraging refutation, Frank risked losing some of the positive attraction that he had before.[8] When these considerations are allied with the strong probability that these listeners would receive arguments about other causes of heart disease, it is clear that Frank had strong reasons to go beyond a one-sided case.

Although Frank did not handle all the categories in item 4 of the questionnaire, he touched on most of them as he

[6] Research indicates that a listener exposed to both sides is more resistant to counterpersuasion. See A. A. Lumsdaine and I. L. Janis, "Resistance to Counter-Propaganda Produced by a One-Sided versus a Two-Sided Propaganda Presentation," *Public Opinion Quarterly,* **17** (1953), 311–318; C. A. Insko, "One-Sided versus Two-Sided Communications and Counter Communications," *Journal of Abnormal and Social Psychology,* **65** (1962), 203–206.

[7] Hovland, Lumsdaine, and Sheffield, loc. cit.

[8] Frank's ethos was clearly positive in the class. For exploration of related material see G. C. Chu, "Prior Familiarity, Perceived Bias, and One-Sided Versus Two-Sided Communications," *Journal of Experimental Social Psychology,* **3** (1967), 243–254.

proceeded with his cholesterol–chlorine arguments. Since Frank showed strength in the primary components of his case as well as a sensitive awareness of the other factors involved, his ethos remained highly positive and his receivers were not tempted to bring forward separate, pet contentions; in the free-for-all period after the speech, for example, all the questions and comments focused on the chlorine–cholesterol points.

The experimental research and the class's reaction show that Frank was right in choosing the both-sides approach. Now one can ask, which side should come first? The responses in item 4 show nobody ready to take the chlorinated-water side and 11 on the cholesterol side. Obviously, Frank did not have the popular side.

To be sensitive in interpersonal communication is to move slowly and carefully when the discrepancy is great. To leap right into his side of the fray would seem to have been unproductive for Frank, his cause, and his audience. The experimental research available does not speak directly to this question; nevertheless, certain findings seem, at least indirectly, to support the fitness of Frank's approach. Janis and Fierbend hypothesized that if the topic were nonsalient and the source highly credible, a placement of arguments favoring the source's position before those opposed to it (in Frank's case, talking of chlorinated water as the culprit before questioning the cholesterol theory) would be more effective than the reverse.[9] Their results supported this hypothesis. If Frank could have assumed at the start of his presentation that heart disease was an insignificant (nonsalient) concern for the students and that he would be viewed as an expert on the subject, he could have followed the chlorine–cholesterol order that the Janis–Fierbend findings would support. But eight respondents had a friend or relative die of a heart attack or stroke (item 3), and the

[9] Irving L. Janis and R. L. Fierbend, "Effects of Alternative Ways of Ordering Pro and Con Arguments in Persuasive Communication," in *The Order of Presentation in Persuasion,* C. L. Hovland et al., eds., op. cit., pp. 115–128.

others had probably been significantly affected by heart disease. Furthermore, the responses to item 4 indicate that the class was familiar with current theories about heart disease, and this perhaps shows that the matter was salient for them. The nonsalience condition did not hold, then, nor did the highly credible source requirement. To be sure, Frank's ethos was highly positive, yet he was still a fellow student, and college students are not likely to credit another undergraduate as an expert on heart disease. Ethos is topic-bound (see pp. 81–85).

Since the reverse of Janis and Fierbend's conditions prevailed, one is probably safe in assuming that the reverse strategy should have been adopted. Frank should have begun by questioning the established cholesterol theory, gradually building his credit as a spokesman in the specialized area of heart disease. Once the cholesterol theory had been shaken and Frank's attraction had been extended to the heart disease area, he could have broached the radically new, at least for this audience, chlorinated-water hypothesis. [Note that Frank allied himself at this critical juncture (lines 152–153) with *Dr.* Joseph Price, *M.D.*—an effective, time-honored means of shoring up one's assertion and ethos by drawing on the attractiveness of another person or institution.]

We have argued that Frank's discussion of heart disease in the cholesterol–chlorine order represents the both-sides approach. We note in leaving this point that Frank might have been more both-sided than he was. The theory and research favoring the cholesterol side could have received fuller treatment, thus gaining a more balanced perspective on cholesterol's role. Similarly, the pro-chlorine argumentation could have been balanced by some discussion of arguments on the opposing side. If Frank's time for preparation and presentation had been more extensive, he probably could have done this; thus he might have established a more persuasive case for a well-educated audience. Given the time limits Frank faced, however, he did unusually well.

PRIMACY-RECENCY ORGANIZATION

Primacy-recency research has tried to determine whether material presented first (primary) has a greater impact than material presented last (recency). For example, if you read first a paragraph suggesting that someone is an introvert and read next a paragraph suggesting the same person to be an extrovert, which of the two versions will show up more strongly if you are asked for your impressions of this person?[10]

The notion that first impressions are the more potent has been fairly current. Advice and effort to show up as well as possible in a first encounter are widespread. Probably the first impression is emphasized because it is felt that this impression establishes the framework (perceptual set) within which subsequent messages about the person will be assimilated.[11] Besides, one may be especially concerned about first impressions because at least in some cases the first impression, if not a good one, could also be the last—the application letter, the job and scholarship interview, and the first date are examples that come quickly to mind.

Early research seemed to bear out a universal primacy effect.[12] But later research showed that the "Law of Primacy"

[10] Abraham S. Luchins, "Experimental Attempts to Minimize the Impact of First Impressions," *The Order of Presentation in Persuasion,* Carl I. Hovland, ed., New Haven, Conn., Yale University Press, 1957, pp. 62–75.

[11] S. E. Asch, "Forming Impressions of Personality," *Journal of Abnormal and Social Psychology,* **41** (1946), 258–290; A. S. Luchins, "Definitiveness of Impression and Primacy-Recency in Communications," *Journal of Social Psychology,* **48** (1958), 275–290; A. S. Luchins, "Primacy-Recency in Impression Formation," in *The Order of Presentation in Persuasion,* op. cit., pp. 33–61.

[12] F. H. Lund, "The Psychology of Belief: A Study of its Emotional and Volitional Determinants," *Journal of Abnormal and Social Psychology,* **20** (1925), 174–196; A. T. Jersild, "Primacy, Recency, Frequency and Vividness," *Journal of Experimental Psychology,* **12** (1929), 58–70; F. H. Knower, "Experimental Studies of Changes in Attitudes: II. A Study of the Effect of Printed Arguments on Changes in Attitude," *Journal of Abnormal and Social Psychology,* **30** (1936), 522–532.

was by no means always true.[13] Following an extensive study of the primacy–recency question, Hovland and Mandell concluded that no universal law of primacy or recency could be stated.[14] Apparently a number of other variables must be considered before one can make a confident prediction of a primacy or recency effect.

The research on primacy–recency, on the whole, seems to have more relevance for mass-audience situations such as an advertiser faces than for more ordinary interpersonal communication; nevertheless, we can mention two insights that are useful in the more typical encounters.

To begin, the dispute over primacy–recency effects does not deny that both the first and last positions are important places in a message. Gulley and Berlo found that either the first or last position brought a stronger impact than middle placement.[15] Their findings suggest that a communicator's more important points should be given first and last billing, while the less important material (perhaps a point or points the communicator would prefer to downgrade) should be "buried" in the middle. This advice is somewhat similar to the emphasis rhetorical theorists traditionally have placed on introductions and conclusions.

If we divide Frank's speech into three major segments (heart disease, lines 1–47; cholesterol side, lines 48–147; and chlorinated water side, lines 148–286, we can see that Frank's organization follows the prescriptions of this theory. Frank's major purpose was to persuade his audience to stop drinking chlorinated water because of its apparent link to

---

[13] R. Ehrensberger, "An Experimental Study of the Relative Effectiveness of Certain Forms of Emphasis in Public Speaking," *Speech Monographs,* **12** (1945), 94–111; H. Cromwell, "The Persistency of the Effect of the First versus the Second Argumentative Speech of a Series," *Speech Monographs,* **21** (1954), 280–284.

[14] C. I. Hovland and W. Mandell, "Is There a 'Law of Primacy' in Persuasion?" in *The Order of Presentation in Persuasion,* op. cit., pp. 13–22.

[15] H. E. Gulley and D. K. Berlo, "Effects of Intercellular and Intracellular Speech Structure on Attitude Change and Listening," *Speech Monographs,* **23** (1956), 14–25.

heart attacks. Frank's major aim was probably well served when he began: "Heart disease is an epidemic . . .," to introduce the heart disease segment, and when he ends: "I will continue to boil my water," after the chlorinated water segment.

Second, primacy–recency research indicates that if the subject is very interesting for the listener, a primacy effect is likely. On the other hand, if the subject is uninteresting, a recency effect will tend to occur.[16] This research advises you to place your most important point first if you are sure that audience interest in your subject is high. If interest appears to be low, your most important point should probably come last. Perhaps interest can be aroused by that time or, at the least, the most important point will not be crowded off the stage by less important aspects of the admittedly uninteresting material. Of course, each of us hopes never to treat material that is uninteresting to an audience, but each probably will be forced to do so on occasion.

DEDUCTIVE–INDUCTIVE ORGANIZATION

Talking as a brusque philosopher (one who is concerned only with speaking the truth, thus not to be troubled by a distraction such as ordering materials to suit an audience), Aristotle says that only two parts and one order are needed for a speech: The communicator should first state the point to be proved and second should go on to prove it (*Rhetoric,* 1414b). To state or preview the point and then to prove or develop it is called deductive organization. Vince's speech at the end of Chapter 1 is an example of the deductive format. Vince tells us in the first two paragraphs what the speech is about; then he develops this preview in the rest of the speech.

Talking as a rhetorician or communication theorist (one who is concerned not only with speaking the truth but also with creating identification as effectively as possible), Aris-

---

[16] R. E. Lana, "Interest, Media and Order Effects in Persuasive Communications," *Journal of Psychology,* **56** (1963), 9–13.

totle allows that an inductive approach has a place in speech organization (*Rhetoric,* 1394a). Mario's speech in Chapter 3 gives an example of inductive organization. Mario begins by relating an extended example that leads eventually to his central theme (see pp. 39–41). To begin with an example or examples and then to draw a conclusion (or to let the audience infer the claim for itself) is to use an inductive order.

Aristotle observes that if one starts with examples, thus suggesting an induction, many examples may be needed to demonstrate the claim. On the other hand, Aristotle says, if one begins deductively by stating a claim, probably only one good example has to be added to testify that the claim is acceptable (*Rhetoric,* 1394a). Certainly this point on deduction is valuable, and the assertion–example method is often used with efficiency and effectiveness. Still, Aristotle's overall point—that the inductive order is less efficient and applicable in general communication than is the deductive order—is questionable. The inductive approach has often been used efficiently and effectively. Gulley and Berlo did not find a significant difference in the effectiveness of the two orders.[17] A number of source, receiver, and scenic variables probably should be considered in deciding which of these orders to use in a particular communication.

If you are wondering which order to use, you can ask yourself questions like these to get at some of the variables: Does the inductive or deductive order seem to be more natural to me? Would I be comfortable and achieve some desirable variety if I were to use both of these arrangements in various parts of the presentation? Which placement will be more interesting for audience? What will happen to the audience's perception of my ethos in either order? How well will the audience be able to follow the movement from point to point with the inductive and deductive formats? Does my material seem to be particularly fit-

[17] Gulley and Berlo, "Effects of Intercellular and Intracellular Speech Structure . . .," loc. cit.

ted to one order or the other? Are there requirements in the situation or occasion that indicate a greater fitness for one of these orders?

Often the two orders can be interwoven in a message. Mario begins inductively, but after his claim is explicitly stated, he adds a number of examples (deductive order) that are listed as backing for the warrant in Mario's argument model (see p. 45). If a communicator masters deductive and inductive ordering, a considered use can be made of them, separately or in some mixture. Such control gives one another tool to use in seeking identification.

CLIMAX-ANTICLIMAX ORGANIZATION

Given a series of arguments (illustrations, anecdotes, episodes), if one places the weakest or least important first, then moves to the strongest or most important, the climax arrangement would be exemplified. Anticlimax reverses the order: the strongest or most important comes first, then the speaker moves to the weakest or least important.

No doubt most readers would agree that Vince's three confrontations with death (President Kennedy's, the young girl's, and Grampa's) are arranged in climax order. Probably, most also would agree that Mario's arrangement is anticlimatic: The eating of sparrows comes first and has the most impact; the subsequent illustrations, ending with the anger over the television commercials, are less significant. Both speeches work well with the chosen orders. As it happens, Vince's can be changed to anticlimactic and Mario's to climactic; however, both speeches seem to suffer in the process. This indicates that both climax order and anticlimax order have a place, and no general rule can be set out for preferring one over the other.

Experimental research bears out this estimate. Climax order was more effective in one study,[18] but anticlimax

---

[18] H. Cromwell, "The Persistency . . .," loc. cit.

seemed better in another.[19] Three other studies revealed no difference in effectiveness.[20] Thus the comment made in evaluating the deductive and inductive orderings can be repeated here: A number of source, receiver, and scenic variables should be considered in deciding whether to use climax or anticlimax order.

Again, you will have to ask questions like the following: How do I respond to this or that arrangement? Where am I most intensely involved? Could I best achieve this level of intensity early or late in my communication? Can I carry this smoothly from point to point in either order? How much audience involvement can I expect, and at which junctures of this speech? Would certain intensity levels be uncomfortable at some times but not at others? How well will the audience be able to follow the material in the climax order? In the anticlimax order? Does my material seem to be particularly fitted to one or the other? Do any requirements in the situation or occasion indicate the greater fitness of one of these orders?

Although no clear advantage can be given to either the climax or anticlimax order, knowing about them and sensitively weighing the pros and cons of their use will give the communicator another tool for achieving identification. A related comment should be made about our overall treatment of organization. The various placement strategies we have discussed are not equally relevant to all communications; for example, problem–solution ordering is a signifi-

---

[19] H. Sponberg, "A Study of the Relative Effectiveness of Climax and Anti-Climax Order in an Argumentative Speech," *Speech Monographs*, **18** (1951), 292–300.

[20] H. Gilkinson, S. Paulson, and D. Sikkink, "Effects of Order and Authority in an Argumentative Speech," *Quarterly Journal of Speech*, **49** (1954), 183–192; D. Sikkink, "An Experimental Study of the Effects on the Listener of Anti-Climax Order and Authority in an Argumentative Speech," *Southern Speech Journal*, **22** (1956), 73–78; D. L. Thistlethwaite, J. Kamenetsky, and H. Schmidt, "Factors Influencing Attitude Change Through Refutative Communication," *Speech Monographs*, **23** (1956), 14–25.

cant consideration in Frank's speech but is irrelevant in Mario's. When one knows the various organizational patterns and is sensitive to the complexities bearing on their use, one can choose and employ these tools intelligently.

SUMMARY

Source-, scene-, and receiver-centered organizations are all used to bring coherence to our communication. Any one of these is better than nothing, and often all three contribute to the arrangement of a message. As a rule, however, receiver-centered organization is the most efficient and effective means of bringing the identification. Thus, while continuing to note the impact of variables in all three centerings, we have focused on audience-centered arrangement.

Frank Barron's speech is primarily receiver-centered. Frank carefully orders his arguments in response to what he knows of the auditors' interests, knowledge, attitudes, and personalities. He correctly chooses the problem–solution arrangement. He consistently makes wise choices in the one-side–both-sides arena.

The primacy–recency research seems to be less applicable to the more standard forms of interpersonal communication than it is to the advertiser–mass-audience matrix; we note, though, two findings that have a more standard application. Deductive–inductive orders and climax–anticlimax arrangement are discussed and related to some of the speeches included in previous chapters. Each pattern gives the communicator a potentially useful tool.

QUESTIONS FOR THOUGHT AND DISCUSSION

1. Do you believe that Frank Barron's speech is organized effectively? What about the other speeches presented in this book?
2. Is it possible that clear organization may hinder the desired identification?

3. Select and outline a magazine article. Can you identify a clear organizational pattern? Now experiment with several alternative organizational patterns. How do these changes affect the article?
4. How important is organization when writing an essay examination? Does the organization affect the grade one receives?

SUGGESTED READINGS

Anderson, Loren, "A Summary of Research on Order Effects in Communication," *Concepts in Communication,* Boston, Allyn & Bacon, 1973.

Hovland, Carl I., et al., *The Order of Presentation in Persuasion,* New Haven, Conn., Yale University Press, 1957.

Mills, Glen E., *Message Preparation,* Indianapolis, Bobbs-Merrill, 1966.

identification through style

Kurt Goldstein reports that certain victims of brain damage do not have the capacity to deal with abstract concepts. They can name separate bears as polar bear and brown bear, but they seem to have no concept of "bear." Apple parer and bread knife get names, but no "knife" concept emerges.[1]

Such an unusual affliction is surprising because we all take for granted the human capacity to abstract a general concept from separate instances. The child who is just learning to talk may apply the term "bus" to any motor vehicle larger than a car; the vocabulary will soon become more precise, but the drawing out of a general concept is clearly evident. The ability to think and communicate symbols that stand for groups or classes of phenomena is a large part of what we call language capacity.

Aside from rare instances like the ones Goldstein describes and a few other minor exceptions, human beings are one by virtue of sharing language capability.[2] Having noted this consubstantial bond, we recognize immediately that the many are represented too by different languages, by

---

[1] "The Nature of Language," in *Language: An Enquiry into its Meaning and Function*, Ruth N. Anshen, ed., New York, Harper & Row, 1957, p. 32.

[2] For support and development of this see John B. Carroll, ed., *Language, Thought, and Reality: Selected Writings of Benjamin Lee Whorf,* Cambridge, Mass., M.I.T. Press, 1956, esp. p. 263; Kenneth Burke, *A Rhetoric of Motives,* Berkeley, University of California Press, 1969, p. 43; Roger Brown, *Words and Things,* New York, Free Press, 1958, esp. p. 135.

variety and change in a given language, and by many individual or "egocentric" uses of a native or foreign language.[3]

Granted that humans are one in the capacity for language, yet many in the ways each uses a given language, we can proceed to discuss the role of style in the search for identification. The subjects of language and style are, of course, large and complex. Philosophers, psychologists, linguists, literary critics, communication theorists, as well as contributors from other disciplines, have explored these subjects with some depth and great length. We can only touch on certain facets of these subjects that seem to be particularly relevant for the communicator to consider.

The canon of style, as we treat it, has to do with the words and sentences used in communication. Nonverbal symbolization is also part of the general language capacity and of individual language use. We discuss these factors of language in Chapter 9.

WORDS AS MAPS

In his *Essay Concerning Human Understanding*, John Locke contends that words are not symbols of things; rather, words represent the ideas one has of things. Twentieth-century semanticists have emphasized this point by using a device like the triangle shown in Figure 11.

Notice that no direct connection exists between the symbol and the *referent*, the thing to which the idea is connected.[4] "The map is not the territory" has become a familiar refrain for promoting this position on language usage. The word "dog," for instance, is a label that the English language com-

---

[3] Piaget and Vygotsky give different interpretations to "egocentric" speech. See Jean Piaget, *The Language and Thought of the Child*, 2nd ed., 1930, trans. Marjorie Gabain, Cleveland, World, 1955, Lev Vygotsky, *Thought and Language*, ed. and trans. by Eugenia Hanfmann and Gertrude Vakar, Cambridge, Mass., M.I.T. Press, 1962.

Figure 11.

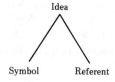

munity *arbitrarily* attaches to the concept of a certain type of animal. No direct, natural tie exists between a specific animal and the general label that is used.[5] Such a view of language usage can yield important insights for improving communication; however, some qualification of the basic position ("The map is not the territory!") should be considered before we discuss these potential benefits.

Understanding Symbolic Distance

Anu, a student from India, spoke on the theme: "Cow is holy." Not "A cow is holy," nor "The cow is holy," but simply "Cow is holy." The expression without the definite or an indefinite article is a bit strange. The strangeness could be written off as a slip by someone working with a second language, but Anu's facility with English seemed to belie this explanation. Overlooking the lack of an article for a moment, one could make the hasty assumption that this sentence is readily understandable. It is widely known that some Indians revere the cow, thus one might think of Anu's statement as describing such reverence. Steak-loving Americans probably have some difficulty appreciating the vision

[4] For some related discussion in Plato's works, see Donald Byker, "Plato's Philosophy of Natural Law as a Key to His View of Persuasion." Doctoral dissertation, University of Michigan, 1969, pp. 60–64.

[5] See C. K. Ogden and I. A. Richards, *The Meaning of Meaning,* New York, Harcourt Brace Jovanovich, 1938.

of privileged beef existing in a land familiar with famine, but such a value is still comprehensible.

If one takes apart the sentence with the triangle from Figure 11 in mind, one sees that "cow" refers to the species concept that can be broken down into other, less abstract terms: Holstein, Guernsey, Jersey, Black Angus, Hereford, etc. "Holy" refers to the concept of the sacred. (The near-tautology here shows something of the overall problem we address in this section.) The "is" of course, is a familiar linking device between subject and predicate.

Returning to the absent article, we can observe that Americans frequently use such constructions in sentences such as, "Mom is good to me," and "God is one." Probably what one confronts here is a naming capacity of language that is not exactly like the thinking and communicating of symbols that stand for groups or classes of phenomena (see p. 176). The commentary following Anu's speech was un-satisfying for the class and seemed to be unusually upsetting and difficult for Anu. We suspect the difficulty came be-cause the class as a whole was using "cow" in the more general mode of manipulating symbols, whereas Anu was using the more particular naming function of language.

Perhaps we can explore this complex matter of dif-ferentiating the language functions by using a device such as Plato employs in *The Republic*. In seeking to prove that jus-tice is superior to injustice for individuals, Plato has Socrates conduct a search for the principle "Justice is supe-rior to injustice," in an imaginary community. The com-munity is larger than the individual, of course; therefore the principle should be larger; thus easier to see. (Plato assumes that the individual is a microcosm of the community.) The enlarged illustration allows one to see the principle clearly; thereafter, the application to the individual case should be less difficult. We can try, likewise, to draw the distinction between the abstract symbolizing and the particular naming functions of language as largely as possible.

Jacques Maritain writes that some primitive people "make the name into a real equivalent of the thing named," and a patient is "as confident in swallowing the prescription as in swallowing the medicine itself."[6] When the name (symbol) and the referent are fused like this, we have what Ernst Cassirer calls a "mythic" use of language.[7] Cassirer claims:

> The notion that name and essence bear a necessary and internal relation to each other, that the name does not merely denote but actually is the essence of its object, that the potency of the real thing is contained in the name—that is one of the fundamental assumptions of the mythmaking consciousness itself.[8]

Bronislaw Malinowski's work with the Trobriand Islanders yields a similar observation:

> We found this very magical attitude towards words. The word gives power, allows one to exercise an influence over an object or an action. . . . The word acts on the thing and the thing releases the word in the human mind. This indeed is nothing more or less than the essence of the theory which underlies the use of verbal magic.[9]

In this mythic view of language's naming function, one's own name is "indissolubly linked" with one's person.[10] To know a person's real name is to have a special hold on that person; since such a hold could be used to bring harm, only a few trusted intimates should know one's real name.[11]

This discussion of the mythic use of language has been an

---

[6] Maritain, "Language and the Theory of Sign," in Anshen, ed., op. cit., p. 94.

[7] Cassirer, *Language and Myth*, trans. Susanne K. Langer, New York, Dover, 1946.

[8] Ibid., p. 3.

[9] Malinowski, *Magic, Science and Religion and Other Essays*, New York, Free Press, 1948, p. 259.

[10] See Cassirer, op. cit., p. 49.

[11] Leonard W. Doob, *Communication in Africa*, New Haven, Conn., Yale University Press, 1961, p. 196.

attempt to show as largely as possible the difference between the particular naming function of language and the abstract symbolizing function: Cassirer calls the latter a "discursive" use. Possibly the mythic use is so foreign that any connection to current language behavior is lost. Certainly most Americans are far more at home with the discursive mode than with the mythic; still, one would not be wise to turn away from an examination of mythic elements in his own language use. Malinowski points out: "The agnostics'fear of blasphemy or at least reluctance to use it, the active dislike of obscene language, the power of swearing—all this shows that in the normal use of words the bond between symbol and referent is more than a mere convention."[12] Probably Malinowski's observation is out of date for some members of our society, but it surely does not seem to be invalid for others.

And even if the particular references Malinowski makes are inapplicable for some, each of us perhaps invests other names with like potency. W. H. Auden reminisced about such a naming:

> I had read the technological prose of my favorite books in a peculiar way. A word like *pyrites*, [metallic-looking sulfides; fool's gold is a pyritic compound] for example, was for me, not simply an indicative sign; it was the Proper Name of a Sacred Being, so that, when I heard an aunt pronounce it *pirrits*, I was shocked. Her pronunciation was more than wrong, it was ugly. Ignorance was impiety.[13]

One wonders, for oneself and for others, which subjects and which words have had and perhaps still have such qualities?

Auden suggests later that his readers suppose someone says to a child: "'Look at the moon!' The child looks and for him this is a sacred encounter. In his mind the word 'moon' is not a name of a sacred object but one of its most im-

[12] *Magic, Science and Religion,* op. cit., p. 258.

[13] Auden, *The Dyer's Hand and Other Essays,* New York, Random House, 1948, p. 34.

portant properties. . . ."[14] Auden's example has special significance for one of the authors of this book. When my (D.B.) son, Patrick was 2 and 3 years old, we lived in a second-floor apartment that had a small deck just outside the living room's sliding-glass doors. Almost every evening I carried Pat out on the deck so he could say "Goodnight Moon" before I put him in his crib. Often we would have to go down the stairs to the other side of the apartment building to see whether the moon was waiting there for the nighttime ritual. When the clouds were too thick, the weather too bad, or the moon elsewhere in the heavens, Pat would say, "Goodnight Nana, Goodnight Poppa, Goodnight Moon," while standing inside his crib. And the same look seemed to be on his face and in his eyes, whether we were on the deck looking up at a glorious full moon or whether we were standing together in the bedroom.

Pat stayed up late one night and sat close to the TV with unusual stillness as the astronauts first walked on the moon. When the program ended, he turned to us with a bewildered look that no one could possibly capture or answer. He was upset because he was sure his Moon was broken. And it was. The magic had departed.

Pat is several years older now. He no longer says goodnight to the moon, but I wonder how much of his present enchantment with the sun and the planets (Saturn is his favorite because it has so many moons) harks back to the cherishing of "Moon" in those early years? Putting the question generally, how much of the child is in each of us?

Auden muses:

It was Edward Lear, I believe, who said that the true test of imagination is the ability to name a cat, and we are told in the first chapter of Genesis that the Lord brought to unfallen Adam all the creatures that he might name them and whatsoever Adam called every living creature, that was the name thereof, which is to say, its Proper Name. Here Adam plays the role of the Proto-poet, not the Proto-prose-writer. . . . Like a line of poetry, a

[14] Ibid., pp. 57–58.

Proper Name is untranslatable. Language is prosaic to the degree that "It does not matter what particular word is associated with an idea, provided the association once made is permanent." Language is poetic to the degree that it does matter.[15]

One wonders, again, how much of the poetic is in oneself and in those with whom one communicates?

To a large extent, each person has to answer on a personal level these related questions about the role of the mythic and the poetic in language use; still, we can present a few observations. Note that Vince uses "grandfather," a discursive, prosaic, rather general symbol, most of the time in his speech. "Grampa," a more mythic, poetic name, is used twice (once in line 65 during Vince's pleasurable reliving of Grampa's storytelling, and once in line 106 when Vince is struck by the full weight of loss; see Chapter 1, pp. 6–7). These particular uses seem to show that the proper name "Grampa" has a special potency for Vince.

Someone else could feel mythic-poetic qualities in "Grampa," yet this person might be comfortable with a more frequent use, or a less frequent use. Perhaps this person would not use the intimate "Grampa" at all with the audience Vince addressed in the classroom setting. Mythic language use is governed by subtle requirements of the speaker, audience, and occasion, and one has to be more careful in its use than in the use of the more generally acceptable discursive code. The warmer, more poetic "Grampa" can be extraordinarily moving if used just right; it can be especially irritating if used improperly.[16] The cooler, more prosaic "grandfather" is less likely to be moving or irritating.

---

[15] Ibid., pp. 34–35. For a similar point see T. S. Eliot, *On Poetry and Poets*, London, Faber & Faber, 1957, p. 19.

[16] Wilbur Schramm makes a similar point in *Mass Media and National Development*, Stanford, Calif., Stanford University Press, 1964, p. 188. For further discussion see Doob, op. cit. pp. 285–286.

"Dad," "Mom," and kindred specific names used in our more intimate encounters are distanced to "father" and "mother" in less intimate discussions. Complex factors in the source, receiver, and scene will determine which sort of naming is used. For example, in the first-round assignment a girl talked about the influence of her father in her life. Her father had died just a few days before, and the material was very warm (almost too warm) to handle at this time and with this group. Maxine consistently used "father" as she spoke. "Dad" or "Daddy" probably would have been too potent for her to use while keeping a desirable level of control. In another speech, a senior talked openly, easily, and for most of his audience, effectively, about the loving relationship between "Jackie" (his wife) and himself. One classmate said he was "turned off" by the speech because "my lady and I are close, too, but it's not proper to talk about it as you do." "Jackie" is clearly the particular-name, mythic usage; "my lady" is the abstract, discursive usage. Watch also the distancing (perhaps the swagger) with which some teenagers talk of the "old man" and the "old lady."

Some Jewish students write G-d rather than God in their papers. Many Jewish people will not say or write the Hebrew word that has been Anglicized as Jehovah. Both practices are probably tied to the Third Commandment: "Thou shalt not take the name of the Lord thy God in vain." Many Christians exhibit a related carefulness in their use of the words God, Jesus, and Christ. A mythic use of language seems clearly evident.

This section, you may have noticed, has taken an inductive approach in developing its title, Symbolic Distance. The section was introduced as a qualifying of the proclamation: "The map is not the territory!" The qualified claim could be, "The map is *usually* not the territory." If this limitation of the dictum is granted, the triangle of Figure 11 will have to be redrawn to represent the particular-naming, mythic functioning of language. A link must be pictured between the symbol (name) and the referent (see Figure 12).

Figure 12.

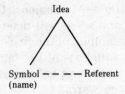

When language use is absolutely discursive (the general, abstract symbolic sort), Figure 12 is incorrect, since no direct tie exists between the arbitrary symbol and the referent, and one returns to Figure 11. When some shade of mythic usage (the particular, Proper Naming sort) is present, Figure 11 is incorrect, because a direct tie exists between symbol (name) and referent. If this tie is very close and strong for a person, a culture, or a subculture, the dotted line would seem to be too weak as a representation. In other cases the link may be present but tenuous; for these cases the line would have to be faintly drawn. Many other kinds of drawing would be needed to depict the precise strength and closeness of other bonds between the referent and its name.

If a community is tightly knit, each member probably will learn how and when to use the discursive and mythic elements of the shared language. One would expect this, for instance, in Augustine's City of God and in Plato's ideal community, where all laugh and cry over the same things. As the society becomes more fragmented, the individuals are increasingly hard put to judge whether the discursive or mythic approach is called for, and to assess, if the mythic posture is decided on, just what distance would be proper. Uses and distances are likely to clash for cultures, subcultures, generations, and individuals; thus humans build their towers of Babel.[17]

[17] Kenneth Burke's *A Grammar of Motives*, Berkeley, University of California Press, 1969, and *A Rhetoric of Motives,* op. cit., are again and again relevant to the thought of this paragraph. See, especially, *A Rhetoric,* pp. 23, 183–286.

The urge to avoid Babel leads to a fervent preaching of the gospel: "The map is not the territory!" The avid proponents of this gospel want all to believe this message and to use language in accord with this belief; then, they reason, the confusion could be held back. But as we have tried to show in this section, the particular-naming, mythical use of language does exist. No amount of preaching will banish it completely. Even if the "error" could be eradicated, human beings would not necessarily be happy for doing so, because they would be left with a language that is "an algebra, and there could exist only one poem, of absolute banality, expressing the system."[18]

Instead of seeking to exorcise mythic usage, we have sought to call attention to its existence. If we all become sensitive to the particular-naming function of language, we can act with greater skill as sources and receivers. Then everyone can profit by using both the narrow, intense light of the mythic naming and the general, diffuse light of the discursive symbols.[19]

Using Word Maps

One can read a book by using the intense, narrow beam of a small flashlight, but one reads more easily with the diffuse light given off by the incandescent or fluorescent bulb. The analogy between lighting systems and mythic and discursive language functions cannot be applied too rigorously; however, the one facet of comparison indicated here should hold for these two sections. The section on symbolic distance dealt with a narrow yet nevertheless important area and gave, we trust, some useful light. The following section treats a wider area of our language usage, and the lighting should be more broadly available and useful.

[18] Auden, *The Dyer's Hand*, op. cit., p. 66.
[19] See Cassirer, op. cit., pp. 83–99.

THE MAP AS A REDUCTION OR SHORTHAND

One can easily carry a map of a state, country, or planet with him; to take along the territory itself is another matter. The map serves as a reduction or shorthand that allows one to function more easily and productively than would be possible without this device.

Words, too, act as maps in giving one an easily used, productive shorthand. John Locke's enormously influential *Essay Concerning Human Understanding*, first published in 1690, takes for granted the existence of an orderly physical universe governed by laws of nature. Stimuli from this physical universe flow, almost as if they were alive, to be picked up by the human being's senses. The sensations produced make impressions in the mind. These impressions—Locke calls them "ideas"—are images of the original physical objects. If we take a common domestic animal as our example, simple ideas such as black, white, height, length, and width, combine with one another and with other ideas to form a complex idea of this animal. We all agree as English language users to call this complex idea a cow. The complex idea and the arbitrary symbol, cow, are reductions. One can walk about carrying the idea with him and one can toss around the word in discussions. One could, of course, do neither with the actual animal.

Locke threw out the Platonic notion of innate ideas, that is, that each human soul (mind) comes equipped with an idea or form that the specific cow fits into. Plato used this scheme of innate ideas to explain how it is that one person's sensations, perceptions, memories, and reflections will be similar to another person's, therefore yielding some confidence that people are talking about the same things in their communications with one another.[20] Locke lops off this scheme as excess baggage, and he proceeds by taking for granted that human minds sense, perceive, remember, and reflect in homogeneous ways.

[20] See Byker, op. cit., esp. pp. 47–57, 60–64.

Even if we were able to do so, this is not the place to explore all the byways of the dispute between the rationalists (Plato et al.) and the empiricists (Locke et al.). We set up this much of Locke's system to draw certain important lessons from it for the use of words maps.

The first lesson has been intimated already throughout this section.[21] The word is a shorthand or reduction of the referent. The shorthand will have to leave out great amounts of detail. If one were to attempt a thorough analysis and description of a specific cow, he would fill volumes and probably never complete the task. Condensation is usually necessary and desirable. One has to be careful, though, not to act as if he knows the whole story of the domestic animal just because he can affix the convenient tag, "cow." E. B. White's delightful essay "Irtnog" satirizes the complacency that can come with condensation too cheaply purchased: An entire Hemingway novel is condensed to one word, "Bang," and its placid readers are satisfied—efficient, certainly, but something is lost in the process. The student who smugly announces that he has read *Crime and Punishment* in two hours should not be accorded high praise.

A second lesson should be drawn when one believes that the word refers to the idea or image that begins with experience from the outside world. The experiences one person has with our domestic animal will not be the same as those of another person. All members of our language community agree to affix the symbol, cow, to these manifold images that exist, and the map is general enough to cover a wide range of individual images. Often this looseness of fit will not matter very much, although it can at times cause some confusion. For instance, if one urbanite has the limited reference of a black and white Holstein for the label, cow, and another urbanite has the limited reference of the much

---

[21] This shows a Lockean or empiricist's bias that is difficult, if not impossible, for our age to avoid. For a sophisticated chastening of this view, see Kenneth Burke, "What Are the Signs of What?" In *Language as Symbolic Action*, Berkeley, University of California Press, 1966, pp. 359–379.

smaller, fawn-colored Jersey, each may find the other ill
educated if the discussion turns to milk producing. Fortunately, cows are not likely to be a prime subject for the ur-
banites, and confusion and denigration will seldom occur, at
least over this subject. One tends, of course, to have more
complete images and more precise vocabularies for
experiences that are frequent and important to him.[22] Even
on familiar ground, however, we all confront communication
difficulties because the ideas or images each of us has will
not be exactly alike, even though the words used seem to be
the same; thus one should keep reminding himself that each
person has various experiences as inputs for the images.
These differences are then summed over by the maps that
are imposed. Words, remember, will usually be more alike
than thoughts. One may find this lesson easier to recall if he
thinks of it in terms of cow_1 not being cow_2, and so on. One
cannot put the index numbers into all writing and speaking,
but we all should profit if we are sensitive to the point before
a communication and if we can call attention to its disrup-
tive force in a coaction that seems to be foundering.

Lesson one warns that words, like maps, can cover a lot of
territory without necessarily telling us many significant
details about what is there. Lesson two says that if ideas
(references in people's heads) begin with experience and if
one grants that experiences vary, one must be careful to remember that two persons may use the same word, but each
person has a different reference for the word. One can cur-
tail the possibilities for confusion and estrangement if he ha-
bitually asks: What is the *actual territory* to which this word
and idea refer? What *idea* or *reference* does each person
have in mind in connection with the use of this word?

These two lessons are drawn within the orderly Lockean
framework: (1) a steady physical universe governed by laws
of nature, and (2) human minds sense, perceive, remember,
and reflect in homogeneous ways. When these two assump-

---

[22] For discussion see Roger Brown, *Words and Things,* New York, Free
Press, 1958, pp. 233–237.

tions are shaken, the basic two lessons must be amplified. Lesson three, thus, is an amplification of lesson one. In a changing universe, ideas and words must account for an ever increasing amount of data. The Greek philosopher Heraclitus (c. 535–c. 475 B.C.) observed that no one can dip his foot in the same river twice, since both the foot and the river are changing. Probability theories and a pervasive awareness of relativity are more fashionable today than beliefs in universal natural laws. One way or another, a person is confronted by a world in flux, by ubiquitous change and decay. Yet enduring labels are attached. The black and white animal that furnished the original experience leading to one's mental construct and to the use of the word cow grows old and becomes "extra-lean ground beef," but the idea and the word remain.[23] If the territory expands and changes while the maps remain the same, more and more detail is omitted and the labels affixed become less and less adequate.

Probably the whole matter seems inconsequential to most of us if we remain bound to the cow example. But what happens when the same point is applied to capitalist, communist, Democrat, Republican, Roman Catholic, WASP, existentialist, black activist, or middle-class? Or if we apply the point to terms like free enterprise, socialism, and welfare? To what actual territory does each of these terms refer? What idea or reference does each of us have in mind in connection with the use of each term? Unless one works hard to become and remain informed of the territory in an increasingly complex world, he will have increasingly fuzzy notions of such matters, and he will be more and more prone to mislabel people and programs. The ignorance will be particularly unfortunate if one clings dogmatically to the misconceptions and misapplications. Fuzziness, inaccuracy, and dogmatism repeatedly disrupt the creating of mutually beneficial identifications.

[23] The permanence of the idea is an important aspect of Plato's philosophy. For comment on this point see Bertrand Russell, *A History of Western Philosophy,* New York, Simon & Schuster, 1945, pp. 121–122.

Lesson four in the use of word maps is an elaboration of lesson two (that experiences vary; therefore, each person can have a different reference for the same word). Even while granting that humans sense, perceive, remember, and reflect in homogeneous ways, confusion can come, for instance, if one of us has had experience only with Holsteins and the other only with Guernseys. Suppose, now, that we shake this assumption of the homogeneous processing of experience.

We all realize that our attention focuses on certain facets of an environment while ignoring other facets. Two persons thus can be placed in the same environment, and ostensibly each will have the same experience; but each will come away with different impressions just because each will pay attention to different parts of the total set of available stimuli. Therefore, disparate ideas or references are formed because of discrepancies at the attention level.

Perception is closely allied with attention. The sensory data that have been picked up and sent along to the brain are processed according to, or into, some pattern; otherwise the data would remain as just so many separate nerve impulses. Each person has a special way of perceiving the messages coming in from the senses. Sinclair Lewis has Carol Kennicott and Bea Sorenson walk down the same street of Gopher Prairie in *Main Street*. Each woman looks at the same things, but each sees (perceives) a very different world.[24] Hadley Cantril discusses findings of experiments using the stereoscope, a device that allows the experimenter to show one picture to the subject's right eye and a different picture to the left eye. In one of the experiments two pictures of statues are shown: one of a madonna with a child and the other of a young female nude. In one of the viewings two visiting professors of psychology are the subjects.

The first looked into the stereoscope and reported that he saw a Madonna with Child. A few seconds later he exclaimed, "But my

---

[24] For supporting research see M. E. Vernon, *The Psychology of Perception*, Baltimore, Penguin, 1962.

God, she is undressing." What had happened so far was that somehow she had lost the baby she was holding and her robe had slipped down from her shoulders and stopped just above the breast line. Then in a few more seconds she lost her robe completely and became the young nude. For this particular professor, the nude never did get dressed again. Then my second friend took his turn. For a few seconds he could see nothing but the nude and then he exclaimed, "But now a robe is wrapping itself around her." And very soon he ended up with Madonna with Child and as far as I know still remains with that vision. Some people will never see the nude; others will never see the Madonna. . . .[25]

We all know from frequent examples that our abilities to remember are not the same, either. Some people seem to possess photographic memories; others take pills for absentmindedness. Moreover, each tends to recall experiences in unique ways. Heterogeneity is also evident in the reflection process. One is again and again surprised by the strange inferences that others draw from the evidence. The tendency to misconstrue a communication (i.e., to see it as being more like or less like one's own position than the communication really is) seems to show that the reflection process is neither precise nor uniform.[26] Theodore Newcomb's findings on the errors due to the urge for congruence (the desire to think that others think as oneself thinks) give additional proof of the tendency to bend reasoning or reflection to suit one's own desires.[27] One can argue

[25] "Perception and Interpersonal Relations," in *Basic Readings in Interpersonal Communications,* K. Giffin and B. R. Patton, eds., New York, Harper & Row, 1971, p. 129. Reprinted from *American Journal of Psychiatry,* **114** (1957), 119–126. Also see W. V. Haney, "Perception and Communication," in Giffin and Patton, eds., op. cit., pp. 139–169.

[26] C. I. Hovland, O. J. Harvey, and M. Sherif, "Assimilation and Contrast Effects in Communication and Attitude Change," *Journal of Abnormal and Social Psychology,* **55** (1957), 242–252. (Also see above, p. 52.)

[27] T. M. Newcomb, R. H. Turner, and P. E. Converse, *Social Psychology,* New York, Holt, Rinehart & Winston, 1965, pp. 173–174.

that the misconstructions reported by these researchers could fit in the discussion of perceptual biases. Whether one places such considerations under perception or reflection makes little difference for our overall argument that human beings show considerable heterogeneity in their sensations, perceptions, memories, and reflections.[28]

When the second assumption—that humans have homogeneous ways of building concepts or ideas—is shaken, one should become yet more wary of thinking that people have similar ideas in mind just because they speak the same words. The questions we urged before become still more important for each of us to ask: To what actual territories do our words refer? What ideas or references do each of us have in mind for the words we use?

Figure 13 may help you visualize some central thoughts in this section on the map as a reduction or shorthand. The two-way arrows between Idea and Referent indicate that each person is active in assimilating the territory, thus bringing to bear individual tendencies in attention, perception, memory, and reflection. As a result, the word is a

Figure 13.

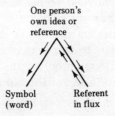

One person's
own idea or
reference

Symbol   Referent
(word)   in flux

[28] Thomas Hobbes's *Leviathan*, 1651, was written during the bloody revolution that included the beheading of a king of England. Hobbes saw human reason as an untrustworthy instrument that each person used to serve the passions. This led to anarchy. Locke, on the other hand, wrote during a rather peaceful changing of power in England, and his view of human reasoning, as expressed in the *Essay Concerning Human Understanding* and in the political works, is far more optimistic.

map or shorthand that has a degree of unavoidably indi-
vidualized usage.[29] This is another piece of evidence of the
many in human communication.

The foregoing lessons are needed as antidotes to the common practice of using words as easy, accurate counters for
the territory under consideration; however, if taken too far
the lessons may make one's hopes for effective communication more bleak than they should be. Human beings are,
after all, both many and one in their use of words as well as
in other matters relevant to interpersonal communication.

One can profit, then, from a combination of the Platonic-
rationalist and the empiricist positions. The former stresses
the human capacity to perceive, remember, and reflect in
similar, thus communicable, ways. The empiricist positions,
on the other hand, can be traced out to underscore the
diversity in human experience and thought, thus warning
one not to take accurate, meaningful communication for
granted.[30] Both inputs are valuable in the study of style.

Of course, words do not just exist as separate units in communication; people usually talk in sentences. Later sections
of this chapter treat the role of sentences in attempts to
reach identification through style. We can borrow one point
for the present discussion. Words, typically, act within
sentences; hence words influence the meaning of sentences
and, in turn, have their meaning influenced by other words,
as well as by factors inherent in sentences. For example,
"Bill hit the ball," "Bill, hit the ball!" and "Bill, was that a
hit?" are three different kinds of sentence, each one using

[29] Semanticists have concentrated on developing these and related points.
For an influential early effort see Alfred Korzybski, *Science and Sanity,*
Lancaster, Science Press, 1933. For a later, more readable treatment see
Irving J. Lee, *How to Talk with People,* New York, Harper & Row, 1952.

[30] While examining Noam Chomsky's assertions, R. Edgeley notes how the
rationalist and empiricist positions can be seen to overlap at the edges;
see "Innate Ideas," in *Knowledge and Necessity,* (vol. 3), New York,
Macmillan, 1970, p. 2 ff. For indications of a similar line in Plato's
thought see Byker, op. cit., 49–57.

"hit" in a different way. Through a range of uses and contexts one acquires practice in the application of the word, and this practice generally rewards certain uses and discourages others.

Usually, too, a person works with words and sentences to try fit them to his thoughts and to the needs of his coactor. As one does this, the whole matter of the relation of word to idea and of idea to territory can come under review, perhaps heading toward a constructive revision. Thus the process of fitting what one communicates to the demands of coactors, oneself, and the territory one tries to map will chasten one's thoughts, words, and sentences.[31] And the continual chastening should bring a more accurate, meaningful, and effective verbal code. Style, like organization, profits from source, receiver, and scenic orientations (see pp. 139–141). Attending to the requirements of each constituent will strengthen the chances of gaining identification.

One should guard against the temptation to be general in affixing maps. To say, "I had a sandwich, fruit, and some other stuff for lunch," covers considerably more territory than "I had cheese-on-rye, a banana, and raspberry yogurt for lunch." The latter is more vivid and should prove more interesting.[32]

To be concerned with vividness and interest is to utilize a receiver-centered approach to style. This is usually the desirable priority, and it should be sought, provided one does not do injustice to the vision of the source and the reality of the scene. Much of the time all three considerations will be enhanced if the more specific, vivid words are used. Roger Brown points out that to say "A lion is coming!" is much more useful information to give a companion than "An

---

[31] A like discussion occurs in Arthur L. Blumenthal, *Language and Psychology: Historical Aspects of Psycholinguistics*, New York, Wiley, 1970, p. 56 ff.

[32] This point is frequently and justly attributed to George Campbell, who gave it systematic treatment in *The Philosophy of Rhetoric*, 1776, Lloyd F. Bitzer, ed., Carbondale, Southern Illinois University Press, 1963, esp. p. 286 ff.

animal is coming."[33] If a lion is in fact coming, the word "lion" is a decidedly better representation of what one perceives and of the actual territory than is the more general word "animal."

While presenting his first-round speech of introduction, one student talked about "handling farm equipment at a very young age." He probably would have done better to say, "I was driving our John Deere tractor when I was nine." For some audiences he could have said, "I was pushing in the hand clutch with one hand, moving the power-takeoff lever to drop the mounted, three-sixteens plow with my other hand, while steering with my chin, when I was nine." Such specificity probably would confuse other audiences. One can go overboard with the specific, vivid, telling approach. Again, the requirements of the receiver, the source, and the scene should be considered in selecting the best words.

Sometimes a more general treatment is better because specific, vivid detail would take too much time. Meticulously stating, "An unusually large lioness has left her two cubs, is now 30 yards away, and closing rapidly," is not in the best interests of speaker and listener if they are standing in the open. If they were studying wildlife from within an armored car, it would be another matter.

We have tried to show in this section that words serve as a useful shorthand or map of the actual territory. Within the empiricist's framework, we have warned that the shorthand will omit great masses of detail, especially if one grants that the referent is in the process of changing. Within the same framework, we also have warned that each person will have different experiences, hence different ideas or references for words. The difference in ideas becomes more likely if one stops assuming that human beings sense, perceive, remember, and reflect in homogeneous ways. These warnings or lessons are important; yet they should not lead one to de-

---

[33] Brown, op. cit., p. 282. Note Brown's instructive use of "superordinate–subordinate" to cover what is often called the "abstract–concrete" continuum.

spair over the possibility for effective communication. One can, perhaps usually does, believe with the rationalist in certain similarities in human thinking and language behavior. One also can see that contexts and feedback will help one gain surer use of individual words. In addition, the advice to display the degree of specificity appropriate to receiver, source, and scenic variables should help one use verbal shorthand with productive efficiency. We all need the warnings and the faith to wrestle with words, to align them as well as possible to the demands of receiver, source, and scene. One will often be disappointed with the result, but one is not doomed always to hear the sad refrain, "'That is not it at all.'"[34]

BIASING WORD MAPS

When Joe works on his telegram in Chapter 2, he seeks words that will testify to his need while revealing neither the poor stewardship of the past nor the less than praiseworthy plans for the future (see pp. 24–25). A black eye can be explained by: "I got it playing basketball." The recipient of the shiner hopes that this report suggests a scrapper who hits the boards after rebounds; he would prefer that the report not give away the distasteful fracas started over a foul. The kindergarten teacher prepares a series of euphemisms for the report cards of students who have done poorly. One knows from these and many like instances that word maps do not always present the territory precisely as it exists.

Jeremy Bentham was exceptionally alert to such biasing. He hoped to lessen its effect (at least insofar as it was helpful to his opponents) by teaching his readers the eulogistic and dyslogistic biasing used in key areas of human concern. For example, in the area of supplying material needs, a neutral or accurate mapping would be given by the "desire of subsistence." This could be biased positively (*eulogistically*) by words such as "frugality" and "thrift." To

---

[34] T. S. Eliot, "The Love Song of J. Alfred Prufrock."

bias it negatively (*dyslogistically*), one would call it "cu-pidity," "avarice," or "lust for gain." Similarly, the desire for information (neutral) can be labeled "love of knowledge" or "scientific" (eulogistic) or painted as "impertinence" and "meddlesomeness" (dyslogistic). The belief in God or hope in God (neutral) can be "eulogized as piety, devotion, holiness, sanctity; dyslogized as superstition, bigotry, fanaticism, sanctimoniousness, hypocrisy."[35]

We all bias our maps, consciously or otherwise; each is perhaps more likely to notice the bias in the communications of others. Suppose your school's basketball team loses, 74–69. You may object righteously to the slanting in the headline "Warriors Crush Hornets," but you may not even notice the bias in the headline "Warriors Turn Back Gallant Hornets."

A more conscious awareness of the biasing of word maps should give one better control of responses to the maneuvers of others, as well as surer command of one's own attempts at coloring. Humans probably cannot eradicate the practice; Burke points out that Bentham did not do so while pressing his cause.[36] Besides, similarities of biasing by the coactors are important factors in the creation of identification. A surer knowledge and control of biasing should enable communicators to gain identification more efficiently. Aristotle gives this example of a skilled craftsman:

> Thus Simonides, when the victor in the mule-race offered him a small fee for an ode, declined to write one—"did not care to write poetry about *half-asses*"; but on receiving a proper fee, he wrote:
>
> All hail, ye daughters of storm-footed mares!
> (*Rhetoric* 1405b)[37]

---

[35] Kenneth Burke, *A Rhetoric of Motives,* op. cit., pp. 90–101.

[36] Ibid., pp. 95–96.

[37] Translated by Lane Cooper, New York, Appleton-Century-Crofts, 1932, p. 189.

CULTURAL CRITERIA FOR BIASING WORD MAPS

One cannot observe or select eulogistic, dyslogistic, or neutral wording all by himself. Standards or criteria in the language using group help to determine what words are neutral and which have positive or negative slants. These criteria usually mirror the ordering principles of a society. For example: If one of the ordering principles of society is wealth (i.e., those who have more money are placed higher in the social order than those who have less money), then labels that affirm the monetary principle (diligent, thrifty, astute businessman) will be eulogistic; labels that counter the monetary principle (lazy, prodigal, incompetent) will be dyslogistic.[38] If legitimacy is an ordering principle, "bastard" is obviously a pejorative term. If color of skin is an ordering principle, similarly loaded uses of "light" and "dark" will show up in the vocabulary.

If all members of the group were true believers in their culture's ordering principles, the correlating eulogistic, neutral, and dyslogistic maps would be affixed without any critical misgivings, since they would be part of the unquestioned "furniture of the mind." As belief in a system becomes less universal and fervent, the principles and the corresponding word maps are taken out into the open, criticized, discounted through ironic usage, and perhaps disavowed.[39] One ought not be surprised to find that Bentham was a relative outsider in making his penetrating critique of the eulogistic and dyslogistic mapping of his time. One ought not be surprised, either, to learn that blacks (and others who are disenchanted with the principles on which American society operates) are very sensitive to the slantings

[38] Burke's *Rhetoric of Motives* returns again and again to this point. See esp. pp. 141–142, 187–192, 208–244, 259–267.

[39] Thomas Hardy was keenly aware of this. See, for example, "In Time of 'The Breaking of Nations,'" and "The Mother Mourns." For a perceptive comparison of the Cynics in Athens with the Yippies of contemporary America, see Theodore O. Windt, Jr., "The Diatribe: Last Resort for Protest," *Quarterly Journal of Speech,* **58** (1972), 1–14.

accepted as standard by those comfortably in the mainstream of American life.

Another perspective on the cultural biasing of word maps is frequently called the Whorfian hypothesis. Benjamin Whorf maintained that the language of a culture is shaped by the world-and-life-view of that culture; as children are born into a language-using group, they are indoctrinated into its world-view while they learn the language. Whorf contrasts the world-views of certain American Indian tribes and their languages with the world-views of what he calls the Standard Average European (SAE) language community.[40] According to Whorf, the Hopi Indians' world-view and vocabulary make the understanding of certain concepts in modern physics easier for them than it is for those who have learned to think in one of the SAE languages.[41]

Plato had a view that was similar to the Whorfian hypothesis, but his vexation with the contemporary Greek language was rather the opposite of the fretting of Whorf, Chase, McLuhan, and others over SAE languages. Plato suggested that the Greek language of his day was predisposed toward the notion that everything was in a state of flux (*Cratylus*, 416 ff.). Because of this biasing of the word maps, Plato thought the expression and belief of his views on timeless reality were made more difficult.

One need not take all the speculations in "superlinguistics" without a grain of salt. Within limits, though, the notion of a language passing along a certain view of life seems to be acceptable. Thus one should expect a given language to be weighted in favor of the world-and-life-view and the ordering principles that have been accepted by the group that uses the language. Ferreting out the manifold biasings that occur should help communicators become more sensitive coactors in their sharing of information.

[40] Carroll, *Language Thought and Reality: Selected Writings of Benjamin Lee Whorf,* op. cit., esp. pp. 262–263.

[41] Ibid. Also see Stuart Chase, *Power of Words,* New York, Harcourt Brace Jovanovich, 1953, p. 100 ff; Marshall McLuhan, *Understanding Media,* New York, McGraw-Hill, 1964, p. 86.

CHANGING MAPS

We remarked in Chapter 4 that the word "dilettante" once served as a positive label for one who had refined sensitivities in many different areas. Today the term has a negative slant and refers to someone who refuses to specialize and become a true expert in any field. Eric Havelock traces the extension of the Greek word "cosmos." Originally, "cosmos" referred to decorative clusters on a woman's headdress or on a horse's harness. Later it was stretched to refer to the ranks of an army—here the notion of order becomes more apparent. Later still it came to cover the thought of a world order, and finally it was extended as far as possible by naming the ordered universe.[42] You may have noticed that our third sentence, "Bill, was that a hit?" (p. 183) could refer to part of a ballgame, to a recorded song, or to a number of other possibilities, including the recent extension in television portrayals of gangland talk in which a hit is an assassination on demand.

These examples illustrate that word maps change. Positive and negative loadings shift, the maps can be extended to cover more or other territory, some words now cover less ground than they once did, and others swell the ranks of words that have become obsolete. With a little thought and some attention to the dictionary (especially works like the *Oxford English Dictionary*, which list definitions that have been current in different time periods), each of us could compile an impressive catalog showing our changing maps. This would be particularly apparent in the rapidly changing "hip" language of various groups.

Despite the rather obvious fact of changing word maps, one still meets those who use their erudition to point out that the Latin roots are such and such, therefore the meaning must be. . . . And the English teacher will hold up for ridicule the fellow in the service station who put up the sign: "Let us install your antifreeze." (The poor bloke should have known that "install" has to do with solids, not liquids.)

[42] Brown, op. cit., p. 274.

English teachers and other preservers of the language wish that the dictionary would stand as a strict judge of any wandering from traditional usage; however, dictionaries of American English do not dictate an unalterable application of word maps. Vast additions to knowledge in specialized fields have spawned a host of new terms and have brought in esoteric applications for terms used before to map different territories. The preface to *Webster's Third New International Dictionary* reports:

> Members of the editorial staff began in 1936 a systematic reading of books, magazines, newspapers, pamphlets, catalogs, and learned journals. By the time of going to press the collection contained just under 4,500,000 such new examples of recorded usage, to be added to more than 1,665,000 citations already in the files for previous editions.[43]

And when *The Oxford English Dictionary, The Dictionary of American English,* and *The Dictionary of Americanisms* (all of which had appeared after the second edition of Webster in 1934) had been consulted, there were more than 10 million citations to draw upon. The new Webster has 450,000 entries. "By itself, the number of entries is, however, not of first importance. The number of words available is always far in excess of and, for a one-volume dictionary, many times the number that can possibly be included."[44]

With such a proliferation of words and usages to draw on, the editorial staff must make far-reaching decisions on what criteria to apply in selecting entries and definitions. *Webster's Third* paid more attention to current usage in making these decisions than many members of English departments and other scholars would have liked. Consternation arose when the volume was published, and even after more than 10 years have passed, the "new book" raises hackles.

[43] Philip B. Gove, ed., *Webster's Third New International Dictionary,* Springfield, Mass., Merriam, 1961, p. 6a.

[44] Ibid., p. 7a.

In general, English department members who teach literature and composition courses want the language to remain stable. They fondly point to the work done by John Dryden (1631–1700) and other seventeenth- and eighteenth-century English scholars to discipline and stabilize the language. The English teachers reason that, without this effort, Shakespeare would be far less readable today. For us to read Shakespeare in the English of the early seventeenth century would be analogous to reading Chaucer in middle English: A relatively strange language would have to be mastered.

Linguists, on the other hand, are likely to disparage efforts by a given class or age to impose standards on a language. They point out that the English language was evolving into a more and more supple instrument for communication in the sixteenth and seventeenth centuries; further changes would not have been major, and the neoclassical belief that the eighteenth century had achieved the best possible language was an unfortunate exhibition of an all-too-prevalent hubris.[45] The linguists also point out that American English should not be compared too closely with British English. In Great Britain the language spoken and written in the London area became the standard for correct usage. America has no such standard group or area to use as a reference point. The various dialect areas in America (now being eroded by mass media and mobility) evolved because of the migration patterns of English-speaking settlers and because of the special influences of other cultures.[46] American English borrowed extensively from the Indian, French, Dutch, and Spanish cultures that existed in various parts of the country, as well as from the many different immigrant groups that arrived later.[47] To elevate the speech of

---

[45] For discussion of the prevalence of this belief in the eighteenth century, see Frederick W. Bateson, *English Poetry and the English Language,* New York, Russell & Russell, 1961, p. 49 ff.

[46] See Donald J. Lloyd and Harry R. Warfel, *American English in its Cultural Setting,* New York, Knopf, 1956.

[47] Albert H. Marckwardt, *American English,* New York, Oxford University Press, 1958, pp. 21–58.

a given group or area as a standard strikes the linguist as profoundly un-American.[48]

Those interested in the study of interpersonal communication will have some sympathy for both sides of this controversy. A measure of uniformity and stability in word maps is needed if communication is to be comprehensible. At the same time, creative usage is needed for the sake of individuality and interest. Here again, one sees a place for the one and for the many. Appreciation of the one should make us careful that changes in maps do not bring anarchy in language usage. Recognition of the many should help us cherish a certain level of freedom; at least one can try not to become so pedantic in his concern for "correct" usage that worthwhile identifications are hindered.

THE USES OF SENTENCES

We have been treating certain aspects of words in an attempt to improve the ability for achieving desired identifications. Words play a significant role in communication, of course, but an exploration of the canon of style cannot focus on words alone. Words usually are used in sentences; hence the structure of the sentence and the context furnished by other words and sentences are important considerations.

We were not able to treat words as entirely separate from sentences in the preceding sections, and occasionally in the coming sections we will touch on individual words. This shows that our division is not absolute. We should also note, as we did before embarking on the discussion of words, that this section is not a complete analysis of sentences. As we did in our treatment of words, we explore only certain facets of sentences that seem to be particularly relevant in our study of identification through style.[49]

[48] Raven I. McDavid, "Sense and Nonsense about American Dialects," *Proceedings of the Modern Language Association,* **81** (1966), 7–17.

[49] For a more extensive discussion, see Paul Henle, ed., *Language, Thought, and Culture,* Ann Arbor, University of Michigan Press, 1958, esp. pp. 121–195; Blumenthal, op. cit., esp. pp. 143–236.

Roger Brown emphasizes:

> The linguist means something when he says: "Language is a
> system." Very simply, he means that when someone knows a
> language, he knows a set of rules. . . . These rules can generate
> an indefinite number of utterances. Learning a language is more
> than the rehearsal of particular sentences. From particular
> sentences we induce a governing set of rules, and the proof is
> that we can say new things, never heard and never rehearsed,
> which nevertheless conform to the rules and are comprehensible
> to people who know the rules.[50]

Granting that each of us can compose any number of different, comprehensible sentences, we can go on to consider
some ways of making our sentences more effective instruments for communication. We discuss means for improving
sentences under two major headings: clarity and appropriateness. (Aristotle has the same two major concerns in his
discussion of style. See *Rhetoric*, 1404b ff.)

Achieving Clarity

Nouns (simple subjects) and verbs (simple predicates) are
the workhorses of clear sentences. Other parts of speech are
necessary, but they should not be allowed to clutter and
confuse. Let us now deal with five common problems.

1. Words, phrases, and clauses intrude between subject
and verb (or between parts of the verb). The sentence becomes difficult for one's coactor to interpret. Mark Twain
gives this example while discussing reforms he would like to
make in the German language:

> I might gladly the separable verb also a little bit reform. I
> might none let do what Schiller did: he has the whole history of
> the Thirty Years' War between the two members of a separate
> verb in-pushed. That has even Germany itself aroused, and one

[50] Brown, op. cit., p. viii.

has Schiller the permission refused the History of the Hundred Years' War to compose—God be it thanked! After all these reforms established be will, will the German language the noblest and the prettiest on the world be.[51]

2. A related problem arises when parenthetical expressions or other interludes ramble on within a sentence, making the main thought hard to grasp. Aristotle quotes these lines to warn against such interruptions:

> "A man contrives ill for himself when ill he
>   contrives for another;
> A long-winded interlude does harm to us all—
>   but harms, above all, the interluder."
>
> (*Rhetoric*, 1409b)[52]

Both parties suffer because of the lack of clarity; the source (interluder) is harmed not only because the desired identification is sidetracked but also because of a loss in attractiveness.

3. Confusion comes if pronouns are not clearly tied to their antecedents. Everyone is aware of tricky cases such as: "Joe has problems with his dad. He wants to know how much he thinks a year at school costs. He also wonders if he could tell him if he ever worries over financial problems other than his own." A reader cannot say for sure which pronouns refer to Dad and which to Joe. The problem is often more acute in oral than in written communication. Unless interruptions are possible, the listener usually has less time than a reader to puzzle over the sentences to figure out the connections. If the listener does stop to determine the probable linkage, the subsequent sentences will get less attention than they should.

---

[51] Cited in Brown, op. cit., p. 232. Taken from Samuel L. Clemens, "The Horrors of the German Language," in *Mark Twain's Speeches*, New York, Harper & Row, 1910, pp. 43–52.

[52] Translated by Lane Cooper, op. cit., p. 203. We have taken the liberty of changing "prelude" and "preluder" to "interlude" and "interluder."

The "indefinite you" presents another pronoun problem. For instance, "You feel kind of funny asking for a raise after a financial report like that." The "you" could refer to the person talking, to the person addressed, or to people in general. The antecedent may be clear from the context, but frequently it is not. The indefinite you occurs very often in oral communication as a substitute for the first person pronouns. The replacement probably is attempted because the indefinite you is cooler and more distant, thus more comfortable, than I, me, my, mine, we, us, and our. With some persons the distancing of the indefinite you becomes habitual. As a consequence, the intimate, first-person revelations are deprived of desirable intensity. Suppose that instead of remaining precisely with the first person, Vince had sprinkled the indefinite you in his last two sentences: "And I saw then, and see now, how it [death] can rob you of the most precious thing that you have—time with people you love. And you fear it." (See lines 118–120 on p. 8.) Certainly, some of the force has been taken away. The example is not far-fetched. In fact, some speakers go so far with the indefinite you that one would not be surprised completely to hear the following proposal: "You love you. Please marry you."

This could be taken as an actual marriage proposal or as an accusation of narcissism. Herein lies a final problem with the indefinite you. A communicator wishes to address a listener or listeners directly with the second-person pronoun, you. If the indefinite you has been strewn about with abandon, the direct address has less chance of being effective—a lamentable harm to an important tool for reaching identification.

"They," "people," and "it" are also used with indefinite antecedents. The problems caused are sufficiently like those just described to allow us to omit a separate treatment. Most of the pronoun problems we have mentioned, as well as others that may have escaped notice for the moment, will be curbed if we try to keep pronouns as close as possible to the nouns to which the pronouns refer. Furthermore, one can aid effective communication by cutting down the profusion of pronouns, remembering the opening dictum: Nouns and verbs are the workhorses of clear sentences. This pronouncement holds doubly true for oral communication.

4. Adjectives and adverbs should modify or sharpen nouns and verbs. Used sparingly and carefully, adjectives and adverbs aid communication by carrying out these functions; when the modifiers are too frequent and imprecise, however, they become verbiage that clutters the message. "Very" and 'really" are prime offenders. Some persons use these and other supposed intensifiers so liberally that others become irritated and refuse to concentrate on the sentences. In another age one could advise the "very" and "really" addict to think "damn" instead of the overworked words. The automatic censor would have disallowed the profanity, the speaker would have proceeded with the untrammeled nouns and verbs. Given present standards, one hesitates to suggest such a measure because profanity itself is so often the clutter.

5. "You know" and "I mean" are so prevalent as to call for separate castigation. These monuments to inarticulateness sometimes crush any spark of clarity or life that a sentence might have. Had Dante faced such an evil, he might have reserved a special niche in his Inferno for the offenders. A gentler, salutary punishment would be to read Strunk and White's little book on style, especially the thundering refrain: "'Omit needless words! Omit needless words! Omit needless words!'"[53]

In English letters, an emphasis on clarity is usually associated with Ben Jonson (1572?–1637) and the classical

[53] William Strunk, Jr., and E. B. White, *The Elements of Style,* 2nd ed., New York, Macmillan, 1972, p. ix. This excellent "little book" is an enjoyable and extremely valuable aid for improving one's style. The book leans more toward written communication, just as this chapter does toward oral. The two modes are not the same, yet they are similar enough to permit us to profit from an intertwined treatment.

school of writing. Jonson was recognized by his contemporaries as "the prophet of classicism."[54] Not only was Jonson's influence great in his lifetime, but his stature grew in subsequent decades. His position on style and the examples he furnished became seventeenth- and eighteenth-century standards. Concerning clarity, Jonson wrote: "The chief virtue of a style is perspicuity [clarity or lucidity], and nothing so vicious in it as to need an interpreter."[55]

Readers of Jonson's prose know how rigorously he adhered to his own standard, but most people become aware of Jonson's classical style through reading his poetry. Without doubt, Jonson's best known poem is the "Song, to Celia," which begins:

> Drink to me only with thine eyes,
> And I will pledge with mine;
> Or leave a kiss but in the cup,
> And I'll not look for wine.

Jonson's classicism was an important influence in the seventeenth century, as well as the dominant force in the neoclassical period of the eighteenth century. John Locke and other prose writers were working in the same periods to improve the clarity of scientific writing.[56] Many rhetoric textbooks and teachers from those eras to the present have preached the classical school's cardinal postulate. Few of us have escaped the classicist's rod of correction, and all are likely to need its discipline again and again.

---

[54] Alexander M. Witherspoon and Frank J. Warnke, eds., *Seventeenth-Century Prose and Poetry*, 2nd ed., New York, Harcourt Brace Jovanovich, 1963, p. 116.

[55] From "De Orationis Dignitate," one of the essays in *Timber: Or Discoveries Made Upon Men and Matter*, 1641, in Witherspoon and Warnke, op. cit., p. 124.

[56] Wilbur S. Howell, "John Locke and the New Rhetoric," *Quarterly Journal of Speech*, **53** (1967), 319–333.

Reservations on Clarity

We return to the source, scene, and receiver perspectives to register our first reservation. In an orderly world, a clear statement would represent precisely what the source wanted to say; the same clear statement would accurately depict the scene; it would be lucid in similar ways for the receiver. But in less orderly worlds a coactor can think and say "I understand exactly what you are saying," while having an interpretation very different from the one the source has. And the source may see what would be a clear statement for the listener, yet this statement would be true neither to the scene nor to the source's vision.

The struggle for clarity must be fought on at least three fronts. Those accustomed to this several-sided conflict will appreciate an exchange in Plato's *Statesman* (307D-E). Plato's spokesman, a wise, old teacher, says: "I wonder if I can express to you in words what I have in mind." The brash, young respondent chimes: "Why not?" And the old teacher responds sadly: "You seem to think that is an easy thing to do."[57] When we deal elsewhere in this book with the source, scene, and receiver perspectives, we emphasize the receiver as the primary concern. We do so again here, but as before, we do not wish to eliminate the other concerns. For some communications, an unhappy compromise is the best available outcome. Other attempts at identification will find a pleasant unanimity in the clarity requirements inherent in each of the three aspects. The sensitive communicator knows that the latter cannot always be taken for granted.

The second reservation warns against placing too much value on mere clarity. George Miller tells about a professor of Romance languages who suffered a stroke when he was 49 years old. He still could read and think in English, French, Spanish, and other languages, but his ability for oral and

---

[57] This translation is by H. N. Fowler, *Loeb Classical Library*, vol. 3, London, Heinemann, 1925.

written expression was seriously curtailed. "In writing he formed simple sentences and complained that he had to use "schoolgirl English." The following letter is an illustration:

> Dear Anne:
>   I like the flowers very much and I feel perfcetly wild about them. Send some up to-morrow. I feel a right today, but I am anxious to go out the next Saturday."[58]

Aside from minor problems with spelling and syntax, the sentences are clear; but creative life is gone, and the reader experiences no excitement over a joint attempt to share ideas.

This excitement in sharing, of sensing that one is thinking *with* another, is a rich, highly prized pleasure. When readers or listeners notice that all has been done for them by the writer or speaker, the excitement and pleasure of a mutual effort are lost. Robert Frost recognized this possible loss writing "Mending Wall":

> ". . . Something there is that doesn't love a wall,
> That wants it down." I could say "Elves" to him,
> But it's not elves exactly, and I'd rather
> He said it for himself. . . .

Frost wants his neighbor to accept the challenge of working to say "exactly" together. For each to bring his own input and yet to say "exactly" together would affirm the value of each (the many), while at the same time giving heartening proof of kinship (the one).

T. S. Eliot used his theory of an "objective correlative" to explain how he tried to achieve this working together in the sharing of an emotion. Eliot expressed the objective correlative as "'a set of objects, a situation, a chain of events which shall be the formula of that *particular* emotion; such that when the external facts, which must terminate in

---

[58] George A. Miller, *Language and Communication,* New York, McGraw-Hill, 1951, p. 242.

sensory experience are given, the emotion is immediately invoked.'"[59] We can illustrate Eliot's objective correlative by comparing Vince's thesis with his speech. Vince's thesis is: "I live with a fear of death in my subconscious and conscious mind—of its suddenness—a fear that it will eternally separate me from someone I love, and rob me of time." Here Vince, as the outlining assignment required, summarizes his speech in one sentence. The sentence does the job clearly, but the sentence alone cannot evoke the same emotion that the speech brings, since the sentence states nearly everything *for* the reader or listener, whereas the speech presents "'a set of objects, a situation, a chain of events . . .'"—that is, an objective correlative. By identifying with Vince and telling your own story along with his (i.e., reliving and projecting your own experiences as you attend to Vince's) you and Vince work together to attain a memorable identification.

In style, then, one should seek not only clarity, but also a mode of expression that will invite one's coactors to participate in the building and sharing of insights. This mandate for style holds whether one considers narrative poetry, didactic prose, formal speeches, or everyday conversations. Perhaps one can escape the rule for certain occasions and audiences, especially when the transactions are brief and immediately practical (e.g., "Please pass the salt."). One will not be attended for long with interest, however, nor returned to with pleasure, if one's sentences usually fail to attain this sharing quality.[60]

---

[59] Reported in F. O. Matthiessen, *The Achievement of T. S. Eliot,* New York, Oxford University Press, 1958, p. 58.

[60] Shannon and Weaver show that the English language is well fitted for both clarity and intrigue, since it is about 50 percent predictable. Claude E. Shannon and Warren Weaver, *The Mathematical Theory of Communication,* Urbana, University of Illinois Press, 1964, esp. pp. 13–14.

Constructing Appropriate Sentences

The appropriateness of sentences is a heading that covers many interrelated subjects, and almost any one of them could be expounded on for many pages. We shall have to be brief in calling attention to each of them.

THE NEED FOR GRAMMATICAL CORRECTNESS

Sentences should be grammatically correct. Most auditors and readers will notice bad grammar, usually viewing it as inappropriate, some forms of humor and the speech of young children being examples of possible exceptions. Each of us has persevered through all sorts of grammar books and lessons, yet we still catch ourselves in various slips and have our errors corrected by others. A particularly frequent slip crops up in a sentence like this one: "There is many problems with county government." The error is so frequent because constructions beginning with "there" are often wordy; hence they are not moving precisely to state the thought, and the extra verbiage gets in the way of good grammar. Few have trouble with the grammar when the same idea is stated as: "County governments have many problems." A similar grammatical difficulty comes with a sentence such as: "Everyone of us are going to go." Usually one would not be uncertain if the pronoun came just before the verb in a crisper sentence: "Everyone is going."

CHOOSING ACTIVE OR PASSIVE CONSTRUCTIONS

When you choose active instead of passive constructions, you give yourself an easier time with grammar. The active voice uses fewer words; thus you have less opportunity to slip. The following sentences are illustrative: "Our next-door neighbors' dog bit him." "He was bitten by the dog which belongs to the neighbors who live in the house that is next to ours."[61] The active voice may be impossible for some state-

[61] Sheridan Baker vigorously expunges passive verbiage and any other wordiness in *The Practical Stylist,* New York, Crowell, 1962, esp. p. 25 ff.

ments, and it may be inappropriate for others; but you do well to drop the passive and use the active whenever possible and appropriate.

The active voice helps to gain and hold attention by bringing brevity and vividness to our sentences, yet brevity is not always a virtue.[62] Doubtless, some subjects and audiences require a more elaborate style, but one should be careful to wax expansive only when it is clearly desirable. Vividness, too, can be overdone, but most of the time one stumbles in the opposite direction.

VIVIDNESS

Precise detail that rivets attention on the word pictures is a large part of vivid expression. In Stephen Crane's novel, *The Red Badge of Courage*, Henry has run away from the battle:

> At length he reached a place where the high arching boughs made a chapel. He softly pushed the green doors aside and entered. Pine needles were a gentle brown carpet. There was a religious half light.
>
> Near the threshold he stopped, horror-stricken at the sight of a thing.
>
> He was being looked at by a dead man who was seated with his back against a columnlike tree. The corpse was dressed in a uniform that once had been blue, but was now faded to a melancholy shade of green. The eyes, staring at the youth, had changed to the dull hue to be seen on the side of a dead fish. The mouth was open. Its red had changed to an appalling yellow. Over the gray skin of the face ran little ants. One was trundling some sort of a bundle along the upper lip.[63]

Stephen Crane had had no firsthand experience with war when he wrote that passage. Crane's imagination created the vivid description by bringing together other experiences that he *had* had. Few of us are as creative as Stephen Crane, yet each one has a measure of creativity. Each can build word

---

[62] See Jonson, in *Witherspoon and Warnke,* op. cit., p. 125.

[63] Crane, *The Red Badge of Courage*, New York, Washington Square Press, 1959, pp. 53–54. First published in 1895.

pictures that will gain and hold attention. One can create new composites from disparate experiences, but one is more likely to re-create scenes from distinct happenings that are vividly etched in memory. Such re-creation provides a strong base for vivid expression. If we look back, we can see that Vince, Mario, Juanita, and Steve gain much of the vividness in their speeches from reliving significant experiences.

If one desires vividness in sentences that are not primarily descriptive, one should start by knowing the material well, by wanting to communicate about it, and by learning what language would be appropriately vivid for a given audience. These starting points require effort and practice. Neither precise rules nor pat expressions can cover the multitude of available subjects and situations. One should, however, understand that specificity in the nouns, the coloration of the verbs, and brevity in the sentences make a difference in the vividness. Note, for example, the difference between, "Their competition will underprice them and take away a part of their market share," and "DuPont will beat their price and grab a chunk of their business." The former can be made less vivid still, and the latter more vivid. A skilled communicator should know how and when to make the appropriate changes.[64]

USING METAPHOR

Metaphorical expressions are widely used to gain vividness. Strictly defined, a metaphor gives something a name that belongs to something else.[65] Some common examples are to call someone who is crafty a "fox," someone who is disreputable a "snake," or someone who is big a "tank." Usually a metaphor is differentiated from a simile—a kindred device except for its use of "like" or "as" in making

[64] George Campbell's analysis of vivacity may appear to be a bit dated for some, still it provides a thorough, useful treatment. See *The Philosophy of Rhetoric,* op. cit., p. 285, ff.

[65] Aristotle, *Poetics,* 1457b. Also see Henle, ed., op. cit., pp. 173–195.

the comparison. Note that both metaphor and simile appear in the last stanza of Longfellow's "The Day is Done." The poetry being read metaphorically becomes "music," and the cares "steal away" in the "Arab" simile:

> And the night shall be filled with music,
>   And the cares, that infest the day
> Shall fold their tents, like the Arabs,
>   And as silently steal away.

Simile is used alone in Lord Byron's famous line, "The Assyrian came down like the wolf on the fold," from "The Destruction of Sennacherib."

Metaphors and similes can be pointed to easily in prose, poetry, and everyday speech. Observing them is, however, only an early step toward effective usage. We seek to go beyond mere notation by describing how metaphor functions as a central component of style. We will use "metaphor" as our general term for the basic device of naming something with the name of something else,—whether the actual language in a given instance is that of simile is not crucial to the discussion. This exploration takes us away from a specific focus on vividness; still, parts of the following will continue to bear on this important concern.

When one metaphorically gives the name of something to something else, he is seeing the one *in terms of* the other; that is, he is seeing the one from the perspective furnished by his view of the other.[66] To call someone "a rotten, stinking skunk" brings a stance of intense dislike that is set up by one's reaction to this animal—more precisely, to the odor one associates with the black, white, and red mess left by previous cars. To speak of "my angel" is to bless this person within the point of view established for these heavenly beings. Unless the audience perceives some labored twisting of the words by the source or notes some distinct inappropriateness in the label that is transposed, the metaphor will etch its slant on the matter.

---

[66] This definition and the following discussion owe a great deal to Kenneth Burke. See especially, *A Grammar of Motives,* op. cit., p. 503.

To present a thing in terms of something else usually gives a positive or negative tilt to the frame in which the matter is set before the eyes of the audience. Aristotle says: "If you aim to adorn a thing, you must take your metaphor from something better in its class; if to disparage, then from something worse." An example Aristotle gives has to do with asking (the precise name for the activity). To adorn the act of asking, one could name it "praying." To disparage the act of asking, one could name it "begging" (or "whining" or "wheedling"). Or, suppose that we adorn the act of breaking a law by calling it an "error" ("mistake"), or disparage the act of breaking a law by calling it a "crime" (*Rhetoric*, 1405a).[67] This is closely allied to Bentham's analysis of eulogistic, neutral, and dyslogistic terms (see above, pp. 186–189).

The aversion to the skunk's odor seems to furnish a direct basis for the negative slant brought by the metaphorical use of "skunk." Perhaps the newly hatched swan is intrinsically unattractive, thus is aptly called an "ugly duckling" (already a metaphor), and the label is directly useful to affix disparaging connotations on other things. Possibly, similar cases can be argued for making hyenas, vultures, excrement, and other unpleasant things direct furnishers of dyslogistic metaphors. The same direct approach could be argued on the positive side for adult swans, new-fallen snow, blue-green oceans, or turtle doves. Probably, however, most of the positive and negative tilting is done through the mediation of our culture's value system. For example, money is valued in our system; thus we can say that money furnishes an ordering of positive and negative names. To be *rich* is to have a lot of money—to be in an upper class of the money hierarchy; to be *poor* is to have little money—to be in a lower class of the money hierarchy. Metaphorically, then, one can talk of rich fabrics, rich carpets, rich land, rich lawns, rich voices, rich interpretations (of a part in a drama or of a particular work of art), and numerous other positive

[67] Cooper's translation, op. cit., pp. 187–188.

applications. "Poor" could be substituted in most cases to bring the negative slanting. If the coactors have the same value system, the metaphorical extension of "rich" and "poor" will be viewed as appropriate and will aid in creating identifications. (Note that we have ventured here to look on adjectives as being metaphorical. This shows something of the broad range the exploration takes when one uses Burke's conception of metaphor: seeing something *in terms* of something else. Almost any definition, illustration, or representative anecdote becomes open for appraisal as metaphor.)

Robert Zajonc reports that the words representing positively valued things in our culture are used much more frequently and are deemed more pleasant than words that represent negatively valued things. In the Thorndike-Lorge count of 1944 (a study of the words that appear most often in the reading normally done by children and young people), "happiness" occurs 761 times and "unhappiness" 49 times. "Beauty" is used 41 times as often as "ugliness." The counts for certain words have changed since 1944, but the basic point, as shown by Zajonc's current research, holds: Americans value, point toward, and speak often about the positively valued things in their culture.[68] A study of words that appear with unusual frequency and infrequency on Zajonc's tables is very revealing of Americans' positive and negative evaluations.[69] Zajonc sees that these values act as mediators to form positive and negative tilts to statements. The mediation, since it is an extra, imposed step, opens the way for inaccuracy and diversity.[70] Presumably, all persons act with innate, correct unanimity to the potent stink of the skunk, for example, thus with a real consonance in assigning negative character to the metaphorical use of "skunk."

Seldom does the tilting brought about by the mediation of

[68]"The Attitudinal Effects of Mere Exposure," *Journal of Personality and Social Psychology,* Monograph Supplement, 1968, **9,** no. 2, part 2, 1–27.

[69] Ibid., 4–5.

[70] Ibid., 1–3.

a culture's values achieve such unanimity. If a culture's values have an intrinsic coherence and if they are solidly espoused by the individuals who are members of that culture, it is easy to make appropriate use of positive and negative metaphors, and the "exactly" response is found with gratifying regularity. But if values run at cross-purposes and dissenters proliferate, appropriate metaphorical usage is more difficult for the source and less predictably effective for a randomly selected coactor. For instance, if the valuations indicated in our rich–poor example worked in complete harmony with other values of American society, nothing would be at cross-purposes with the amassing of wealth. No dissonance would arise if someone were lauded as a rich mobster or positively valued as a rich miser. One sees immediately that "rich" does not exist as a positive value without reference to other values. Americans, in general, expect that riches be honestly gained (or at least Americans expect a measure of "playing by the rules" in the getting of wealth), and Americans also value generosity in alliance with wealth. Thus the finding of appropriate metaphorical use is made more complicated. Also, as the ordering principles of a society are shaken (athletes refusing to stand at attention when "the land of the free" is being toasted), the effectiveness of metaphorical namings that follow these principles will be less predictable. The increasing diversity makes specific listener analysis more and more necessary before one can proceed to affix labels that appropriately adorn or disparage.

OTHER EFFECTS OF HIERARCHIES

The ordering principles of a society have effects on communication other than the influences we have just discussed in the realm of metaphor. We can indicate one of these effects by returning to the monetary principle. According to a monetary ordering (assuming no contrary influence from other values) person A with more money has higher status than person B who has less. Since A is higher in the accepted order, B is expected to express an appropriate deference to A. And A should express the correct measure of condescension to B.

We all know that status differences based on wealth always have and still do affect what statements are appropriate. But a neat ordering has never been achieved and now is even less possible. Some confusion occurs because the roles change in a society ordered by money. Wealthy person A may own a thriving hardware store and poor B may do odd jobs about town; nevertheless, when B comes to buy, A says, "Can I help you, sir?" Thomas Caryle fumes over this ready changing of roles: "Whoso has sixpence is Sovereign (to the length of sixpence) over all men; commands Cooks to feed him, Philosophers to teach him, Kings to mount guard over him,—to the length of sixpence."[71]

Additional confusion arises because Americans who are monetary unequals are still thought to be equals in ethnic, political, and religious realms. This undermines rigid class structures and does not allow appropriate forms of address between classes to become stable—thus readily studied and learned. Wilbur Howell discusses the existence of standardized modes of address in Venerable Bede's book on rhetoric, presumed to be the first book on rhetoric written by an Englishman (ca. 701 or 702). The modes of address taught require a careful avoidance of the speech of the common folk. Howell writes:

> It is suggestive to speculate upon the cultural implications of a rhetorical theory which equates true elegance and hence true effectiveness with a system of studied departures from the established pattern of everyday speech. Such a theory appears to be the normal concomitant of a social and political situation in which the holders of power are hereditary aristocrats who must be conciliated by the commoners if the latter are to gain privileges for themselves. In a situation like that, persuasive forms of

---

[71] From *Sartor Resartus* as cited in Burke, *A Rhetoric of Motives,* op. cit., p. 119. Also see Hugh D. Duncan, *Communication and Social Order,* New York, Bedminster, 1962, p. 271 ff.

speech would emerge as agreeable forms; and agreeable forms would be those which sound agreeable to the aristocratic holders of power. What forms could sound more agreeable to the aristocrat than those which originated in a repudiation of the speech of the lower classes? Would not such forms remind him of the superiority of his own origin and thus be a way of softening his will by the subtle inducements of flattery? Would not the patterns of ordinary speech, if used by a commoner in seeking advantage from a great lord, be a way of showing contempt for the august person addressed? And would not that implication of contempt be enough to secure the prompt denial of the advantage sought?[72]

Extreme, easily recognized forms of address such as Howell indicates are not readily discerned in contemporary America. Perhaps a member of a lower class attempts to elevate vocabulary and grammar when addressing one who supposedly occupies a higher station. To hit just the right note, so that one does not appear pushy or obsequious, is difficult.[73] Similar problems face the person on the upper end who wants to avoid an irritating note of "talking down."

Since universal public education and the pervasive influence of mass media have homogenized much of the publicly used verbal code, the distinguishing characteristics of these exchanges between classes probably have to be examined as part of the nonverbal code: the spatial distances assumed, the postures and gestures to be used, the tones of voice, and the object language (kinds of houses, furnishings, clothes, cars, vacations, schools, etc.). This is material for Chapter 9 (see pp. 214–220). We remark here that this language is learned through long experience and

[72] Wilbur S. Howell, *Logic and Rhetoric in England, 1500–1700*, New York, Russell & Russell, 1961, p. 117. For the consternation that appears when someone accustomed to such class differentiation meets one who is unaccustomed to it, see Vernon L. Parrington, *The Colonial Mind: 1620–1800*, New York, Harcourt Brace Jovanovich, 1927, esp. pp. 97 and 126.

[73] See Aristotle's *Rhetoric,* 1404b, for the difficulties he saw in the attempts to find proper decorum in communication between those of different social stations.

careful nurture. It is extremely difficult to describe, and it is impossible to manage without a period for practice and without some trauma along the way. Witness the proverbial plight of the "newly rich" as they fumble through inappropriate expressions of their status.

Our society features many ordering principles in addition to the monetary one. Hierarchies are present for old and young, employers and employees, professionals and non-professionals, teachers and students, natives and immigrants. Expressions that are appropriate for some persons in a given hierarchy are inappropriate for others. As interactions occur some of the rules will change, but certain prescriptions and proscriptions are likely to remain. The complexity and fluidity of each situation, plus the paucity of present knowledge in the field, cancel the possibility of any very specific treatment. We wish only to alert the communicator to the ubiquitous effect of hierarchy on interpersonal communication. We hope the warning will bring about greater attention and more sensitive adjustment.[74]

The canon of style is extraordinarily complex. Communicators make countless choices of words and sentences as they coactively share information. The choices made reveal a mind at work, seeking to answer the myriad requirements of source, scene, and receiver. All these interdependences must be handled with sensitivity. As people choose words and sentences and shape from these communications, each person leaves a mark that is distinctly her or his own.[75]

[74] Part III, "Order," of Kenneth Burke's *Rhetoric of Motives* is a sophisticated, general treatment of the presence and working of hierarchy. For a more specific, though breezy, application of Burke's thought see Duncan, op. cit., p. 109 ff.

[75] For a recent discussion of Buffon's famous statement, "The style is the man himself," see Donald C. Bryant, "Of Style: Buffon and Rhetorical Criticism," in *Essays on Rhetorical Criticism,* Thomas R. Nilsen, ed., New York, Random House, 1968, pp. 50–63, esp. p. 56.

QUESTIONS FOR THOUGHT AND DISCUSSION

1. What words have a "mythic" quality for your community? For yourself?
2. What limitations do "word-maps" have? How are these limitations likely to affect communication? How can communications guard against these limitations?
3. Locate some typical biasings in your own use of language? Are your biasings the same as those of your parents?
4. Examine several communications that you have prepared in the past. Has the style varied?
5. How does oral style differ from written style?
6. Do you agree that style should reflect the requirements of source, scene, and receiver? Why or why not?

SUGGESTED READINGS

Anshen, Ruth N., ed., *Language: An Enquiry into its Meaning and Function*, New York, Harper & Row, 1957.

Blankenship, Jane, *Public Speaking: A Rhetorical Perspective*, 2nd ed., Englewood Cliffs, N.J., Prentice-Hall, 1972, chs. 6 and 7.

Brown, Roger, *Words and Things*, New York, Free Press, 1958.

Cassirer, Ernst, *Language and Myth*, trans. Susanne K. Langer, New York, Dover, 1946.

Strunk, William, Jr., and E. B. White, *The Elements of Style*, 2nd ed., New York, Macmillan, 1972.

the non verbal code: identification through delivery

In their efforts to share, communicators must rely on verbal and nonverbal cues. Someone selects and transmits the cues, another picks up and interprets the cues. However, the cues have no meaning in isolation; meanings are attached by the participants in the communication event. Effective communication requires, among other things, that the coactors have a somewhat similar understanding of the cues employed. This shared understanding of verbal and nonverbal codes constitutes one element of the consubstantial: It makes communication possible.

No two people, however, share exactly the same meanings. An action that the communicator intends to be a friendly wave may be interpreted by some as a sign of condescension or ridicule. Someone who means to appear relaxed by leaning back in a chair may be seen by someone else as uninterested and indifferent. These differing interpretations of nonverbal cues reflect individuality and are often a source of misunderstanding.

In Chapter 8 we focused on the role of verbal cues (words) in interpersonal communication. In this chapter we turn our attention to nonverbal cues and the manner in which they may expedite or impede the identification process.

THE NONVERBAL CODE

When human beings prepare for communication, their focus is usually on the verbal code. As they select, develop, and arrange their ideas, they search for the right words, words that will express ideas accurately, meaningfully, and effectively. When communication occurs, however, the verbal cues are only part of the coactive sharing. During the coaction, the chosen locations, postures, gestures, facial expressions, and vocal inflections are important factors in creating identification. Harrison estimates that only 35 percent of the shared meaning may be attributed to the verbal code. The remaining 65 percent is the result of cues other than words—that is, nonverbal cues.[1] This breakdown does not, of course, apply to all communications. Some communication events, such as the hitchhiker signaling to a passing motorist or the policeman directing traffic, are totally nonverbal. The number of nonverbal cues, on the other hand, is limited in telephone and written communications.

The nonverbal elements can impede effective interpersonal communication. Because communicators tend to focus on the use of verbal symbols, they often are unaware that nonverbal behavior provides a continual series of cues. These cues may stimulate meanings that are unrelated to the verbal message, or they may affect greatly the interpretation and understanding of verbal cues. In either case, nonverbal cues are an important part of interpersonal encounters. So while we all carefully plan and attend to verbal cues, our control of the nonverbal message is limited because, as Ekman points out, "Information about what is occurring is not customarily within awareness."[2]

---

[1] Randall Harrison, "Nonverbal Communication: Explorations into Time, Space, Action, and Object," in *Dimensions in Communication,* 2nd ed., James H. Campbell and Hal W. Hepler, eds., Belmont, Calif., Wadsworth, 1970, p. 258.

[2] P. Ekman and W. V. Friesen, "Nonverbal Behavior in Psychotherapy Research," *Psychotherapy,* **3** (1968), 179–216.

Nonverbal cues may impede desired identifications because the source and the receiver tend to interpret these cues from different perspectives. *"The inclination . . . is to define personal action as natural and spontaneous and to view the nonverbal acts of others as deliberate and intentionally motivated."*[3] A student in class may smile at the instructor, and the instructor may interpret this action as a failure to take the class seriously. You may unintentionally pass a good friend on the sidewalk without speaking or nodding. Your action may be seen as an expression of unfriendliness and hostility. The receiver tends to attribute motive and intention, while the source assumes the action is natural.

If listeners note a conflict between the verbal and nonverbal cues sent by someone, they tend to believe the nonverbal rather than the verbal. People usually sense that the nonverbal message is more difficult to manipulate; thus the nonverbal behavior is closer to the true motive and intention of the source. If one does not like the looks and mannerisms of the salesman, one will probably discredit his "pitch." If a person looks and sounds coolly distant while being introduced, few are likely to believe the cordial words.

We have said that the meanings attributed to nonverbal behavior are variable. This assertion holds for different cultures as well as for individual persons. Both verbal and nonverbal behavior are learned, but as people move from one culture to another, they will be well aware of the verbal differences, tending to forget that the nonverbal code changes too. Edward T. Hall illustrates this in describing the different sense of interpersonal distance in North American and Latin American cultures:

> In Latin America the interaction distance is much less than it is in the United States. . . . The result is that when they move close, we withdraw and back away. As a consequence, they think that we are distant or cold, withdrawn and unfriendly. We, on

---

[3] David Mortenson, *Communication: The Study of Human Interaction,* New York, McGraw-Hill, 1972, p. 212.

the other hand, are constantly accusing them of breathing down our necks, crowding us, and spraying our faces.[4]

Within our own culture, we all have encountered individuals who have a sense of interpersonal distance different from our own. When talking with these individuals, one is likely to find oneself continually retreating or advancing and feeling strangely uncomfortable.

In rural America it is not uncommon to see farmers dispose of their cigarette ashes by placing them in the cuffs of their overalls. Nor is it uncommon to see them place their ashes on their overalls and vigorously rub them into the fabric. Although these behaviors can go largely unnoticed in a small rural community, they will arouse much interest in an urban setting. Many, many examples like these can be used to illustrate the variability and, consequently, the complexity of the nonverbal code.

TYPES OF NONVERBAL COMMUNICATION

Nonverbal cues of several types may affect interpersonal communication. Perhaps the most abundant cues relate to body position or movement, *kinesics*. Ray L. Birdwhistell estimated that more than 700,000 body positions can be observed by others.[5] These cues range from our basic posture (slouched, reclining, leaning forward, etc.) to the position of our fingers (curled, straight, up, down, etc.). How can one precisely number all these positions and movements? Perhaps Gilbert Austin's elaborate efforts to sketch postures and gestures (as a means of recording the visual aspects of

[4] Edward T. Hall, *The Silent Language,* Garden City, N.Y., Doubleday, 1959, p. 164.

[5] Ray L. Birdwhistell, *Introduction to Kinesics,* Louisville, Ky., University of Louisville Press, 1952.

communication) give a precedent for such a system.[6] Leonard Doob suggests that these bodily cues may be classified as voluntary or involuntary. Relatively involuntary movements refer to actions that are difficult to control such as pupil dilation, facial expressions, blushing, and perspiring. Voluntary movements are somewhat easy to control and include such cues as gestures, posture, position, and contrived facial gestures.[7]

In rather large one-to-many communication settings, the source depends heavily on these cues in gauging audience response. A general lack of movement, erect posture, and direct eye contact are usually taken as positive signs. Restlessness, slouched posture, and avoidance of direct eye contact usually suggest that the speaker has lost the audience's attention. In one-to-one communication settings, the participants can notice less obvious behaviors. One can see that the other is trembling, that a slight flush appears in the neck and face, that an eyebrow raises slightly. Cues of this sort are a vital part of an interpersonal transaction.

For most Americans the eyes play an especially important role in interpersonal communication. Erving Goffman describes how eyes are used to acknowledge the presence of another person.[8] When people do not wish to communicate with each other, they purposely avoid eye contact. Thus, for example, each may quickly glance at the other approaching on the sidewalk, then each will look downward in passing. If persons wish to engage each other in communication, they are likely to sustain the eye contact. In Goffman's words, "Eye-to-eye looks . . . play a special role in the communi-

---

[6] *Chironomia or a Treatise on Rhetorical Delivery, 1806,* Mary Robb and Lester Thonssen, eds., Carbondale, Southern Illinois University Press, 1966.

[7] Leonard W. Doob, *Communication in Africa,* New Haven, Conn., Yale University Press, 1961, pp. 68–69.

[8] Erving Goffman, *Behavior in Public Places,* New York, Free Press, 1963, pp. 83–111. ·

cation life of a community, ritually establishing . . . openness to verbal statements. . . ."[9]

The participants' eyes help regulate the flow of communication during coaction. If someone wishes to continue talking, he may look away from the other. When he finishes his statement, he uses his eyes to signal, "I am finished, now it is your turn." When someone wants a chance to talk, he tries to establish eye contact with the speaker. The importance of eye contact is also evident from the use of teleprompters and "idiot cards" in television broadcasting. These devices are arranged so that the communicator may be prompted while appearing to maintain direct eye contact with the viewers. Eye contact seems to assure that the participants are in touch with one another. This is an essential element in interpersonal interaction, especially when feedback is readily available and the participants expect to switch back and forth in the roles of source and receiver.

Meaning is also affected by *vocalics:* the rate, pitch, volume, quality, and inflection of the voice. You perhaps have heard someone with quavering voice proclaim, "I'm not nervous." Or, observe how the meaning of a simple sentence such as "This building is red" can be changed by alternate emphases: "*This* building is red," "This *building* is red," or "This building is *red*." Each of us notes frequently that someone sounds pleased, displeased, or lukewarm about the opportunity to talk to him. Listeners attend to vocalics to discern whether interaction or boredom, condescension or deference, hostility or affection, are being intimated. Research indicates that a source's social status can be judged on the basis of vocal cues.[10] Studies also show that the speaker's emotional state can be gauged by listening to the voice.[11]

---

[9] Ibid., p. 92.

[10] L. S. Harms, "Listener Judgments of Status Cues in Speech," *Quarterly Journal of Speech,* **47** (1961), 164–168.

[11] Joel R. Davitz, *The Communication of Emotional Meaning,* New York, McGraw-Hill, 1964.

The meaning shared through interpersonal communication is also influenced by space, *proxemics*. The earlier example of Latin and North American perceptions regarding interpersonal distance illustrates the role of space in communication. What is judged to be appropriate distance in communication depends, of course, on a number of factors. A person retains a greater distance when talking with strangers than with close friends. Also, each of us probably maintains closer spatial relationships with peers than with persons of higher status. Observe for example, that if a class is arranged in a circle, the students tend to avoid sitting next to the instructor. Note, too, that offices tend to become larger as one moves to higher echelons in an organization, and subordinates usually observe appropriate distances when entering a superior's office. The judgment of "appropriate distance" is also affected by the environment. In an elevator people may remain fairly comfortable even though they are very close to one another. If they were talking in a large room, they probably would be uncomfortable unless they stayed farther apart. The perception of proper interpersonal distance is flexible, but this does not diminish the great significance of proxemics in nonverbal communication.

Reusch and Kees label another type of nonverbal communication *object language*.[12] This term refers to observable material possessions that will influence the communication. When meeting someone or entering a home or office for the first time, everyone uses object language. We evaluate clothes and personal possessions. In home or office we may note the thickness of the carpet, concluding that the homeowner is wealthy or that the dentist's bill will be unusually large. (Kenneth Burke comments that the medical equipment in a doctor's office has a lot to do with our being persuaded that we are expertly cared for.)[13] Noting a Bible on

[12] Jurgen Ruesch and Weldon Kees, *Nonverbal Communication*, Berkeley, University of California Press, 1964.

[13] Kenneth Burke, *A Rhetoric of Motives*, Berkeley, University of California Press, 1969, p. 171.

a table, we may conclude that the person who put it there is religious. Observing an ample supply of records, we may infer that the occupant of the room likes music. These are just a few of the sorts of object that influence our communication.

Nonverbal communication also includes time considerations—for instance, who keeps whom waiting, and for how long. In our culture, being forced to wait for another is often a serious affront and can be very damaging to subsequent communications. This factor is variable, however, since persons in prestigious positions sometimes keep others waiting. Other cultures place more or less emphasis on the time element.

Touching behavior is also a part of nonverbal communication, for greetings, farewells, and for many other communications. Individuals and groups differ in the kind and amount of touching that is used. (One student talked very memorably about his problems with the touching part of the nonverbal code. The larger family unit on his father's side was Italian, and a great deal of touching was natural for them. His mother's side was Scottish, and very little touching was appropriate with them.) The subjects of time and touching could be discussed at greater length; we judge, however, that kinesics, vocalics, proxemics, and object language describe the types of nonverbal communication that most frequently affect human interaction. Still, all the types help suggest the breadth of the nonverbal code, and they all show the importance of a sensitivity to the nonverbal code in seeking identification.

THE RELATIONSHIP OF VERBAL AND NONVERBAL COMMUNICATIONS

Nonverbal and verbal communications cannot be separated into mutually exclusive categories. In interpersonal communication the sharing is, usually, based on both codes.

Knapp described the interrelationship of the two codes as:

Repeating.   When making a verbal statement, one may repeat it nonverbally. One may tell the lost traveler to "turn right," and point to the right at the same time.

Substituting.   One may use a nonverbal rather than a verbal message. When the lost traveler asks directions, one may simply point to the right.

Accenting.   Nonverbal behavior may function as punctuation for verbal messages. Vocalics are commonly used in the accenting role.

Complementing.   One uses nonverbal behaviors to express attitudes toward others.

Regulating.   Nonverbal cues are employed to regulate the communication flow.

Contradicting.   While stating one message verbally, nonverbal behavior may be saying the opposite.[14]

When nonverbal behaviors serve the repeating, regulating, accenting, substituting, and complementing functions they may contribute to successful interpersonal communication. However, when the nonverbal cues contradict the verbal message, desirable identification seems likely to be impeded.

NONVERBAL COMMUNICATION AND THE DELIVERY CANON

The nonverbal behaviors that we have described as kinesics, vocalics, and proxemics are commonly treated in the canon of delivery, the presentation of the message. Good delivery implies that our nonverbal cues contribute to our verbal communication; they do not contradict or in other ways

[14] Mark L. Knapp, *Nonverbal Communication in Human Interaction,* New York, Holt, Rinehart & Winston, 1972, pp. 9–12.

detract from it. Good delivery does not call attention to itself; it focuses the listener's attention on the verbal message. We all have listened to a speaker and lamented that invention, organization, and style were acceptable, but delivery was so poor that nearly all effect was lost. Delivery can also fail if the vocal and visual cues are so remarkably fine (in a showy sense) that they obscure what the participants ought to have shared.

Effective presentation is an important element in interpersonal communication. A well-presented message can help achieve the goals of interaction. Effective delivery may enhance the communicator's ethos,[15] improve comprehension of the message,[16] and facilitate attitude change.[17] But skillful delivery is not a substitute for thoughtful work with the earlier canons. Effective delivery must be thought of as a facilitator in that it allows a message to function. Arnold and McCroskey report that good delivery may increase attitude change when coupled with good content. Good delivery did not increase attitude change when the message contained poor content.[18] These findings support our view that the verbal message is primary: Effective nonverbal behavior compliments the verbal message.

[15] Gerald R. Miller and Murray A. Hewgill, "The Effect of Variation in Nonfluency on Audience Ratings of Source Credibility," *Quarterly Journal of Speech,* **50** (1964), 36–44; Kenneth K. Sereno and Gary J. Hawkins, "The Effects of Variations in Speaker's Non-fluency upon Audience Ratings of Attitude toward the Speech Topic and Speaker Credibility," *Speech Monographs,* **34** (1967), 58–64.

[16] Kenneth C. Beighley, "An Experimental Study of the Effect of Four Speech Variables on Listener Comprehension," *Speech Monographs,* **19** (1952), 249–258; Kenneth C. Beighley, "An Experimental Study of Three Speech Variables on Listener Comprehension," *Speech Monographs,* **21** (1954), 248–253.

[17] James C. McCroskey and R. Samuel Mehrley, "The Effects of Disorganization and Nonfluency on Attitude Change and Source Credibility," *Speech Monographs,* **36** (1969), 13–21.

[18] This finding is reported in James C. McCroskey, *Studies of the Effects of Evidence in Persuasive Communication,* East Lansing, Speech Communication Research Laboratory, Michigan State University, 1967.

QUALITIES OF GOOD DELIVERY

James Winans points out that every communication setting is similar to a conversation. Even settings that involve a large number of participants, Winans argues, should be thought of as enlarged conversations. A single communicator addressing a group of listeners may be described as "conversing" with them.[19] This description of communication as conversation suggests the first quality of good delivery, a conversational quality.

Seldom do any of us fall asleep during a small-group discussion. Yet when meeting in larger groups, one may feel bored, disinterested, and even doze off. What accounts for these different reactions? What are the qualities or dimensions of informal conversations that, somehow, are lost in the large group setting?

Probably the key ingredient is a sense of involvement. In the one-to-one or small group situation, the participants are obviously engaged in the coaction. In large group settings, each person's chances for direct verbal participation are greatly reduced. Thus the communicator must attempt to establish a relationship that encourages others to be involved. The need to create a sense of involvement dictates that one person should not monotonously read at some others. Nor can the communicator gaze blankly toward the ceiling and walls while talking. Instead, the speaker should focus directly and obviously on individuals in the audience. (This clear contact should be avoided, of course, when special considerations in the scene, message, or persons make the direct contact inappropriate. Many communicators avoid eye contact more than is desirable, however, and as a result, any special consonance that a specific averting of the eyes might have is partially reduced by the general lack of contact.)

[19] James A. Winans, *Speech-Making,* Englewood Cliffs, N.J., Prentice-Hall, 1938, pp. 11–45.

The one-to-one contact should move from one auditor to another, but a mechanical rhythm of doing this should be avoided. As the one-to-one conversations take place with the different listeners, separate bonds and distinct spacial relationships are formed. This is an easy way to bring visual and vocal variety to the presentation, since people tend to adjust these nonverbal factors automatically as the relationships change. In addition, coactive loops are overtly established that should help strengthen involvement and interest for all participants.

The argument for conversational delivery also suggests that delivery should be natural, not artificial. We all know individuals who commonly violate the criterion of naturalness. These individuals apparently regard every communication as a performance and "just love to hear themselves talk." Their delivery behaviors usually are exaggerated and artificial.

In the nineteenth and early twentieth centuries, certain teachers called "elocutionists" offered extensive training in delivery. Their prescriptions and coaching led to very formal and pompous delivery mannerisms. This kind of delivery is still practiced by "old-line platform orators." Today, however, this gilded mode of presentation survives mainly in certain television commercials and in the performances of comedians who caricature these foibles of the past. Fortunately, the microphone and television (which is a one-to-one medium that can reach out to millions at a time) have virtually eliminated any need that once might have existed for extreme emphasis on delivery.

If a communicator's delivery is truly natural, distracting nonverbal behaviors are unlikely. The communicator's voice, gestures, and bodily action usually reinforce the verbal message. This is true because most of us have developed habits that effectively blend the verbal and nonverbal codes. Nevertheless, we all should keep a conscious ability to monitor nonverbal cues. This ability is important (1) because distracting vocal, gestural, and bodily cues may creep in, and these need to be recognized to be changed; and

(2) because we all should try to maximize our awareness of what occurs in our interpersonal communication. Some distracting nonverbal habits may be harder to change than others; vocalics, for instance, typically will be harder to adjust than kinesics. New habits can be learned, though, and the more effective behaviors will blend in naturally to aid the verbal code.

Effective delivery is also characterized by directness. Directness is, in large measure, a function of eye contact, treated already. In addition, directness requires that the communicator project what Winans has labeled a "lively sense of communication."[20] This requires that you have something you really want to say and that you be actively involved with formulating your message at the moment of expression. Other things being equal, a memorized presentation lacks the liveliness of an impromptu communication. When the message is memorized, you are too likely to appear detached and uninterested. (Maintaining a lively sense of communication would seem to be a particular problem for the stage actor or actress who, night after night, must perform the same role.) Directness, then, demands that you have and project active involvement with the ideas you express.

MODES OF DELIVERY

One very practical concern about delivery involves the modes of preparation and presentation. A message may be prepared and delivered (1) memorized, (2) manuscripted, (3) impromptu, or (4) extemporaneously. This section considers the merits and weaknesses associated with each approach. No single "best" mode of delivery exists. The choice should be influenced by the communication setting, the audience requirements, and the personal preference of the communicator.

[20] Ibid., pp. 26–30.

The memorized message is learned word for word and delivered without notes. As a result, eye contact may be maximized and possible distractions from papers or notes are avoided. On the negative side, a memorized presentation often lacks the sense of directness mentioned previously because the primary effort of creation (or re-creation) is in the preparation stage. When the presentation occurs, perhaps the source is superficially involved, since the effort is past and only a role is left to be played out. This leads to the "canned" flavor that most listeners dislike. Memorizing a message probably will also limit the communicator's ability to adapt to listener feedback: This can be a critical flaw in certain memorized presentations. On the other hand, the memorized mode is just what is needed, or even required, for some occasions. When it is used, exceptional care is needed to foresee sensitively what should be said and to practice so well that control is achieved without leaving the "canned" impression.

The manuscripted message is delivered from a completely written text. The manuscript mode of delivery usually serves in formal communication settings where language choices are particularly important. Manuscripts have the disadvantage of limiting eye contact and restricting the source's ability to adapt to feedback. Two pitfalls frequently trap those who use manuscripts. The first is similar to one problem mentioned for the memorized mode: The major effort has occurred during the writing stages; hence the source is merely going through the motions in the actual presentation, producing a far too rapidly paced, uninvolving event. The second pitfall is that the manuscript gives one a false sense of security, and the reading is attempted with little or no practice. The resulting disaster can visit the neophyte as well as the person who has had a lot of experience with manuscripts.

Disciplined practice with the manuscript is always desirable. The speaker should seek clear mastery over the intellectual and emotional flow of the material to read with lively and appropriate coloration. The communicator will do well to use a typed manuscript rather than a handwritten one. Triple spacing is advisable. Sometimes the use of upper-case type throughout with added underlining and highlighting are desirable. Even the exceptionally large type available in special typewriters built for preparing speech manuscripts can be a great aid.

The impromptu communication is delivered after little or no specific preparation and without notes. Informal conversations are commonly impromptu. Although impromptu delivery can help the conversational, natural, and direct qualities of presentation, the message may suffer from a lack of adequate preparation in the canons of invention, organization, and style.

Careful study and practice in the first three canons should bring gradual, steady improvement in one's impromptu communication efforts. Sensitive assessment of delivery elements usually leads to beneficial changes in the impromptu behavior. Disciplined experience with the other delivery modes will probably yield transfer benefits for the impromptu mode.

These effects are obviously by-products of an approach to improving communication that focuses on assigned speeches, with considerable time and energy spent in preparing, presenting, and responding to significant communications. We believe this to be a more efficient way of improving communication skills than a teaching method that only elicits and discusses impromptu remarks. This does not mean that impromptu statements receive no attention. On the contrary, extremely important impromptu remarks come in response to the prepared communication. These remarks are weighed and responded to in turn. This seems to be a very productive way of treating both the impromptu and the other modes of delivery.

The extemporaneous mode of delivery is appropriate for a wide variety of communication settings. The communicator prepares specifically for the interaction. Invention receives paramount consideration as various arguments are prepared, tested, changed, tossed aside, or selected. An outline is used to organize the selected materials. While practicing from the outline, the speaker polishes the wording to some extent, but practice should stop before a memorized, mechanical note is reached. The number or practice runs required will vary from person to person, and fewer practices seem to be needed as the speaker gains experience. The speaker should try to imagine the actual setting with each practice (perhaps by talking to a mirror or to a roommate) and should seek as much concentrated involvement as possible. Intense practice sessions are far more helpful than a lackadaisical run-through of the material.

During the organization, style, and delivery stages of preparation, the speaker may wish to double back to do further work with invention or the other canons. Probably though, he is wise to allow for one or more practices with the final, rather stable outline.

Even in the presentation, however, one should be able to make adjustments in all canon areas as the occasion and feedback seem to show that changes are desirable. Effective on-the-spot adaptation requires depth of preparation in all the canons, and it requires sure control of self and subject. To realize that you have this depth and control while sensitively adjusting the communication is an exciting experience.

Notes for reference purposes can be extensive or nonexistent. If notes are used, cards are probably better than sheets of paper. The cards are less distracting and allow more freedom to adjust the delivery. Papers are likely to restrict you to one position (frequently behind a lectern), whereas note cards can be used easily while sitting, standing, or moving about; that is, the cards give greater latitude for harmonizing proxemics and kinesics with the occasion, verbal code, and other factors.

In these descriptions we have set out the criteria for evaluating various modes of delivery. We believe that effective communication is most likely to occur (1) when the communicators have prepared thoroughly, (2) when a conversational quality fits efficiently with this sort of preparation, and (3) when the speaker is able to adapt to listener feedback. The extemporaneous mode of delivery is usually most consistent with these criteria.

SUMMARY

Nonverbal behaviors are an important part of interpersonal communication. Like words, nonverbal cues are learned, and the meanings assigned vary with individuals. Thus nonverbal cues may result in misunderstanding.

Among the kinds of nonverbal cues available, those that relate to body position and movement (kinesics), to the use of the voice (vocalics), to the use of space (proxemics), and to object language are most important in interpersonal communication. These cues may reinforce or weaken the verbal message. Good delivery involves behaviors that reinforce our verbal symbols.

Effective delivery is receiver-centered. Receiver-centered delivery may be described as conversational, natural, and direct. When delivering a message, the source should sensitively seek nonverbal actions that are consonant with the verbal message.

A message may be delivered from memory or from a manuscript. The presentation can also be impromptu or extemporaneous. The extemporaneous mode of delivery begins with careful preparation, encourages a conversational style, and allows the speaker to adapt to audience feedback.

QUESTIONS FOR THOUGHT AND DISCUSSION

1. What special problems inhere in nonverbal communication that are not typical of verbal communication?
2. List situations in which nonverbal messages have contradicted verbal messages. How could these situations have been avoided?

3. Why are nonverbal messages of particular importance in cross-cultural communication?
4. Why will the extemporaneous mode usually bring the most effective delivery?
5. If a listener remembers fine delivery but has little knowledge of what the speaker said, do you think the communication was successful?

SUGGESTED READINGS

Hall, Edward T., *The Silent Language,* Garden City, N.Y., Doubleday, 1959.

Knapp, Mark L., *Nonverbal Communication in Human Interaction*, New York, Holt, Rinehart & Winston, 1972.

Mehrabian, Albert, *Silent Messages,* Belmont, Calif., Wadsworth, 1971.

Ruesch, Jurgen, and Weldon Kees, *Nonverbal Communication,* Berkeley, University of California Press, 1969.

Epilogue: the forgiveness quotient

> No virtuous act is quite as virtuous from the standpoint of our friend or foe as it is from our standpoint. Therefore we must be saved by the final form of love which is forgiveness."[1]

To believe that each person always values his or her act more positively than another values that act is probably too pessimistic; nevertheless, few would contest the assertion that each person usually wishes for a more positive valuation than is received. The gap between what each would like to receive from others and what each does receive can be called an unmet social need (see above, pp. 62–68). Niebuhr's statement, "No virtuous act is quite as virtuous from the standpoint of our friend or foe as it is from our standpoint," then, is consonant with our common knowledge that humans again and again have social needs that go unsatisfied.[2]

When one is disappointed by the treatment others give, one can lash out in anger (probably creating even less rewarding relationships); or one can try to exercise the final form of love, forgiveness, thereby opening possibilities for rebuilding and improving interpersonal relationships. Leo

[1] Reinhold Niebuhr, *The Irony of American History*, New York, Scribner, 1952, p. 63.

[2] See, for example, Virginia Satir, "Communication: A Verbal and Nonverbal Process of Making Requests of the Receiver," in *Basic Readings in Interpersonal Communication*, Kim Giffin and Bobby R. Patton, eds., New York, Harper & Row, 1971, pp. 37–38; reprinted from *Conjoint Family Therapy*, rev. ed., Palo Alto, Calif., Science and Behavior Books, 1967, pp. 75–90.

Tolstoy's short story "The Long Exile" can help us see how forgiveness is the final form of love and how forgiveness improves interpersonal relationships.[3]

Here is a précis of the story. Aksenof was a happy young Russian merchant who lived in the city of Vladimir. As part of his business, he had to travel to a trade fair in another city. He said a fond farewell to his wife and young children and set forth. The first evening he stopped at an inn to rest, had dinner with a fellow merchant, and went to sleep early. He awoke while it was still dark and told his driver to harness up the horses. They left quickly, drove some distance, and stopped at another inn for lunch. While Aksenof relaxed by playing his guitar, a troika carrying an official and two soldiers suddenly appeared at the inn. The official questioned Aksenof closely about his meeting with the other merchant and the morning's early start. The merchant, Aksenof learned, had been robbed and stabbed to death during the night. The soldiers searched Aksenof's belongings and found a bloody knife in his bag. He was accused of the crime. Aksenof was so shaken by the sudden turn about that he stammered and trembled—this was taken as a sign of guilt. He was bound and put in prison. The court found him guilty; the czar refused an appeal; even Aksenof's wife let slip a doubt about his innocence when she came with the children to see him.

After a tearful goodbye to his wife and children, Aksenof resigned himself to ask truth and mercy only of God. Aksenof was beaten, and when the wounds had healed, he was sent to hard labor in the mines of Siberia. He worked in the mines for 26 years. He earned a little money by making boots; with this money he bought the *Book of Martyrs* to read. His hair turned white, and he had a long gray beard. He became bent, spoke little, never laughed, and prayed much. The authorities saw him as a model prisoner; his fellow prisoners called him a "man of God," and they asked him to adjudicate disputes they had among themselves.

[3] Sometimes the title given by the translator is "God Sees the Truth But Waits."

One day some new prisoners were brought inside the walls. The old convicts crowded about them that evening to hear news from the outside. One healthy-looking 60-year-old was from Vladimir. His name was Makar. He complained that he was imprisoned for a trifle while he had done far worse before and had not been caught. As Aksenof, Makar, and the other prisoners talked, Makar revealed that he knew the bag in which the bloody knife was found had been close to Aksenof's head as he slept at the inn. This showed Aksenof that Makar had done the deed for which Aksenof had suffered.

Aksenof walked away to be by himself. He remembered his youth, his young wife, and his little children, from whom he had never heard since going to Siberia. His trail, the beating, and the long years were vividly remembered, and the recollections deepened his melancholy. And he thought of the criminal, Makar. Aksenof struggled with his desire for revenge. He said his prayers over and over, yet he could not sleep. He avoided Makar the next day and spent the next two weeks with indecision, sleeplessness, and depression.

Then one night, as Aksenof wandered about the prison, he saw some freshly dug earth. Makar crawled from beneath a bunk where he had begun to tunnel under the wall. He grabbed Aksenof and threatened to kill him if he told. Aksenof trembled with rage. Makar had killed him many years ago, he said; now any threats were useless.

The next day the guards discovered the hole and the chief of the prison lined up the prisoners for questioning. All the prisoners knew that the punishment for trying to escape was to be flogged nearly to death. Each denied knowledge of the digging. Finally, the chief came to Aksenof and said: "'Old man, you are truthful, tell me before God who did this.'" An agitated Makar stood nearby. Aksenof struggled. He said to himself: "'Why should I forgive him when he has been my ruin?'" After further thought, Aksenof told the chief to treat him as he wished, but he would not tell.

That night Makar came to tell Aksenof about the crime at the inn; Makar knelt to beg:

"Forgive me, forgive me for Christ's sake. I will confess that I killed the merchant—they will pardon you. You will be able to go home." Aksenof said: "It is easy for you to say that, but how could I endure it? Where should I go now? My wife is dead! My children have forgotten me. I have nowhere to go."

Makar did not rise; he beat his head on the ground, and said:

"Forgive me! When they flogged me with the knout, it was easier to bear than it is now to look at you. And you had pity on me after all this—you did not tell on me. Forgive me for Christ's sake! Forgive me though I am a cursed villain!"

And the man began to sob.

When Aksenof heard Makar sobbing, he himself burst into tears, and said:

"God will forgive you; maybe I am a hundred times worse than you are!"

And suddenly he felt a wonderful peace in his soul. And he ceased to mourn for his home, and had no desire to leave the prison, but only thought of his last hour.

Makar would not listen to Aksenof, and confessed his crime.

When they came to let Aksenof go home, he was dead.[4]

The changes forgiveness brings for Makar, Aksenof, and their relationship are great. Makar, the obnoxious braggart and bully, becomes able to make a willing confession. Aksenof finds peace (eternal peace, in Tolstoy's vision) after years of mourning. Two who had been on the verge of killing each other were able to cry together.

Why is forgiveness the final form of love? We think Niebuhr sees it this way (and Tolstoy would probably have agreed) because this form of love asks no return.[5] If one asks for a return on the forgiveness, the love retains a selfish motive. And if the return proves disappointing, the ability to forgive will dwindle away. Eventually, the relationship comes to a bitter end; or, perhaps worse, it drags along with ever-increasing injury and resentment.

[4] Translated by Nathan Haskell Dole and reprinted in *Greatest Short Stories*, vol. 6, New York, Collier, 1953, pp. 363–376.

[5] For a sensitive examination of different loves—nearly all asking something in return—see Thornton Wilder's *The Bridge of San Luis Rey*.

Constructive interpersonal communication depends on forgiveness. We have discussed the process of communication as well as we are able to at this time. Our efforts, we are sure, fall short in many places. And we cannot always put into efficient operation even the limited understanding we have for ourselves and can write about for others. To think about and to understand are some way from achieving better communication in one's everyday attempts at identification. Sometimes, too, one can know what he should communicate, have the requisite command of skills to do so, yet perversely do otherwise. By not knowing, by not having brought knowledge to skilled operation, or by not caring, we all have abundant occasion to give and receive injury. With forgiveness, we can repair and seek to improve; without it, we will reach a point at which beneficial identifications are impossible.

Furthermore, we have argued throughout that human beings are many as well as one. As a unique individual, each of us is never to be fully understood; hence knowledge, skill, and good intentions can be pressed to their utmost and the desired identifications will not always be gained. The many holds great benefits for human communication, but an irreducible element of disappointment is also part of the bargain. Therefore, as many, human beings are one in the need to forgive and be forgiven.[6]

Suppose, though, that human beings are unalterably evil. Machiavelli (1469–1527) wrote: "All men are bad and ever ready to display their vicious nature, whenever they may find occasion for it."[7] Then forgiving is foolish because the forgiving person is only letting down his guard and becoming more vulnerable to inevitable injury. We note that this view of the world has been popular throughout history. We take

[6] Carl Rogers's language differs from ours, but we believe that Rogers's basic stance in *Client Centered Therapy*, is not very different from ours. Boston, Houghton Mifflin, 1951, esp. pp. 159, 165.

[7] Niccolò Machiavelli, *The Prince and the Discourses*, New York, Random House, 1950, p. 117. Later sections of *The Discourses*, ameliorate this view of absolute depravity, but it is standard fare in *The Prince*.

a brighter view (albeit while recommending some caution), but see no way of presenting a convincing argument to those on the other side. Each side looks to its own evidence, and the citations for each are endless. We pass by the issue, remarking that if all of us are not to be in a small measure forgiving and forgivable, the study of interpersonal communication becomes merely a study of how best to signal our coercive capacities to each other.

Within our more optimistic assessment, we turn again to Niebuhr:

> Erich Fromm in his *Man for Himself*, as also others, defines the capacity to love as a "phenomenon of abundance," but mistakenly he assumes that the abundance of security which enables the self to love is derived from its previous self-seeking. It is more correct to regard the abundance of security as furnished by the love and devotion which others give the self, as Erik Erikson, for example, illustrates with his concept of "basic trust."[8]

Human beings will be able to seek mutually beneficial identifications as long as they are willing to share with one another. When interpersonal injuries threaten the willingness to share, a constructive coaction will only be possible through forgiveness—the final form of love that does not value oneself above another:

$$\frac{\text{One's estimate of his or her ability to inflict injury (or remembrance of the injuries one has inflicted).}}{\text{What the other has done to give injury}} = +1 \text{ or greater}$$

Aksenof says, "Maybe I am a hundred times worse than you are!" If taken literally, this would yield a quotient of 100. All of us need, however, only a +1 to be able to build again.

[8] Reinhold Niebuhr, *Man's Nature and His Communities*, New York, Scribner, 1965, p. 109.

Index